Nicholas Rescher
The Realm of Facts

Epistemic Studies

—

Philosophy of Science, Cognition and Mind

Edited by
Michael Esfeld, Stephan Hartmann, Albert Newen

Editorial Advisory Board:
Katalin Balog, Claus Beisbart, Craig Callender, Tim Crane, Katja Crone,
Ophelia Deroy, Mauro Dorato, Alison Fernandes, Jens Harbecke,
Vera Hoffmann-Kolss, Max Kistler, Beate Krickel, Anna Marmodoro, Alyssa Ney,
Hans Rott, Wolfgang Spohn, Gottfried Vosgerau

Volume 39

Nicholas Rescher

The Realm of Facts

Aspects of Philosophical Realism

DE GRUYTER

ISBN 978-3-11-077775-8
e-ISBN (PDF) 978-3-11-067002-8
e-ISBN (EPUB) 978-3-11-067011-0
ISSN 2512-5168

Library of Congress Control Number: 2019955857

Bibliographic information published by the Deutsche Nationalbibliothek
The Deutsche Nationalbibliothek lists this publication in the Deutsche Nationalbibliografie;
detailed bibliographic data are available on the Internet at http://dnb.dnb.de.

© 2021 Walter de Gruyter GmbH, Berlin/Boston
This volume is text- and page-identical with the hardback published in 2020.
Printing and binding: CPI books GmbH, Leck

www.degruyter.com

Professor Jamie Morgan
in cordial friendship

Preface

Logicians study which facts follow from or contradict others. Epistemologists and cognitive theorists study how we arrive at knowledge or conjecture regarding the facts. But the basic issue of what facts are has largely fallen between the stools. It is on this issue, however, that the present book will center.

I am grateful to Estelle Burris for her help in preparing my MS for the publisher and to James Baron for his constructive proofreading of my imperfect manuscript.

Nicholas Rescher

Pittsburgh PA
June 2019

Contents

Introduction: Why Facts Matter —— 1
1   The Need for Information —— 1
2   Cognition as an Economic —— 4
3   Wider Vistas —— 7

1   Factual Basics —— 8
1.1   Facts —— 8
1.2   Real Existence Involves Mind-Transcendence —— 9
1.3   Truths vs. Facts —— 11

2   Fact vs. Fiction —— 14
2.1   Existence —— 14
2.2   The Cognitive Opacity of Real Things —— 17
2.3   On the Complexity of Real —— 18
2.4   The Systemic Integrity of Fact —— 23
2.5   How Fictional Possibilities Differ from Real Things —— 27
2.6   Realms of Thought —— 29
2.7   Fiction —— 32
2.8   Fiction vs. Error —— 35
2.9   Possibilities and Merely Possible Objects —— 36
2.10   A Historical Perspective on Thought Experiments and Unreal Possibilities —— 39

3   Reality vs. Appearance —— 45
3.1   Reality vs. Appearance —— 45
3.2   The Historical Perspective —— 48
3.3   An Ontological Fallacy —— 49
3.4   The Impetus of Mind —— 51
3.5   The Reality Postulate —— 52
3.6   Communicative Realism —— 57

4   Conceiving Facts —— 60
4.1   Conceivability —— 60
4.2   Inconceivability —— 62
4.3   Meaninglessness —— 64
4.4   The Corrigibility of Conceptions —— 67
4.5   A "Logic" of Inconceivability —— 68

4.6	Inconceivable Possibilities —— 69	
	Appendix —— 71	
5	**Stating Facts: Formulating Facts in Language —— 72**	
5.1	Facts and Language —— 72	
5.2	Fact Outruns Language —— 73	
5.3	The Vastness of Fact —— 76	
5.4	Facts Are Transdenumerable —— 79	
5.5	The Comprehensiveness and Integrity of Fact —— 81	
6	**Knowledge of Fact —— 84**	
6.1	Cognition —— 84	
6.2	Cognitive Principles —— 84	
6.3	Science and Reality —— 90	
6.4	The Potential Diversity of "Science" —— 94	
6.5	The One World, One Science Argument —— 97	
6.6	A Quantitative Perspective —— 100	
6.7	Comparability and Judgments of Relative Advancement or Backwardness —— 106	
6.8	Cosmic Limitations —— 110	
6.9	Hidden Depths: The Impetus to Realism —— 116	
7	**The Ramifications of Ignorance —— 120**	
7.1	Modes of Error: Ignorance —— 120	
7.2	Ignorance About Our Own Ignorance Is Fundamental —— 122	
7.3	Some Prime Sources of Ignorance —— 125	
	The Unavailable Future —— 125	
	The Statistical Fog —— 125	
	The Stochastic Universe of Chance —— 126	
	The Ravages of Time —— 126	
	The Ways of The World —— 126	
7.4	Culpable vs. Venial Ignorance: Invincible vs. Vincible Ignorance —— 126	
7.5	Presumption as Gap-Filler for Ignorance —— 128	
7.6	The Extent of Ignorance —— 130	
8	**Access to Fact (The Rational Intelligibility of Nature) —— 132**	
8.1	On The Claims of Majority Judgment —— 132	
8.2	Explaining the Possibility of Natural Science —— 135	
8.3	"Our" Side —— 138	

8.4	Nature's Side in Evolutionary Perspective —— 140
8.5	Synthesis —— 143
8.6	Implications —— 146
8.7	Coda —— 148

9 Our Limited Knowledge of Fact —— 149
9.1	Cognitive Incapacity —— 149
9.2	Insolubilia Then and Now —— 150
9.3	Cognitive Limits —— 152
9.4	Surd Facts and Unknowability —— 154
9.5	Identifying Insolubilia —— 157
9.6	Relating Knowledge to Ignorance —— 159
9.7	Unknowability —— 162
9.8	Unknowable Facts vs. Unanswerable Questions —— 164

10 On Existence, Reality, and Facts —— 167
10.1	Is Man the Measure? —— 167
10.2	Realism and Incapacity —— 170
10.3	Cognitive Dynamics —— 172
10.4	Conceptual Basis of Realism as a Postulate —— 174

Bibliography —— 180

Index —— 184

Introduction: Why Facts Matter

1 The Need for Information

The changeable nature of human knowledge about the world's facts has been recognized since classical antiquity.[1] The history of science and of inquiry in all its forms clearly shows that facts, theories, concepts, and methods are not endowed with a fixed permanence, but reflect an ever-changing cognitive state of the art with variation in time, place, and cultural *modus operandi*. Science is not an object of some sort, a thing-like "body of knowledge"—it is an activity, a dynamic cognitive enterprise geared to the creation and active manipulation of information. Human cognition is a process that actively develops and with this development we not only have change but also the emergence of a novelty that radically divides the present from what has gone before. Our cognitive endeavors are involved in a constant process of transformation. Since the rise of science, no two human generations have viewed the world and its contents in just the same way. Science, properly understood, is not a body of theories, but a process—an ongoing project of inquiry whose products are ever changing.

The development of knowledge—and of science in particular—is thus a human activity which, like any other, involves the expenditure of time, effort, and other resources—and accordingly has an ineliminable economic dimension. Knowledge possesses an ineliminable economic dimension because of its nature as an activity which, as such, has a substantial involvement with costs and benefits. Virtually every aspect of the way we acquire, maintain, and use our knowledge can be properly understood and explained only from an economic point of view. Throughout the entire range of our endeavors in this world, we are involved in the expenditure of limited resources, and knowledge is no exception to this rule. Its acquisition, processing, storage, retrieval, and utilization are activities which, like any other human endeavor, engender costs. Over and above this practical dimension there are also certain purely cognitive disabilities and negativities—that is, costs—involved in the lack of knowledge, in ignorance, error, and confusion. And on the positive side, it has come to be increasingly apparent in recent years that knowledge is *cognitive capital*, and that its extraction and consolidation involves the creation of intellectual assets, in which both produc-

---

[1] *Veniet tempus quo posteri nostri tam aperta nos nescisse mirentur:* "There will come a time when our descendants will be amazed that we did not know things that are so plain to them." (Seneca, *Natural Questions*, vol. 2: *Books 4–7*, Cambridge, MA: Harvard University Press, 1972, VII, 25, 5.)

ers and users have a very real interest. Any theory of knowledge that ignores this economic aspect of the matter does so to the detriment of its own adequacy.

That greatest of American philosophers Charles Sanders Peirce (1839–1914) proposed to construe the "economy of research" at issue in knowledge development in terms of the sort of balance of assets and liabilities that we today would call cost-benefit analysis.[2] Peirce insisted that one must recognize the inevitably economic nature of any human enterprise—inquiry included:

> The value of knowledge is, for the purpose of science, in one sense absolute. It is not to be measured, it may be said, in money; in one sense that is true. But knowledge that leads to other knowledge is more valuable in proportion to the trouble it saves in the way of expenditure to get that other knowledge. Having a certain fund of energy, time, money, etc., all of which are merchantable articles to spend upon research, the question is how much is to be allowed to each investigation; and the value of that investigation is how much it will pay for us to spend upon it. Relatively, therefore, knowledge, even of a purely scientific kind, has a money value.[3]

On the side of benefits of scientific claims, Peirce also recognized a wide variety of epistemic factors: closeness of fit to data, explanatory value, novelty, simplicity, accuracy of detail, precision, parsimony, concordance with other accepted theories, even antecedent likelihood and intuitive appeal. And he placed in the liability column those cost-geared factors of "the dismal science": the expenditure of time, effort, energy, and money needed to secure and substantiate our claims. And this view of the matter is entirely appropriate, although the introduction of such an economic perspective does not, of course, detract from the value of the quest for knowledge as an intrinsically worthy venture endowed with a perfectly valid *l'art pour l'art* aspect.

Philosophical epistemologists subsequent to Peirce have paid regrettably little attention to these matters.[4] Indeed, they often proceed on the tacit assumption that information is something that is economically costless—a free good that comes to rational inquirers without expenditure and effort. But even casual consideration shows that such a view is totally erroneous and unrealistic.

---

[2] On Peirce's project on economy of research, see the author's *Peirce's Philosophy of Science* (Notre Dame and London: Notre Dame Press, 1976), as well as Cornelius F. Delaney, "Peirce on 'Simplicity' and the Conditions of the Possibility of Science," in: Linus J. Thro (ed.), *History of Philosophy in the Making* (Washington, D.C.: University Press of America, 1982), pp. 177–194.
[3] Charles Sanders Peirce, *Collected Papers*, ed. by Charles Hartshorne and Paul Weiss, vol. 1 (Cambridge, MA: Harvard University Press, 1931), sect. 1.122 [c. 1896].
[4] One valuable contribution in this area is Fritz Machlup, *The Production and Distribution of Knowledge in the United States* (Princeton: Princeton University Press, 1962).

For sure, knowledge brings great benefits. The relief of ignorance is foremost among them. Man has evolved within nature into the ecological niche of an intelligent being. In consequence, the need for understanding, for "knowing one's way about," is one of the most fundamental demands of the human condition. Man is *Homo quaerens*. The need for knowledge is part and parcel of our nature. A deep-rooted demand for information and understanding presses in upon us, and we have little choice but to satisfy it. Once the ball is set rolling it keeps on under its own momentum—far beyond the limits of strictly practical necessity. The great Norwegian polar explorer Fridtjof Nansen put it well. What drives men to the polar regions, he said, is:

> ... the power of the unknown over the human spirit. As ideas have cleared with the ages, so has this power extended its might, and driven Man willy-nilly onwards along the path of progress. It drives us in to Nature's hidden powers and secrets, down to the immeasurably little world of the microscopic, and out into the unprobed expanses of the Universe ... it gives us no peace until we know this planet on which we live, from the greatest depth of the ocean to the highest layers of the atmosphere. This Power runs like a strand through the whole history of polar exploration. In spite of all declarations of possible profit in one way or another, it was that which, in our hearts, has always driven us back there again, despite all setbacks and suffering.[5]

The discomfort of unknowing is a natural component of human sensibility. To be ignorant of what goes on about us is almost physically painful for us—no doubt because it is so dangerous from an evolutionary point of view. It is a situational imperative for us humans to acquire information about the world. We have questions and we need answers. *Homo sapiens* is a creature who must, by his very nature, feel cognitively at home in the world. The requirement for information, for cognitive orientation within our environment, is as pressing a human need as that for food itself. We are rational animals and must feed our minds even as we must feed our bodies. Relief from ignorance, puzzlement, and cognitive dissonance is one of cognition's most important benefits. These benefits are both positive (pleasures of understanding) and negative (reducing intellectual discomfort through the removal of unknowing and ignorance and the diminution of cognitive dissonance). The basic human urge to make sense of things is a characteristic aspect of our make-up—we cannot live a satisfactory life in an environment we do not understand. For us intelligent creatures, cognitive orientation is itself a practical need: cognitive disorientation is physically stressful and distressing. As William James observed: "It is of the utmost practical importance

---

[5] Fridtjof Nansen as quoted in Roland Huntford, *The Last Place on Earth* (New York, 1985), p. 200.

to an animal that he should have prevision of the qualities of the objects that surround him."[6]

2 Cognition as an Economic

The benefits of knowledge are twofold: theoretical (or purely cognitive) and practical (or applied). The theoretical/cognitive benefits of knowledge relate to its satisfactions in and for itself, for understanding is an end unto itself and, as such, is the bearer of important and substantial benefits—benefits which are purely cognitive, relating to the informativeness of knowledge as such. The practical benefits of knowledge, on the other hand, relate to its role in guiding the processes by which we satisfy our (noncognitive) needs and wants. The satisfaction of our needs for food, shelter, protection against the elements, and security against natural and human hazards all require information. And the satisfaction of mere desiderata comes into it as well. We can, do, and must put knowledge to work to facilitate the attainment of our goals, guiding our actions and activities in this world into productive and rewarding lines. And this is where the practical payoff of knowledge comes into play.

The costs (and benefits) of knowledge acquisition will, of course, vary with people's conditions and circumstances. Time is of the essence here. The medical knowledge of the twentieth century was not available to patients in the eighteenth century—"not for all the tea in China." In pursuing information, as in pursuing food, we have to settle for the best we can obtain at the time. We have questions and need answers—the best answers we can get here and now, regardless of their imperfections. We cannot wait until all returns are in. Our needs and wants impel us to resolve our questions by means of the best available answers we can get. What matters for us is not ideal and certain knowledge in the light of complete and perfect information, but getting the best estimate that is actually obtainable here and now.

The impetus to inquiry—to investigation, research, and acquisition of information about the world we live in—can accordingly be validated in strictly economic terms with a view to potential costs and benefits of both theoretical and practical sorts. We humans need to achieve both an intellectual and a physical accommodation to our environment.

---

[6] William James, "The Sentiment of Rationality," in: *The Will to Believe and Other Essays in Popular Philosophy* (New York and London: Putnam, 1897), pp. 62–88 [see pp. 78–79].

2 Cognition as an Economic

The Ancients saw man as the rational animal *(zoōn logon echōn)*, set apart from other creatures by capacities for speech and deliberation. Under the precedent of Greek philosophy, Western thinkers have generally deemed the use of thought for the guidance of our actions to be at once the glory and the duty of *Homo sapiens*.

To behave rationally is to make use of one's intelligence to figure out the best thing to do in the circumstances. Rationality is a matter of the intelligent pursuit of appropriate objectives; it consists in the use of reason to resolve choices in the best feasible way. Above all, it calls for the intelligent pursuit of appropriate ends, for the effective and efficient cultivation of appropriately appreciated benefits. Rationality requires doing the best one can with the means at one's disposal, striving for the best results that one can expect to achieve within the range of one's resources, specifically including one's intellectual resources. Be it in matters of belief, action, or evaluation, its mission centers about the deliberate endeavor to secure an optimally favorable balance of benefits relative to expenditure.

Accordingly, rationality has an ineliminable economic dimension. The optimal use of resources is, after all, a crucial aspect of rationality. It is against reason to expend more resources on the realization of a given end than one needs to.[7] And it is against reason to expend more resources on the pursuit of a goal than it is worth—to do things in a more complex, inefficient, or ineffective way than is necessary in the circumstances. But it is also against reason to expend fewer resources in the pursuit of a goal than it is worth, unless these resources can be used to even better effect elsewhere. Cost effectiveness—the proper coordination of costs and benefits in the pursuit of our ends—is an indispensable requisite of rationality.

Economy of effort is a cardinal principle of rationality that helps to explain many aspects of the way in which we transact our cognitive business. Why are encyclopedias organized alphabetically rather than topically? Because this simplifies the search process. Why are accounts of people's doings or a nation's transactions standardly presented historically, with biographies and histories presented in chronological order? Because an account that moves from causes to effect simplifies understanding. Why do libraries group books together by topic and language rather than, say, alphabetically by author? Because this minimizes the difficulties of search and access. We are in a better position to under-

---

[7] But is it indeed irrational to give a gift more costly than the social situation requires? By no means! It all depends on one's aims and ends, which may, on such an occasion, lie in a desire to cause the recipient surprise and pleasure, rather than merely doing the customary thing. There is an important difference between wastefulness and generosity.

stand innumerable features of the way in which people conduct their cognitive business once we take the economic aspect into account.

It is particularly noteworthy from such an economic point of view that there will be some conditions and circumstances in which the cost of acquiring information—even assuming that it is to be had at all in the prevailing state of the cognitive art—is simply too high relative to its value. There are (and are bound to be) circumstances in which the acquisition costs of information exceed the benefits or returns on its possession. In this regard, too, information is just like any other commodity. The price is sometimes more than we can afford and often greater than any conceivable benefit that would ensue. (This is why people generally do not count the number of hairs in their eyebrows.)

Rationality and economy are thus inextricably interconnected. Rational inquiry is a matter of epistemic optimizations, of achieving the best overall balance of cognitive benefits relative to cognitive costs. Cost-benefit calculation is the crux of the economy of effort at issue. The principle of least effort—construed in a duly intellectualized manner—is bound to be a salient feature of cognitive rationality.[8] A version of Occam's Razor obtains throughout the sphere of cognitive rationality: *complicationes non multiplicandae sunt praeter necessitatem*. Efforts to secure and enlarge knowledge are worthwhile only insofar as they are cost effective in that the resources we expend for these purposes are more than compensated for through benefits obtained—as is indeed very generally the case. But not always. We are, after all, finite beings who have only limited time and energy at our disposal. And even the development of knowledge, important though it is, is nevertheless of limited value—it is not worth the expenditure of every minute of every day at our disposal.

The standard economic process of cost-effectiveness tropism is operative throughout the cognitive domain. Rational inquiry is rigorously subject to the economic impetus to securing maximal product for minimal expenditure. Concern for answering our questions in the most straightforward, most cost-effective way is a crucial aspect of cognitive rationality in its economic dimension.

The long and short of it is that knowledge acquisition is a purposive human activity—like most of our endeavors. And as such it involves the ongoing expenditure of resources for the realization of the objectives—description, explanation, prediction, and control—that represent the defining characteristics of our cogni-

---

[8] On this theme, see the important investigations of George K. Zipf, *Human Behavior and the Principle of Least Effort* (Cambridge, MA: Addison-Wesley, 1949). Zipf's investigations furnish a wide variety of interesting examples of how various aspects of our cognitive proceedings exemplify a tendency to minimize the expenditure of energy.

tive endeavors. The balance of costs and benefits becomes critical here, and endows the cognitive enterprise with an unavoidably economic aspect.[9]

3 Wider Vistas

Some creatures survive and thrive in the world by means of speed that enables them to outrun their enemies. Some have hard shells that render them unreachable. Some are so prolific that their predators cannot avert the survival of another generation. But the survival instrumentality of our species is in fact intelligence. We humans survive and thrive by figuring out how best to go about it. We exploit information for the guidance of action.

In order to do this, however, we need to secure or at least approximate the facts. For us, access to the facts is as important as food—indeed arguably more so since we could not survive the latter save by means of the former.

Accordingly, the following considerations are critical in addressing the question of why facts matter:
1. We humans must make our way in the world on a basis of our beliefs regarding the prevailing facts.
2. For the most part we are reactive rather than productive in relation to facts: we are for the most part situationally required to adjust to facts whose nature is outside the range of our creative control.
3. We can accommodate our proceedings to the facts only by learning about them. An appropriate understanding of relevant fact is indispensable for the efficacy of our effects and indeed for our very survival.

All in all, achieving an adequate knowledge of relevant fact is an indispensable instrumentality for us. The facts matter because we cannot survive without adequate access to them.

---

[9] On this theme, see also the author's *Cognitive Economy* (Pittsburgh: University of Pittsburgh Press, 1989).

1 Factual Basics

1.1 Facts

Facts constitute the conditions of reality: they manifest the way in which things actually are and configure the nature of actuality. As such, they stand in contrast to mere possibilities—the way things might be—and also to suppositions, assumptions, and surmises regarding the way things might be.

Facts can be classified according to the subject-matters at issue. Paramount here is the pivotal distinction between *empirical* facts regarding the natural world, and *formal* facts regarding the abstract domain of structure, symbolism, and language. Empirical facts relate to the substantial existence of the physical realm; formal facts relate to the realms of abstract idealizations. Our cognitive access to empirical fact is principally observational; our cognitive access to formal fact is primarily theoretical.

There are no false facts. But in this context—as in all others—people can be wrong. There are mistaken facts no more than there are triangular circles. Beliefs mistakenly taken as factual by people. It is not the facts that are mistaken by the situation of being taken for a fact by people. Here the mistake is on the part of the taker: that facts as such stand mistake-free. Still, there is a real prospect of error here. But then one cannot speak of false or mistaken facts but only of apparent facts or putative facts that turn out to be mistaken.

Facts as such—i.e., as authentic facts—are subject to various principles:
1. Factual truth: Individual facts must agree with the truth of things.
2. Factual consistency: Collectively, facts must be consistent with each other—they cannot conflict.
3. Factual integrity: The systemic integrity of fact as will be discussed below.

Only true claims can state facts. But this does not mean that only accurate and precise facts can do so. Saying that George Washington was over six feet tall states a fact. It is a fact that the Eiffel Tower is roughly 400 meters high. It is true that John D. Rockefeller was very wealthy. Yet none of these assertions has any precision to it. Every precise fact spans a multitude of imprecise ones. But when you are in possession of the precise facts on the matter, you are in a position to determine the rest: they yield no further instructive information.

A temporally indefinite statement such as "It is raining" does not state a fact unless and until the time at issue is indicated—either via an indefinite index (such as "now" or "here") or via of a definite dating (such as "in Paris on 22 July 1980").

Facts can come into existence in time. The fact of "George Washington's being the first president of the United States" only became so at his inauguration.

Facts can be necessary or contingent. The former (necessity) is a matter of a fact's obtaining on logico-conceptual grounds. (Swords—complete unbroken swords—must have blades; causes must have effects.) There are matters of conceptual inevitability. We would not call something a sword that did not have a blade. However, the Statue of Liberty's presence in New York is a matter of contingency. Its French donors could have given it to Boston instead. Contingency is matter of reality's conceivably variable arrangements. Even the laws of nature—gravitation, for example—are contingent.

But while the facts of the natural realm are contingent and could in theory stand differently, the facts of the formal domain are conditionally necessary. Once the communicative conventions are in place, they could not be different from what they are. Given that forks are the sort of things at issue with our terminology, it is necessary that forks (whole and unbroken) must have tines.

Facts can also be distinguished by the manner in which we obtain cognitive access to them. Three categories are principally at issue here. With facts regarding the world's nature and workings, we must rely on observation and interactive experience. Such facts are accordingly characterized as *empirical*.

Then too there are facts engendering the products of our own artifice—language, laws, manners, and the like. These may be characterized as *normative*. They relate to the proper management of our own productions.

Finally, there are facts regarding abstractions—numbers, shapes, structures, etc. These facts—primarily logico-mathematical in substance—may be characterized as *theoretical*.

1.2 Real Existence Involves Mind-Transcendence

The facts constitute reality. But what is it to be real? These are two very different questions. The former is a substantive question that is best left to investigative inquiry. To find out what is real in the world we must investigate it. But the latter is a conceptual question that should be addressed by rational analysis. And only this second question falls within the purview of philosophy.

So, what is it to be real, to actually exist? In addressing this question, it seems sensible to begin with the straightforward existence of things in space and time in the manner of trees, dogs, and automobiles. And we then thus proceed reiteratively somewhat as follows, specifying that something exists if:

1. it exists unproblematically in the just-specified manner of playing an active causal role in this real world of ours in which our life and our experience unfolds, or else;
2. it is something whose actual existence must be invoked in providing a satisfactory explanatory account of the features of something that exists. (And here it does not matter if the explanatory account at issue is efficiently causal, or functionally finalistic, or conceptually explicative.)

Such a meaning-specification is essentially recursive. It proceeds by sequential steps or stages, maintaining first that ordinary material objects are existentially real, and thereupon extending this stepwise to anything whatsoever that is bound up with the existent by way of explanatory linkages.

Approached in this manner, one quintessential way of being real is by figuring in human experience through being something with which we can get into perceptual contact. This is a special concern of item (1) and is certainly a paradigmatic way of establishing a claim to reality. In fact, Immanuel Kant was sufficiently in the grip of the empiricist tradition to think this experiential route to afford the *only* viable pathway to reality. But this view of the matter is too narrow. For we do well to include in "reality" not only those things that we experience, but also those processes and factors needed to explain them.

Accordingly, "to exist" in the physical mode is to feature as a component or aspect of the causal commerce real world. And some jargon expression such as "to subsist" needs to be coined for contextualized existence within a framework of supposition at issue with fictions or hypotheses. Thus, merely possible objects —or *possibilia*, for short—are things that merely "exist" in the sense of subsistence within a hypothetical realm in a fictional make-believe world. They are not part of the real world's actual furnishings.

To be sure, such a view of existence is anathema to a considerable array of philosophers for whom our commonplace world is not reality but mere appearance whose furnishings do not really exist. For them, what "really exists" is something that entirely transcends this world of everyday experience (Plato's realm of ideas, for example), or that imperceptibly underlies it (such as Democritus's atoms and the void). With such theorists, what is basic to the conception of reality is not existence as we standardly have it, but a somehow concealed manifold of being that is thought somehow to account for those familiar things. In contrast to such doctrines, the present approach to the issue of realism takes the line that in understanding real existence, as in so much else, we must begin from where we are.

Viewing matters in this light casts experience in a leading role as our cognitive gateway to reality. Experiential encounter is the basic and primary way in which one can learn about reality and experience in our inevitable starting point here. But—dogmatic empiricism to the contrary notwithstanding—this is only the beginning and not the whole story. For in the process of a theoretical systematization that seeks to explain what we experience, the horizons of our reality will inevitably expand. And as they do so, we are led to the conviction that there is always some as yet experience-transcending room for them to expand into.

Such a metaphysical realism represents the doctrine that the world exists in a way that is substantially independent of the thinking beings it contains that can inquire into it, and that its nature—its having the characteristics it does actually have—is also comparably knowledge-transcending. In saying of something that it is "a real thing," a concrete object existing as part of the world's furniture, we commit ourselves to various (obviously interrelated) points:

1. *Self-subsistence.* Being a "something" (an entity or process) with its own unity of being. Having an enduring identity of its own.
2. *Physicality or world-boundedness.* Existing within the causal order of things. Having a place on the world's physical scene as a participant of some sort.
3. *Publicity or accessibility.* Admitting universality of access. Being something that different investigators proceeding from different points of departure can get hold of.
4. *Autonomy or independence.* Being independent of mind. Being something that observers find rather than create, and *learn about* rather than *define* in the course of their cognitive endeavors.
5. *Experience-transcendence.* Having more facets and features than do—or indeed even can—manifest themselves in experience.

These, then, are the core features of the metaphysical conception of reality. The fact is that our conception of a real thing has at its very core the idea of its projecting beyond the cognitive reach of mind. The governing idea is that there is more to reality than "meets the eye"—that reality somehow transcends appearance.

1.3 Truths vs. Facts

Some important distinctions must be drawn in the interests of clarity and precision about claims that something is the case:

1. *Assertion/statement:* the verbal formulation of a claim. This is a matter of how the claim is articulated. For example, "The cat is on the mat."
2. *Contention/proposition:* the informative meaning of a claim—what it purports; its affirmatory substance. This is a matter of what the claim claims.

It admits of many formulations, e.g., by holding (in any of various ways) that the cat is positioned on the mat.
3. *Claimed circumstances:* the supposed or putative state of affairs which the claim affirms—how things would stand if the claim were true. This is a matter of how things will have to stand if the claim is to be true: viz. that there must be a mat and a cat emplaced upon it.
4. *The fact of the matter:* the state of affairs that actually obtains. This is a matter of how things actually stand in relation to the matters at issue with the claim.

When an assertion (statement) accords with the fact of the matter, we have a *truth*. The realization condition for this circumstance is that the claimed condition agrees with the fact of the matter. For truth (and also accuracy, correctness, and the like), harmonization with the facts of the matter will be pivotal.

Whatever is a fact is so timelessly.

That it's raining now in Peoria is a fact, but only if the time at issue is specific. And once this is done, the fact is so timelessly. On this basis, what is factual obtains not always and omni-temporally but timelessly and extra-temporally.

The facts are what they are. There is no time dependency here. When people grow old, it is they that age and not the facts of their age possession.

It is misleading and inappropriate to say that "It was a fact that he entered High School four years before it was a fact that he graduated from High School." This is simply an improper and misleading way of saying "It is a fact that he entered High School four years before graduating from it." The relation at issue obtains between events and not facts.

Facts are states of affairs; truths are language-formulated statements that make correct claims about the facts.

There is an infinite and indeed even trans-countable multitude of facts. For there are trans-countably many real objects (e.g., real numbers), and each admits of specifically characteristic facts. But language is recursively developed and thereby admits of only a countable infinitude of statements, and thus of true statements. Accordingly, reality can never be fully and adequately encompassed in language. There are just not sufficiently many statements available.

One fact encompasses another when this other is a logico-conceptual consequence of the former. This means that each fact encompasses an infinitude of others. For whenever p is a fact, so is p-or-q for any q whatsoever.

Different and distinct truths can indicate the same fact with equal accuracy. Thus, consider:
- The cat is on the mat.
- The mat has a cat on it.
- A cat is currently atop the mat.

In this way, any number of different statements represent (indicate, formulate, state) the same fact.

However, barring equivocation, a specific statement can present only a single fact.

However, a vague statement can be consistent with different and distinct facts. Thus, consider the statements:
- There are 5,403 beans in the jar.
- There are 5,402 beans in the jar.

The facts at issue here are distinct, different, and discordant. However, the statement "There are roughly 5,400 beans in the jar" does justice to all of them. Different facts can be conveyed (at least approximately) by one single common statement.

2 Fact vs. Fiction

2.1 Existence

"To be" is to be an item of some kind. Such taxonomic sortality is crucial for being since different sorts of things exist in very different ways. There is physical being in the order of space, time, and causality, mathematical being in the realm of quantities or structures, sensory being in the spectrum of colors or the catalogue of odors, and so on. To be, in the most general sense of the term, is to play a part in such a realm, and there are as many modes of being as there are such realms.

Since being is realm-correlative, the idea at large is inherently contextualized. Strictly considered, then, we should not speak of being categorically and without qualification. It is always a matter of being-as-something-or-other: being as a physical object, as a number, as a shade of color, or the like. Being is accordingly not homogenous but categorically differentiated: different kinds of items are beings in their own characteristic way.

To exist (in the broadest sense of this term) is to function as a constituent of a realm, to play a role in a domain of identifiable items of some sort. In principle, there are thus as many modes of existence as there are types of interrelated items, and to exist is to exist as an item of the correlative kind. There is physical existence in space and time, mathematical existence in the realm of quantities or structures, sensory existence in the spectrum of colors or the catalogue of odors, and so on. This means that existence is realm-correlative and thus contextualized. Strictly considered, we should not speak of existence categorically and without qualification. It is always a matter of "existence as": as a physical object, as a number, as a character in a Shakespeare play, or the like. Existence is accordingly not homogenous but categorically differentiated: different kinds of existing things exist in their own characteristic way. To attribute to numbers the same kind of existence that colors or that mammals have is to commit a serious category mistake.

All the same, when philosophers talk of existence they generally mean *physical existence* in the natural world. And here the term admits both a narrower and a broader construction. In its narrower construction, to exist physically is to be an object in space and time: to occupy a place here in the manner in which cats and trees and water molecules do. But to exist physically in the broader sense of the term is to play a role in the causal commerce of such things—to exist in the manner in which droughts or headaches or human desires do, and thereby to figure as part of the world's processual development. It is

https://doi.org/10.1515/9783110670028-005

such actual, real-world existence—narrow and broad alike—that will be our principal object of concern here. And the overall range of such existences can be specified in an essentially recursive manner as follows:
1. the things we experience with our internal and external senses exist;
2. the things whose existence we need to postulate in order to realize an adequate causal explanation of things that exist also exist.

This view really takes the approach of a *causal* realism, a theory maintaining that to be a real existent is to be part of the world's causal commerce. On this basis, existence is best characterized recursively. We would thus begin with the unproblematic existence of things in space and time in the manner of trees, dogs, and automobiles.

Various generalizations can be made about being collectively—for example, the previous contention that to be is to play a significant role in a realm of interrelated items. But there is very little that can be said in general about being distributively throughout the whole range of its possible applicability. The variety of different ways in which something can correctly be said to be means that little of substantive purport can be said about beings at large.

Radical empiricism in ontology goes beyond the unproblematic idea of observability as a sufficient condition for existing ("If one can actually observe it, then it really exists") to set it up as a necessary condition as well ("If one can't somehow observe it, then it just doesn't really exist"). This imposes rather drastic limits. However, a more liberal mode of realism in ontology is also prepared to admit those things whose acceptance as real facilitates the project of understanding—anything whose assumed existence figures in our best available explanation of the real. Thus, not observation alone but conception is also seen to qualify in suitable circumstances as a viable cognitive pathway to existence. But there are limits to what can be achieved in this way.

Figuring in works of fiction and imagination does not suffice to establish a claim upon being more strictly understood. For to be is to function on one's own thought-independent footing as a constituent of a realm—to have a place and play some self-subsistingly functional role in a domain of interrelated items of some sort. It will not do to say, "To be is to be thought of—to be an object of consideration." To be thought about, talked about, imagined, is not to play a part on one's own but simply to figure in the ideas of some mind or other. This does not suffice for the self-sufficiency needed to ratify a claim to existence.

To construe existence in the presently contemplated manner goes beyond the doctrinal stance that D. M. Armstrong calls *naturalism*: the position that the only objects that exist are those physically constituting this real world of ours.[10] For as the present, more liberal account sees it, there are also items that are merely features of objects in nature rather than objects as such: properties, relationships, force-fields, etc. And while these do not themselves constitute objects in the world, they too can stake a claim for existence—albeit only insofar as they do or can serve to account for some features of the world's objects.

Jargon expressions such as "to subsist" or the like have been coined to stand for contextualized "existence" within a framework of supposition at issue with assumptions, hypotheses, and fictions. But this is a questionable usage because such items are, by hypothesis, no more than mere fictions and thereby unreal. And so, the issue arises of how much ontological weight such supposed quasi-being can bear.

The well-known dictum "To be is to be the value of a variable" is not much help in matters of ontology. For "to be" in *this* sense is simply to be an object of discussion, since we will—or certainly can—put anything we care to discuss into the domain of discourse at issue with our variables. One can quantify over fictional characters without endorsing their actual existence in any way, shape, or manner. Thus, mere qualification as such does not mean all that much. The statement "There are nonexistent persons at issue in Shakespeare's comedies" is not to be understood as "Nonexistent persons exist and figure as characters in Shakespeare's comedies." It has to be interpreted as "Shakespeare's comedies project to be about certain persons who actually do not exist at all." The one who is committed to the possible existence of Puck and Ganymede is not our self but (at best) Shakespeare. Of course, a conscientious theorist who takes seriously the idea that an *existential* quantifier is at issue and keeps in mind the dictum that "To be is to be the value of a variable" will be mindful to keep his ontology—the range of items he actually views as existing—in consideration with his quantifier domain. But this is a matter of metaphysical conscientiousness, not of logical principle. And so mere possibilia—merely possible objects and worlds—lack the credentials for being considered as authentic beings.

After all, what sort of reason would we ever have for attributing some sort of attenuated being or quasi-existence to avowedly nonexistent possibilities? The only answer seems to be that we can talk about them in a communicatively intelligible way. For something to be actually real is for it to be able to figure in the world's causal and explanatory commerce, while for something to be quasi-real in the way now being contemplated is for it to be a creature of thought—to figure in the thought and discourse of mind-endowed creatures. However, the only sort

---

[10] See David M. Armstrong, *A Combinatorial Theory of Possibility* (Cambridge: Cambridge University Press), 1989.

of quasi-reality or quasi-existence which something that is a mere nonactual possibility ever has is that which it acquires in the framework of discourse and discussion. Its being consists in being thinkable. (This view of the matter might be called *fictionalism*, to borrow once more from D. M. Armstrong.[11]) On this perspective, fictions "subsist" in the realm of supposition or hypothesis, and here alone. And the crucial fact is that objects of discussion are no more authentic objects than hobby horses are horses or tin soldiers are soldiers. (To *call* something an *X* does not make it an *X!* Verbal legerdemain creates only claims and statements but not objects.) Let us examine more deeply what is really at issue with being real.

2.2 The Cognitive Opacity of Real Things

It is worthwhile to examine somewhat more closely the considerations that indicate the inherent imperfection of our knowledge of things.[12]

For the cognitive depth of objective factual claims, inherent in the fact that their content will always outrun the evidence for making them, means that the endorsement of any such claim always involves some element of evidence-transcending conjecture.

The concepts at issue (viz. "experience" and "manifestation") are such that we can only ever experience those features of a real thing that it actually manifests. But the preceding considerations show that real things always have more experientially manifestable properties that they can ever actually manifest in experience. The experienced portion of a thing is similar to the part of the iceberg that shows above water. All real things are necessarily thought of as having hidden depths that extend beyond the limits, not only of experience but also of experientiality. To say of something that it is an apple or a stone or a tree is to become committed to claims about it that go beyond the data we have—and even beyond those which we can, in the nature of things, ever actually acquire. The "meaning" inherent in the assertoric commitments of our factual statements is never exhausted by its verification. Real things are cognitively opaque—we cannot see to the bottom of them. Our knowledge of such things can thus become more extensive without thereby becoming more complete.

---

11 See Armstrong, *A Combinatorial Theory of Possibility.*
12 For an informative discussion of philosophical issues located in this general area, see Vincent J. Fecher, *Error, Deception, and Incomplete Truth* (Rome: Officium Libri Catholici, 1975).

In this regard, however, real things differ in an interesting and important way from their fictional cousins. To make this difference plain, it is useful to distinguish between two types of information about a thing, namely that which is generic and that which is not. Generic information tells about those features of a thing which it has in common with everything else of its kind or type. For example, a particular snowflake will share with all others certain facts about its structure, its hexagonal form, its chemical composition, its melting point, etc. On the other hand, it will also have various properties which it does not share with other members of its own "lowest species" in the classificatory order—its particular shape, for example, or the angular momentum of its descent. These are its nongeneric features.

Now, a key fact about fictional particulars is that they are of finite cognitive depth. In discoursing about them we shall ultimately run out of steam as regards their nongeneric features. A point will always be reached when one cannot say anything further that is characteristically new about them—presenting nongeneric information that is not inferentially implicit in what has already been said. New generic information can, of course, always be forthcoming through the progress of science. When we learn more about coal in general, then we know more about the coal in Sherlock Holmes' grate. But the finiteness of its cognitive depth means that the presentation of ampliatively novel non-generic information must, by the very nature of the case, come to a stop when fictional things are at issue.

With *real* things, on the other hand, there is no reason of principle why the availability of new nongenerically idiosyncratic information need ever come to an end. On the contrary, we have every reason to presume these things to be cognitively inexhaustible. A precommitment to description-transcending features—no matter how far description is pushed—is essential to our conception of a real thing. Something whose character was exhaustible by linguistic characterization would thereby be marked as fictional rather than real.[13]

2.3 On the Complexity of Real

The paradigmatic existents are the real things of this world. And this reality is endlessly complex in its details. As we standardly think about particulars within

---

[13] This also indicates why the dispute over mathematical realism (Platonism) has little bearing on the issue of physical realism. Mathematical entities are akin to fictional entities in this—that we can only say about them what we can extract by deductive means from what we have explicitly put into their defining characterization. These abstract entities do not have nongeneric properties since each is a "lowest species" unto itself.

the conceptual framework of our factual deliberation and discourse, *any* real concrete particular has more features and facets than it will ever actually manifest in experience. For every objective property of a real thing has consequences of a dispositional character and these can never be surveyed completely because the dispositions which particular concrete things have inevitably have endow them with an infinite aspect that cannot be comprehended within experience.[14] This desk, for example, has a limitless manifold of phenomenal features of the type "having a certain appearance from a particular point of view." It is perfectly clear that most of these will never be actualized. Moreover, a thing *is* what it *does:* entity and lawfulness are coordinated correlates—a good Kantian point. And this consideration that real things must exhibit lawful comportment means that the finitude of experience precludes any prospect of the *exhaustive* manifestation of the descriptive facets of any actual existents.[15]

Moreover, real things are invariably concrete,[16] and concrete things not only have more properties than they ever *will* overtly manifest, but they have more properties than they ever *can* possibly actually manifest. This is so because the dispositional properties of things always involve what might be characterized as *mutually preemptive* conditions of realization. This lump of sugar, for example, has the dispositional property of reacting in a particular way if subjected to a temperature of 10,000 °C and of reacting in a certain way if placed for 100 hours in a large, turbulent body of water. But if either of these conditions is ever realized, it will destroy the lump of sugar as a lump of sugar, and thus block the prospect of *its* ever bringing the other property to manifestation. The severally possible realization of various dispositions may fail to be mutually *compatible*, and so the dispositional properties of a real thing cannot ever be

---

14 To be sure, various *abstract* things, such as colors or numbers, will not have dispositional properties. For being divisible by four is not a *disposition* of sixteen. Plato got the matter right in Book VII of the *Republic:* in the realm of mathematical abstracta there are not genuine *processes*—and process is a requisite of dispositions. Of course, there may be dispositional truths in which numbers (or colors, etc.) figure that do not issue in any dispositional properties of these numbers (of colors, etc.) themselves—a truth, for example, such as my predilection for odd numbers. But if a truth (or supposed truth) does no more than to convey how someone *thinks* about a thing, then it does not indicate any property of the thing itself. (Fictional things, however, *can* have suppositional dispositions: Sherlock Holmes was addicted to cocaine, for example.)

15 This aspect of objectivity was justly stressed in the "Second Analogy" of Kant's *Critique of Pure Reason*, although his discussion rests on ideas already contemplated by Leibniz. See Gottfried Wilhelm Leibniz, *Philosophische Schriften*, ed. by Carl I. Gerhardt, vol. 7 (Berlin: Weidmann, 1890), pp. 319 ff.

16 On the concreteness of the real, see Charles Hartshorne, *Anselm's Discovery* (La Salle, IL: Open Court, 1965), pp. 189–192.

manifested completely—not just in practice, but in principle. Our objective claims about real things always commit us to more than we can actually ever determine about them. Our information about things is always simply the visible part of the iceberg.

The existence of this latent (hidden, occult) sector is a crucial feature of our conception of a real thing. Neither in fact nor in thought can we ever simply put it away. To say of this apple that its only features are those it actually manifests is to run afoul of our conception of an apple. To deny—or even merely to refuse to be committed to—the claim that it *would* manifest certain particular features *if* appropriate conditions came about (for example, that it would have such-and-such a taste if eaten) is to be driven to withdrawing the claim that it is an apple. The latent, implicit ramifications of our objective factual claims about something real are potentially endless, and such judgments are thus "non-terminating" in C. I. Lewis' sense.[17] The totality of facts about a thing—about any real thing whatever—is in principle inexhaustible and the complexity of real things is in consequence descriptively unfathomable. Endlessly many true descriptive remarks can be made about any particular actual concrete object. For example, take a stone. Consider its physical features: its shape, its surface texture, its chemistry, etc. And then consider its causal background: its subsequent genesis and history. Then consider the multitude of functional aspects reflected in its uses by the stonemason, or the architect, or the landscape decorator, etc. There is, after all, no end to the perspectives of consideration that we can bring to bear on things. The botanist, horticulturist, landscape gardener, farmer, painter, and real estate appraiser will operate from different cognitive "points of view" in describing one selfsame vegetable garden. And there is in principle no theoretical limit to the lines of consideration available to provide descriptive perspectives upon a thing.

Our characterization of real things can accordingly become more *extensive* without thereby becoming more *complete*. New descriptive features can and do ongoingly come into view with the progress of knowledge. (Caesar not only did not know, but in the existing state of knowledge also could not have known, that his sword contained tungsten.) Real things are—and by their very nature must be—such that their actual nature outruns any particular description of it that we might venture. From this angle too it is clear that the realm of reality-appertaining fact inevitably outruns the reach of our descriptive information at hand.

---

[17] See C. I. Lewis, *An Analysis of Knowledge and Valuation* (La Salle, IL: Open Court, 1962), pp. 180–181.

It serves the interests of precision to introduce a distinction at this stage. On the standard conception of the matter, a "truth" is to be understood in *linguistic* terms—the representation of a fact through its statement in some actual language. Any correct statement in some actual language formulates a truth. (And the converse obtains as well: a *truth* must be encapsulated in a statement, and cannot exist without linguistic embodiment.) A *fact*, on the other hand, is not a linguistic entity at all, but an actual circumstance or state of affairs. Anything that is correctly stateable in some *possible* language presents a fact.[18] Facts correspond to *potential* truths whose actualization hinges on an appropriate linguistic embodiment.

Every truth must state a fact, but given the limited resources of language it is not only possible but indeed to be expected that there will be facts that elude stateability in any actually available language and thereby fail to be captured as truths. Truths involve a one-parameter possibilization: they encompass whatever can correctly be stated in some actual language. Facts, by contrast, involve a two-parameter possibilization, including whatever *can* be stated truly in some *possible* language. Truths are *actualistically* language-correlative, while facts are *possibilistically* language-correlative.[19]

There are unquestionably more possible states of affairs than there are statements available for their formulation. For statements are linguistically formulated and this means that the set of possible statements is, at most, countably infinite. But we live in a world that is not digital but analogue and the manifold of possible states of affairs will thus be transenumerably infinite. Accordingly, it must be presumed that there are facts that we will never manage to formulate as truths, though it is obviously impossible to give concrete examples of this phenomenon.[20]

---

18 Our position thus takes no issue with Peter F. Strawson's precept that "facts are what statements (when true) state." ("Truth," *Proceedings of the Aristotelian Society*. New Series 59 [1958–1959], pp. 141–162). Difficulty would ensue with Strawson's thesis only if an "only" were added.
19 But can any sense be made of the idea of *merely* possible (i.e., possible but nonactual) languages? Of course it can! Once we have a generalized conception (or definition) of a certain kind of thing—be it a language or a caterpillar—then we are inevitably in a position to suppose in the *de dicto* mode the possible actuality of things meeting these conditions are over and above those that in fact do so. The prospect of mooting certain "mere" possibilities cannot be denied—that, after all, is just what possibilities are all about. (Of course, the move from possibilities to possibilia is something else again, as the ensuing discussion will show in detail.)
20 Note, however, that if a Davidsonian translation argument to the effect that "If it's sayable at all, then it's sayable in *our* language" were to succeed—which it does not—then the matter would stand on a very different footing. For it would then follow that any possible language can state no more than what can be stated in our own (actual) language. And then the realm of facts (i.e.,

It follows from these considerations that we can never justifiably claim to be in a position to articulate "the whole truth" about a real thing. The domain of thing-characterizing fact inevitably transcends the limits of our capacity to *express* it, and *a fortiori* those of our capacity to canvas it completely. In the description of concrete particulars, we are caught up in an inexhaustible detail: the cardinal feature of reality is its inherent complexity. There are always bound to be more descriptive facts about actual things than we are able to capture with our linguistic machinery: the real encompasses more than we can manage to say about it—now or ever.

After all, the truth regarding any particular actual existent runs off into endlessly proliferating detail. No matter how much is told to us, we can ask for yet more pertinent information and in principle expect a sensible and informative answer. It is a crucial facet of our epistemic stance toward the real world that there is always more to be known than what we explicitly know now. Every part and parcel of reality has features lying beyond our present cognitive reach—at *any* "present" whatsoever.

Consider an example. On a map of the United States, Chicago is but a dot. But when we go to a map of Illinois it begins to take on some substance, and on a map of Cook County it presents a substantial and characteristic shape. Yet the line does not end there. We could, in theory, go on to map it block by block, house by house, room by room, dish by pitcher, molecule by molecule. And with increasing detail, new and different features constantly emerge. Where does the process stop? Not with atoms, certainly—for the impenetrable and unchanging atoms of the ancient Greeks have become increasingly dematerialized and ethereal, in the light of modern physics even composed of ongoingly smaller processes. As we increase the power of our particle accelerators, our view of the make-up of the physical world becomes not only ever different but also ever stranger. There is, as best we can tell, no limit to the world's ever-increasing complexity that comes to view with our ever-increasing grasp of its detail. The realm of fact and reality is endlessly complex.

---

what is (correctly) stateable in some *possible* language) and that of truths (i.e., what is (correctly) stateable in some *actual* language) would necessarily coincide. Accordingly, our thesis that the range of facts is larger than that of truths hinges crucially upon a failure of such a translation argument. (See Donald Davidson, "The Very Ideas of a Conceptual Scheme," *Proceedings and Addresses of the American Philosophical Association* 47 [1973–1974], pp. 5–20, and also the critique of his position in Chapter 2 of the author's *Empirical Inquiry* [Totowa, NJ.: Rowman & Littlefield, 1982]).

2.4 The Systemic Integrity of Fact

Any fact—any state of affairs—has aspects and involvements beyond number and can therefore never be *completely* characterized. Moreover, the web of fact is woven tight.

Thus, suppose that we make only a very small alteration in the descriptive composition of the real, say, by adding one pebble to the river bank. But which pebble? Where are we to get it and what are we to put in its place? And where are we to put the air or the water that this new pebble displaces? And when we put that material in a new spot, just how are we to make room for it? And how are we to make room to the so-displaced material? Moreover, the region within six inches of the new pebble used to hold N pebbles. It now holds $N + 1$. Of which region are we to say that it holds $N - 1$? If it is that region yonder, then how did the pebble get here from there? By a miraculous instantaneous transport? By a little boy picking it up and throwing it? But then, which little boy? And how did he get there? And if he threw it, then what happened to the air that his throw displaced which would otherwise have gone undisturbed? Here, problems arise without end.

The causal and interactive state of things in nature's realm is an interwoven fabric where the severing of any thread unravels the whole, with results and consequences that are virtually impossible to discern in advance.

And this situation obtains at the deeper level of logical general principles. For the fact is that the interlinkage of our beliefs about the real is such that belief-contravening suppositions always function within a wider setting of accepted beliefs $B_1, B_2, \ldots B_n$ of such a sort that when one of them, for simplicity say B_1, is abandoned owing to a hypothetical endorsement of its negation, nevertheless the resulting group $\sim B_1, B_2, \ldots B_n$ still remains collectively inconsistent. And the reason for this lies in the logical principle of *the systemic integrity of fact*. For suppose that we accept B_1. Then let B_2 be some other claim that we flatly reject—one that is such that we accept $\sim B_2$. Initially, however, since we accepted B_1, we will certainly also have accepted B_1 or B_2. But now consider the group of accepted theses: B_1, B_1 or $B_2, \sim B_2$. When we drop B_1 here and insert $\sim B_1$ in its place we obtain $\sim B_1, B_1$ or $B_2, \sim B_2$. And this group is still inconsistent. The structure of fact is an intricately woven fabric. One cannot sever one part of it without unraveling other parts of the real. Facts engender a *dense* structure, as the mathematicians use this term. Every determinable fact is so drastically hemmed in by others that even when we erase it, it can always be restored on the basis of what remains. The fabric of fact is woven tight. Facts are so closely intermeshed with each other as to form a connected network. Any change anywhere has reverberations everywhere. And this condition of things is old news.

Already in his influential *Treatise on Obligations*[21] the medieval scholastic philosopher Walter Burley (ca. 1275–ca. 1345) laid down the rule: *When a false contingent proposition is posited, one can prove any false proposition that is compatible with it.* His reasoning was as follows. Let the facts be that:

(P) You are not in Rome.
(Q) You are not a bishop.

And now, of course, also:

(R) You are not in Rome or you are a bishop. (P or not-Q)

All of these, so we suppose, are true. Let us now posit by way of a (false) supposition that:

Not-(P) You are in Rome.

Obviously, (P) must now be abandoned—"by hypothesis." But nevertheless, from (R) and not-(P) we obtain:

You are a bishop. (Not-Q)

And in view of thesis (Q), this is, of course, false. We have thus obtained not-Q where Q is *an arbitrary true proposition.*

It is clear that this situation obtains in general. For let p and q be any two (arbitrary but nonequivalent) facts. Then all of the following facts will also, of course, obtain: $\sim(\sim p)$, $p \,\&\, q$, $p \vee q$, $p \vee \sim q \vee r$, $\sim p \vee q$, $\sim(\sim p \,\&\, q)$, etc. Let us focus upon just three of these available facts:

(1) p
(2) q
(3) $\sim(\sim p \,\&\, q)$ or equivalently $p \vee \sim q$

Now, let it be that you are going to suppose not-p. Then of course, you must remove (1) from the list of accepted facts and substitute:

---

[21] Translated in part in Norman Kretzman and Eleonore Stump, *The Cambridge Translation of Medieval Philosophical Texts*, vol. 1: *Logic and Philosophy of Language* (Cambridge: Cambridge University Press, 1988), see pp. 389–412.

(1') ~p

But there is now no stopping. For together with (3) this new item at once yields ~q, contrary to (2). Thus, that supposition of ours that runs contrary to accepted fact (viz., not-p) has the direct consequence that *any other arbitrary contingent truth must also be abandoned*. This circumstance is one of the salient aspects of the aforementioned systemic integrity of fact.

And on this basis, Burley's Principle has far-reaching implications. As far as the logic of the situation is concerned, you cannot change anything in the domain of fact without endangering everything. The domain of fact has a systemic integrity that one disturbs at one's own cognitive peril: a change at any point has reverberations everywhere. Once you embark on a reality-modifying assumption, then as far as pure logic is concerned all bets are off. At the level of abstract logic, the introduction of belief-contravening hypotheses puts everything at risk: nothing is safe anymore. To maintain consistency, you must revamp the entire fabric of fact, which is to say that you confront a task of Sisyphean proportions. (This is something that people who make glib use of the idea of other possible worlds all too easily forget.) Reality is something too complex to be remade more than fragmentarily by our thought, which can effectively come to terms only with piecemeal changes *in* reality, but not with comprehensive changes *of* reality. Reality has a grip upon us that it will never entirely relax.

We arrive here at a fundamental diversity of views regarding possible world ontology, a disagreement made explicit in the Hartshorne–Adams controversy.

According to Charles Hartshorne, the actuality of our real world consists exactly in its complete descriptive determinateness. Descriptive indefiniteness carries us into the domain of kinds—of abstraction—so that there simply are not, strictly speaking, any other possible nonexistent *worlds* but only other possible *kinds of worlds*. For Hartshorne "definiteness is the soul of actuality." Were a possibility equally definite, it would be redundant to actualize it since it would then have to be the real world.[22]

For R. M. Adams, by contrast, "there is a plurality of possible worlds."[23] And so it is not just that there are *alternative possibilities for a world*, but there indeed are alternative possible worlds. Bizarre though it may seem, when we toss a coin and get a head, it transpires on such a view not just that there are (or were) alternative possibilities for that toss, but there really "are" (in some sense) alternative toss outcomes.

---

[22] Hartshorne, *Anselm's Discovery*, pp. 189–190.
[23] Robert M. Adams, "Theories of Actuality," *Nous* 8 (1974), pp. 211–231.

In this debate, Hartshorne surely has the better of it. Just what is it that makes *the* world—our world—into *a world*? The world is a manifold of concrete processes—some of which engender and others of which constitute things and beings of different sorts, intelligent beings included. The world is not a collection of facts, although there is doubtless a manifold of facts that characterizes and in its hypothetical totality identifies it. Nor is it a collection or manifold of states of affairs, although such a manifold doubtless serves to characterize and identify it as well. For facts and states of affairs obtain, while the world exists. Facts and states of affairs can only be apprehended by the intellect, whereas the world's doings can be experienced as well. We do not observe facts and states of affairs as such—though we may observe *that* they obtain. But we can observe and experience the world, or at least its features and components.

A *chaotic condition*, as natural scientists nowadays use this term, obtains when we have a situation that is tenable or viable in certain circumstances but where a change in these circumstances—even one that is extremely minute—will destabilize matters with imponderable consequences, producing results that cannot be foreseen in informative detail. When a precarious condition exists, even a small change in the prevailing circumstances can produce results that are at once large and unpredictable.

Historians and students of human affairs generally regard the state of public affairs as existing in a chaotic condition of this sort. Who can say, they are wont to ask, what would have happened had Cleopatra's nose been longer, let alone if one of Hitler's failed assassins had succeeded or if JFK's successful assassin had failed? The result of changes in the historical course of things cannot be assessed with any reliability. Historians—and diplomats as well—are reluctant to enter into what-if speculation because the firm ground not just of reality but of realism is then apt to dissolve beneath their feet.

And much the same case holds among present practitioners of astrophysics and cosmology. Given the structure of fundamental physical law as we have it, they see the universe as existing early on in a highly precarious position with respect to the value of the fundamental physical constants. They view the universe as incredibly fine-tuned, arguing that if its fundamental forces (gravitation, nuclear binding force, etc.) were even the least bit different, a universe of stable objects could never have developed.[24] But exactly what sorts of conditions would have resulted if the universe had to evolve under different conditions (different laws and operating principles) is a matter of risky speculation that permits no confident resolution on the basis of our knowledge about how matters stand.

---

24 See Martin Rees, *Just Six Numbers* (New York: Basic Books, 2000).

Reality, it is fair to say, is a chaotic system in the preceding sense. Every hypothetical change in the physical make-up of the real—however small—sets in motion a vast cascade of further such changes, either in regard to the world's furnishings or in the laws of nature. For as we conjure with those pebbles, what about the structure of the envisioning electromagnetic, thermal, and gravitational fields? Just how are these to be preserved as was, given the removal and/or shift of the pebbles? How is matter to be readjusted to preserve consistency here? Or are we to do so by changing the fundamental laws of physics?

And what is true at the physical level here holds at the ontological level as well. For it is readily seen that we cannot make hypothetical alterations in the make-up of the real without thereby setting out on a course that raises an unending series of questions. And not only do *content redistributions* raise problems but so do even mere *content erasures*, mere cancellations, because reality being as it is, they require redistributions to follow in their wake. If, by hypothesis, we zap that book on the self out of existence, then what is it that supports the others? Just exactly when and how did it disappear? And if it just vanished a moment ago, then what of the law of conservation of matter? And whence the material that is now in that book-denuded space? Once more we embark upon an endless journey.

2.5 How Fictional Possibilities Differ from Real Things

Fact differs crucially from fiction. Fictions, unlike real things, have a finite descriptive depth. For there are no (item-specific) facts of the matter about fictional objects over and above the things said about them in their formative suppositions and their consequences. Accordingly, fictional, unrealized possibilities will differ from actual realities in this respect, that with fictions the course of meaningful questioning soon comes to a stop. Did Sancho Panza trim his mustache short? And just how much of it had turned gray? Seeing that Cervantes did not tell us, there is no way of securing an answer. Fiction has finite cognitive depth: the quest for detail comes to an end of the line.

The world of fiction has informative limits in a way that the real world does not. Once the resources of ostension (of pointing and other modes of self-correlative locating) are available, we can speak simply of that dog (pointing) or "the only globe in this room" and manage to identify an object unambiguously with a bare minimum of descriptive elaboration. Only when dealing with nonexistents —objects beyond the reach of ostension—are we thrown upon descriptive resources all by themselves.

In clarifying the difference at issue, it is useful to distinguish between two types of information about a thing, namely what is *generic* and what is not. Generic information involves those features of the thing that it has in common with everything else of its kind or type. Now, a key fact about *fictional* particulars is that there is only so much one can ever manage to say about them. Thus, there are decided limits to what we can assert nongenerically about Don Quixote: namely, just as much as Cervantes told us. A point will always be reached with regard to fictional individuals when one cannot say anything characteristically new about them—presenting nongeneric information that is not inferentially implicit in what has already been said. With *real* things, on the other hand, there is no reason of principle why this process need ever terminate.

Again, real things always have potentialities—and counterfactual potentialities at that. (His neighbor would certainly have recognized Smith if he had not been wearing that false mustache.) But counterfactual reasoning about fictional objects is something else again—something far more problematic save in the generic case. Who (possibly excepting Cervantes) can say what Don Quixote would have thought of those windmills if he had not mistaken them for giants?

For reality forms a highly integrated ontological system, and the truth—the sum-total of what can correctly be said about it—correspondingly does the same. The systemic integrity of the real is a crucial fact for ontology and epistemology alike. And this fact has far-reaching ramifications.

And so, while fact is often *stranger* than fiction, it is always more *complex*. And the reason for this is straightforward. Fictions are creatures of thought, and the capacity for complexity management that we finite creatures possess is limited. Nature is vastly more complex than our brain—if only because we ourselves are merely a minor constituent of nature itself. The states of affairs that our minds can envision are vastly fewer and simpler than those that nature can present. To give just one rather obvious example, we cannot even begin to conceive the facts and phenomena that will figure on the agenda of the science of the future.

The cognitive depth of fiction is always finite because fiction—unlike reality—is the finite product of a finite mind. It relates to a realm whose constituent detail is the limited creation of a limited intellect. And unlike the real world, the realm of fiction is bounded by the limits of existing thought and language. Because of this, one is bound to reach the end of its road with a finite number of steps. But reality just isn't like that. It is like an unendingly layered onion; in theory, and presumably in practice as well, one can always peel off further layers of detail without ever reaching an end. Thus, reality has more complications, more twists and turns that are impossible to anticipate, than fiction ever could have. It can surprise and astound us in ways more profound than fiction ever could. Reality is to fiction as chess is to tic-tac-toe.

2.6 Realms of Thought

Homo sapiens is an amphibian. We live in the real world through our emplacement in space and time, equipped with bodies that can act upon and interact with the other realities that exist about us. But we also live in a thought world of ideas, beliefs, and suppositions. This thought realm itself divides into two sectors. On the one side there is the realm of thought about reality—of science, philosophy, and scholarship. On the other side there is the realm of conjecture and imagination, where the mind deliberately cuts loose from reality and produces a domain of its own—a realm of fancy, make-believe, and speculation that deals not with real things but with imaginatively devised artifacts of thought. This is the world of literature, and preeminently of fiction, where our thought quite deliberately leaves reality behind.

The possibility of fiction is inherent in language. It is built into the "is not" of negation. Since the negation of any assertion can itself also be asserted, the contentions at our disposal cannot possibly all be about reality alone. Once negation becomes available, we can immediately turn any factual statement into a fiction through its denial.

Why should we concern ourselves with unreal possibilities at all? For many reasons. Fictions can be entertaining and instructive—and useful as well because they enable speculative thought to penetrate to regions where realities do not go. On the negative side they enable us to engage in deceit, but on the positive side they enable us to do planning and contrive precautionary measures through engaging in "what if" thinking. They also enable us to broaden our understanding by means of thought experiments and the exploration of hypotheses.

Virtually every step in the history of human innovation and invention has come about in the wake of someone asking about imaginary possibilities, speculating about what would happen "if..." and reflecting on as yet unrealized and perhaps unrealizable possibilities. Thought about as yet nonactual and often never to be realized possibilities is a pervasive feature of innovation. The domain of the possible plays a prominent part in our thought about the affairs of nature and of man. Deliberation about alternatives, contingency planning, reasoning from hypotheses and assumptions, and thought experiments are but a few instances of our far-flung concern with possibility. The rational guidance of human affairs involves a constant recourse to possibilities: trying to guard against them to prevent them, to bring them to realization, etc. represents a significant part of our understanding of man's ways of thought and action.

To be sure, in the world of experiential fact one inevitably encounters the actual and never the (merely) possible. The range of possible things and states of affairs is not the discovery of acute observers of nature; it is at the bottom of the theoreticians' devising. It is thus not surprising that this conception has usually been displeasing to those who find metaphysical speculation distasteful, ranging from Hume to the logical positivists of the 1930s and their later congeners, such as W. V. O. Quine and Nelson Goodman. In fact, by the end of the 1940s this product of philosophical theorizing was in very bad repute. In recent years, however, the stock of the possible has risen sharply in the wake of the development, initially by Rudolf Carnap, of the "possible world" semantics for modal logic. The resulting conceptual solidification of modal logic—not only in its standard, alethic guise, but also in the direction of such applications as epistemic, temporal, and deontic logic—has made talk about possibilities and possible worlds once again philosophically respectable, not to say fashionable.

And this turn of events should not be seen as surprising. Throughout a long tradition in philosophy, theorists have generally insisted on regarding fictions not as useless falsehoods but as potentially serviceable instrumentalities of inquiry.[25] And rightly so, since they are useful tools of reason in the conduct of those hypothetical inquiries that can, by contrast, illuminate our understanding of the real. For as Hans Vaihinger emphasized,[26] fictions need not simply be playful devices of the speculative imagination, but can provide highly productive instrumentalities of knowledge. Perfectly elastic bodies, completely homogeneous fluids, and isolated bodies in space free of all external influences are all fictions. Such things do not exist in the real world. And yet we could not do physics without them. Nor does the fictional status of such "quasi-objects" (Vaihinger's term) as the North Pole or the equator or the prime meridian counteract against their great utility in helping us to find our way about in the real world. In sum, the contemplation of unreal possibilities facilitates our efforts both in the enjoyment of diverting play and in the accomplishment of useful work.

Moreover, seeing that our only *cognitive* access even to actual reality proceeds by way of what we think about it, it transpires that fact and fiction do not have the cognitive terrain to themselves. For there lies between them the nebulous borderland of error, where that which is taken to be fact is actually fiction

---

[25] The medievals spoke of a *fictio rationis* and even an *entia rationis* with just such ends in view.
[26] Hans Vaihinger, *Philosophie des Als ob* (Berlin: Reuther & Reichard, 1911).

		Something that in fact is:	
		real	unreal
is thought of as being:	real	knowledge	positive errors [illusion and delusion]
	unreal	negative errors [ignorance and oversight]	fiction

Display 1: Ways of Thinking

and that which is no more than fiction is mistaken to be fact. And this also makes room for a zone of uncertainty, where we incline to believe that something is so but are not really sure of it one way or the other.

As a first approximation, then, the domain of what we can consider divides into four sectors:
- the authentically actual or real: what actually exists as it really is,
- the putatively merely actual or merely supposedly real: what is (erroneously) thought to be real but in fact is not,
- the misperceived and unrecognized: what is (erroneously) thought to be unreal but in fact is not,
- the fictional: what is contemplated under the aegis of possibility and yet is neither real nor thought to be so.

The overall situation accordingly stands as per Display 1. In any case, however, thought is our only gateway to unreality. It is conception, not perception, that alone can reach nonexistents, and only in the realm of conjecture and imagination can we encounter things that are unreal and do not exist as such.

What people think is never by itself sufficient to ensure authenticity. They can go astray regarding factual issues exactly because it is not what they think but how matters actually stand that is ultimately decisive here. And even in purely speculative matters, there is more to it than simply what people think, since cogency depends not just on what they think but also on how this conforms to the requirement of logic.

2.7 Fiction

Paradoxical though it may seem, we can think about unicorns—have ideas and beliefs on the subject of unicorns—even though there are no unicorns for such thoughts to be about. Being available as an object of thought and actually existing are two very different things. Our thoughts themselves excepted, we humans can create neither things in the world nor truths about the world by simply thinking them. The reality of things is always something that reaches beyond the range of our thinking. Thought objects *(entia rationis* or *imaginationis)* are not in general actual objects as such. For a fictional or delusional object or individual is really not an object or individual at all—any more than a paper tiger is a tiger or a wooden horse is a horse. Such things are so in name only. The real world, by contrast, is a realm of things and facts—the material of observational experience and the stage-setting for action.

What, then, is to be made of the idea of fictional truth? What is involved in saying "the proposition p is true in the fiction F?" A recursive characterization is in order here which can be set out as follows:
1. F states that p explicitly *(expressis verbis)* and p is not self-contradictory;
2. p is a common-knowledge truth that is uncontradicted by truths in F, or;
3. p follows from propositions that are true in F, provided however that p is uncontradicted by anything that is true in F.

This characterization is recursive because it provides a starter set and then tells us how to work our way beyond it.

But when is it in order to say, "There is a fiction F in which the proposition p is true"? Provided that p is not self-contradictory, this will always be so. For then the fiction whose only assertion is p itself will do the job. In this sense, fiction and (logical) possibility are coordinate.

Fictions have a very limited potential for change. Granted, Arthur Conan Doyle might have made his Sherlock Holmes an eighteenth-century Londoner. But this simply means that we would then have had a different Sherlock Holmes altogether. It certainly does not mean that Sherlock Holmes as we know him had the capacity or potential of backsliding by 100 years. Fictions are defined by what is stipulated in and about them. Alter the stipulations and you alter the fiction itself. (But of course, alteration does not have a uniform size—it admits of lesser and larger.)

What is the status of those fictions? In his *Introduction to Mathematical Philosophy*, Bertrand Russell argued against Alexius Meinong that:

> The sense of reality is vital in logic, and whoever juggles with it by pretending that Hamlet has another kind of reality is doing a disservice to thought. A robust sense of reality is very necessary in forming a correct analysis about unicorns...and other such pseudo-objects.[27]

Russell then goes on to say, "If no one thought about Hamlet, there would be nothing left of him," and to point out that this would not be the case with reals such as Napoleon or The Rock of Gibraltar. And this position is sensible. For it lies in the nature of our concept of authentically real things that they exist independently of thought, but that thought objects should be mind-independent is questionable on the very the face of it. That "robust sense of reality" calls for acknowledging both the mind-independence of real existents and the merely imaginative and thereby mind-dependent nature of the acknowledged unreal.

It is, to be blunt, a very mistaken idea that to speak or think of something is to stand committed to the view that this exists in some manner or other. This, after all, would render it impossible in principle as a contradiction in terms even to question—let alone to deny—that something or other exists in no manner or shape.

Authentic fictions do not characterize actual reality and generally do not even *purport* to do so. They are not about the real world, but about a virtual reality that does not exist at all but only figures in the ideas—the imaginations, if you will—of thinking beings.[28] Imagination is thus the only entryway into the realm of the nonexistent. The sole feasible route for coming to cognitive terms with unreal possibilities is via assumptions, suppositions, and hypotheses. Fictions accordingly root in suppositions and hypotheses that reality makes available.

Although fictions are certainly not true of this world, they are nevertheless its products. Those conjectural fictions that concern us are fictions alright but their link to the real world is never altogether severed by this fact. In this manner, the present position is an existentialism: it prioritizes actuality as the basis

---

27 Bertrand Russell, *Introduction to Mathematical Philosophy* (London: Allen & Unwin, 1919), p. 170. See also Chapter 16, passim.
28 But what about fictions within fictions—fictional fictions, so to speak, that are supposed to be written by the fictional characters of works of fiction? For one thing, their author is indirectly the author of that framework fiction itself—the circumstance that their *supposed* authors are someone else is just another aspect of what makes that work fictional. That fiction produced by a fictional author is (insofar as realized) in fact the product of the actual author of the underlying work. There are, strictly speaking, no fictional fictions; there are no fictions unless real people really make them up. Fiction cannot detach itself from actuality altogether to take on a life of its own.

of possibility. The fictions that concern us are those that can be projected from a vantage point within this world. The limits of fictional possibility are set by the limits of real-world imaginability.

The state that fictions and mere possibilities occupy is not the real world but rather the realm of hypothetical thought. Real things—real objects, properties, events, and processes—are located within the real-world framework of space, time, and causality. To be sure, fictions can be supposed (thought, imagined, etc.) to be located there as well, but they do not actually have such a location and do not actually interact with real things. Nor do real things—minds, in particular—so function as to render fictions real. Minds only produce the ideas, conceptions, images, or pictures of such nonexistent things, and their status is that of thought things *(entia rationis)*, mere thought fictions.

And so, while fictions are merely figments of the imagination, they inevitably have an oblique relation to reality. The claim that something is fictionally true (in the fiction *F*) amounts to claiming that it is actually feasible (in the real world) to project a fiction *F* that has it so. Fictional truths—the truths of fictional worlds—are accordingly obliquely actual truths, truths about fictions realizable from within the realm of the real. Theirs is a dependent, derivative existence.

Accordingly, when D. M. Armstrong maintains[29] that what is needed for a viable semantics is "an Actualist, one-world account of fictional statements," he is entirely on the right track. Fictions are hinged on truths of sorts; specifically, truths about the explicit or tacit commitments of works of fiction or even fictional fictions can only be realized as such where there is someone to project them—an actual author. Fictions do not enjoy an "independent" existence. The being of something fictional lies in its having a role in some fiction or other.[30] A fictional world thus has no independent ontological status of its own; such existential (or quasi-existential) status as it has it derives from the real-world actualities of the fictional work that projects it. Of course, there are actual and possible fictions, and also truths, falsehoods, and possibilities with respect to fictional matters. But such items themselves will invariably have to be rooted in actual fictions. To envision a merely possible fiction is still to subordinate it to an actual supposition. Mere fictions, then, do not belong to the material of ontology proper—concerned as it is with matters of existence, being, and their approximation—but rather to the phenomenology of imagination.[31]

---

[29] Armstrong, *A Combinatorial Theory of Possibility*, pp. 45–50.
[30] But are there not "merely possible" fictions that are never projected as such? Certainly "there are" such fictions—but only insofar as second-order fiction (fictions about fictions) project them.
[31] This enterprise is a relatively under-cultivated area of deliberation. One of the few books on the topic is Edward S. Casey, *Imagining: A Phenomenological Study* (Indianapolis: University of

2.8 Fiction vs. Error

In relation to the actual facts, a supposition can be pro, neutral, or con. That is, it can be:
- *Factual* by way of *adaequatio ad rem*—in agreement with the actual facts. ("Suppose that you are now reading an English sentence.")
- *Agnostic* by way of a noncommittal indifference to the actual facts of the case. ("Suppose it rains in London on 1 January 3000.")
- *Fact-contravening* (or counterfactual)—by way of acknowledged disagreement with the actual facts. ("Suppose Napoleon were still alive.")

In the usual course of things, the texts one calls "fictions" are generally fact-contravening rather than merely agnostic; they proceed in deliberate contrariety to the actual facts. However, a futuristic *utopia* might well be agnostic one way or the other.

Thought and reality can accordingly be in or out of tune with one another in significantly different ways. Specifically, a narrative or account can depart from the truth:
- *inadvertently*, through what we would ordinarily characterize as falling into error,
- *knowingly and deliberately with a malign intent*, through what we would ordinarily characterize as deceptions and lies,
- *knowingly and deliberately with a benign intent*, through endeavoring to amuse, divert, instruct, stimulate (to thought or action), or the like.

The first two of these lie outside the range of the idea of fiction as it concerns us here, namely fiction that is intended and received as such. Note, in particular, that a mistaken account of something that inadvertently fails to present it as it is does not thereby become fictional. For example, suppose that a number of people report an extraordinary happening of some sort (say, a UFO sighting). And let it be that someone accepts these contentions at face value and proceeds to write a history of this putative episode—talking to all those eyewitnesses and weaving their reports into a coherent account. But—so let us also suppose—these individuals are a mixture of blatant liars and self-deceivers. That supposedly "historical" account produced by our author is certainly not fact. But is it fiction? Does failed history constitute fiction? The answer is clearly negative. Failed at-

---

Indiana Press, ²2000). However, its relevancy to the deliberations of the present book is somewhat tenuous.

tempts to represent the real may be "fictions" in substance but do not thereby become actual *fictions;* to call them such is to speak figuratively.

Facts must be consistent with one another. It lies in their nature that one fact cannot actually contradict another. But this is not necessarily so with fictions. A careless author can tell us on page 5 that X is older than Y and on page 183 that Y is older than X. However, the only fictions that matter for serious inquiry are coherent fictions—fictions that honor the principles of logic. Accordingly, the only fictions that need be of concern to us here are logically coherent fictions.

2.9 Possibilities and Merely Possible Objects

How deep does our commitment to fictions run? It certainly goes so far as possibilities—possible states of affairs. But does it extend to possibles—to nonexistent possible objects or even manifolds thereof? Are we committed to the idea that such "possibilia" have some sort of actuality or quasi-existence?

The position that Charles Chihara (1998) characterizes as "Serious Actualism" in *The Worlds of Possibility*[32] is based on much the same line of thought as that of the medieval precept *nihil sunt nullae proprietates*. That is, it takes the line that to be the bearer of a predicate—to have a property of some sort—is possible only for things that exist. The underlying principle may be represented symbolically as:

$(\exists F)Fx \to \exists!x$

On this perspective, to deny that something exists ("the present king of France," say) is thus to deny all properties to this supposed monarch (and so even to deny that a living male is at issue). And to concede that a putative idem is of such-and-such a sort—that is, has some property or other—is now by definition *ipso facto* to concede its existence.

On this approach, all property attributions to a nonexistent item are either flatly false (as in Bertrand Russell's theory of descriptions) or at best semantically meaningless in being indeterminate as between truth and falsity. Such a view is not entirely without its plausibility. For notwithstanding Alvin Plantinga's assertion to the contrary, the statement "Othello was a Moor" is clearly false[33]—if

---

[32] Charles Chihara, *The Worlds of Possibility: Modal Realism and the Semantics of Modal Logic* (Oxford Clarendon Press, 1998).
[33] Plantinga. *The Nature of Necessity* (Oxford: Clarendon Press, 1974), p. 162.

only because its effective equivalent "There was once a Moor named 'Othello' who had many of the properties and did many of the things Shakespeare attributes to his character of that name" is a patent falsehood. What it is true and correct to say is that "Shakespeare's play has it that Othello was a Moor who..." But that, of course, is something else again. Someone's having something be so—be it in fiction or in misimpression—clearly will not make it so as a matter of truth and fact. It is not that fictional things are flatly and simply so, but that they are held to be so in a story or by a supposition.

Oddly, the best way to make coherent sense of "Sherlock Holmes lived in London" is via the counterfactual "If there indeed had been a Sherlock Holmes along the lines envisioned by Conan Doyle, then he would have lived in London." And the warranting basis for this statement is simply that Conan Doyle's story *said* that Sherlock Holmes lived in London.[34]

All the same, however, fictional individuals do not wear their falsity on their sleeves. It is perfectly true to say, "According to Homer's *Iliad*, Odysseus was a king of Ithica who fought against the Trojans." But the status of Odysseus—as fact or fiction—remains totally indeterminate after this truth is conceded. His existence has a fact of the matter to it, and one way or the other is left unresolved. And this means that there need be no specifiable *descriptive* difference between:
- a real burglar,
- a fictional burglar (as someone depicts him),
- a delusional burglar (as someone envisions him).

No specific descriptive property that a real burglar has can be denied flatly to a fictional or delusional burglar. For as philosophers since Kant have stressed, existence itself is *not* a descriptive property. The difference between the real and unreal does not lie in matters of *description* but rather in matters of *condition*. Only the factor of existence separates the two; there need be no difference in point of any descriptive feature.

---

[34] To be sure the situation can get more complicated. We would doubtless accept "Sherlock Holmes had five and not six toes on his left foot." And here our best warranting evidence for the claim "If there indeed had been a ..." is not that Conan Doyle told us so but rather the fact that if one were not to be authorized in thinking it to be so, Conan Doyle would have told us otherwise so as to remove the standing presumption of normalcy that is operative in such contexts.

Fact is thus indistinguishable from fiction at the verbal level.[35] Every (non-paradoxical) statement implicitly purports its own truth, so that we can never tell from a statement itself whether it belongs to a work of fiction rather than some strange or even crazy attempt to present facts. We describe and discuss nonexistents in just the same way as existents. Contemplation alone cannot tell fact from fiction. If we lived in a Borges-reminiscent Logopolis—a library-city whose vast library with its verbally formulated materials were our only accessible reality—we could not tell fact from fiction in any decisive way. We could, to be sure, do statistics and consider what sorts of claims are supported by a majority of sources. But, of course, this could be a very shaky guide to truths as such. Not only can majorities err, but it could easily happen that two-thirds of our sources support P, two-thirds support Q, and two-thirds support *not-(P-and-Q)*. What we then have on our hands is clearly not truth but contradiction. However, as long as consistency is preserved, discourse alone underwrites no workable distinction between fact and fiction.

In consequence, the insistence of Charles Chihara's "Serious Actualism"? that discursive property attribution entails existence is ultimately untenable. For such a view takes us back to the erroneous doctrine of the Parmenides of Plato's dialogue of that name, who held that only the real can be discussed—that where there is meaningful talk, its object must be something actual. But to take this line is to confuse being an object of thought or discourse with being an actual and somehow existing object. Not a good idea!

Consider the following aporia:
1. Unicorns can be talked about meaningfully.
2. Whatever can be talked about meaningfully exists.
3. Unicorns do not exist.

These three theses are logically incompatible so that one of them, at least, must be abandoned. Now, there is little real alternative to retaining (1). We must therefore either join Parmenides and abandon (3) in favor of (2), or else take the reverse course and abandon (2) in favor of (3). And here all considerations of common sense and plausibility argue in favor of (2) abandonment. There is simply no cogent reason to think that to introduce objects of consideration via the attribution of properties requires existence. We need to be able to talk about various things without even the slightest existential or actualistic commitments. After

---

[35] Charles Sanders Peirce rightly observed that "the real world cannot be distinguished from the fictitious world by any description" (*Collected Papers*, ed. by Charles Hartshorne and Paul Weiss, vol. 2 [Cambridge, MA: Harvard University Press, 1931]), sect. 2.337.

all, if this were so, a meaningful denial of existence would be in principle impossible. And we know well that whatever can be affirmed can also be denied.

After all, while much of our thought moves in the realm of unreality, we fortunately do not live in Logopolis but in the realm of action and interaction within the environing world. And while there is much that is easily said, there is much less that is easily done. It is ultimately in the domain of praxis, of the actions and activities of intelligent agents, that the crucial difference between reality and fiction makes itself felt. At the reading room of make-believe. It is when we emerge once more into the open air and engage ourselves in life's affairs that our sturdy sense of reality reasserts itself.

2.10 A Historical Perspective on Thought Experiments and Unreal Possibilities

Unreal and merely possible *objects* are deeply problematic and of very questionable legitimacy. But unrealized *possibilities*—unreal states of affairs—have played a constructive role in Western philosophy since its very start.

The scholastics employed a whole host of terms for gaining entry, one way or another, into the realm of fictional deliberation: supposition, conjecture, presumption, hypothesis, and the like. And to us moderns, raised on imaginative children's nursery rhymes ("If wishes were horses, then beggars would ride") and subsequently accustomed to adult fictions, this sort of belief-suspensive thinking seems altogether natural. But it takes a serious logician to appreciate how complex and sophisticated suspension of disbelief and thought experimentation actually is. For what it involves is *not* simply the drawing of an appropriate conclusion from a given fact, but also the higher-level consideration that a particular thesis (be it fact or mere supposition) engenders various conclusions in its wake wholly irrespective of its own status in point of truth.

Thought experiments have long been common in natural science. Think, for example, of Albert Einstein's deliberations about what the world would look like if one were to travel along a ray of light. Think too of the physicists' assumption of a frictionless rolling body or the economists' assumption of a perfectly efficient market in the interests of establishing the laws of descent or the principles of exchange, respectively. Indeed, thought experiments are far more common in science than one may think. For Ernest Mach made the sound point that any sensibly designed *real* experiment should be preceded by a *thought* experiment that anticipates at any rate the possibility of its outcome.³⁶ The conclusion of *such* a thought experiment will clearly be hypothetical: "If the experiment turns out X-wise, we shall be in a position to conclude..." There is thus good reason to see thought experimentation as an indispensably useful accompaniment to actual experimentation.³⁷

It is noteworthy, moreover, that the use of thought experimentation in philosophy is as old as the subject itself. For in the history of Western thought, the explicit contemplation of possibilities deliberately acknowledged as unreal first became prominent among the Greek nature-philosophers of Presocratic times. It is they who invented thought experimentation as a cognitive procedure and practiced it with great dedication and versatility. It is worthwhile to consider some instances.

Xenophanes of Colophon (b. ca. 570 B.C.) resorted to the *explanatory* use of thought experiments:

> Xenophanes thinks that a mixing of the earth with the sea is going on, and that in time the earth is dissolved by the liquid. [Earlier there was a reverse phase of solidification of the sea.] He says that he has proofs of the following kind: shells are found inland, and in the mountains and in the quarries of Syracuse he says that an impression of a fish and of seaweed can be found, while an impression of a bayleaf was found in Pharos in the depth of the rock, and in Malta flat shapes of all marine object. These, he says, were produced when everything was long ago covered with mud, and the impression was dried in the mud.³⁸

This passage clearly shows that Xenophanes sought to substantiate his doctrine of alternative phases of solidification and dissolution through the use of thought experiments by way of explanatory conjectures.

Moreover, Xenophanes also introduced an important innovation. He inaugurated a style of *skeptical* use of thought experimentation. The salient thesis of Xenophanes affords the classical instance of this sort of reasoning:

---

36 Ernst Mach, "Ueber Gedankenexperimente," in: *Erkenntnis und Irrtum* (Leipzig, 1906), pp. 183–200 [see p. 187].
37 For an interesting discussion of scientific thought experiments, see Thomas S. Kuhn, "A Function for Thought Experiments in Science," in: Ian Hacking (ed.), *Scientific Revolutions* (Oxford: Oxford University Press, 1981), pp. 6–27. Further informative discussions are given in Tamara Horowitz and Geoffrey J. Massey (eds.), *Thought Experiments in Science and Philosophy* (Savage, MD: Rowman & Littlefield, 1991).
38 Hippolytus, *Ref.* I, 14, 5; Geoffrey S. Kirk and John E. Raven, *The Presocratic Philosophers*, 2nd ed. with the collaboration of M. Schofield (Cambridge: Cambridge University Press, 1983), p. 177.

2.10 A Historical Perspective on Thought Experiments and Unreal Possibilities — 41

> But if cattle and horses or lions had hands, or could draw with their hands and do the works that men can do, then horses would draw the forms of the gods like horses, and cattle like cattle, and they would make their bodies such as they each had themselves.[39]

This style of reasoning may be depicted as follows:
- Things being as they are, we incline to accept that P must be true.
- But suppose—by way of a "thought experiment"—that our situation were appropriately different (*as mutatis mutandis* it well might be).
- Then we would not accept P at all, but rather something else that is incompatible with P.
- Hence, we aren't really warranted in our categorical acceptance of P (seeing that, after all, this is merely a contingent aspect of our particular, potentially variable situation).

What we have here is a resort to thought experimentation as an instrumentality of thought that is powerfully skeptical in its impetus.

Yet another example of this process is afforded by the following argument presented by Xenophanes: "If god had not made yellow honey, men would consider figs far sweeter."[40] The reasoning of this last passage answers to the pattern:
1. Things being as they are, honey is "the sweetest thing in the world"—the very epitome of sweetness.
2. But suppose that honey did not exist.
3. Then figs would be the sweetest thing we know of, so that *they* would then be the epitome of sweetness.
4. Hence, we should not maintain that honey is actually the epitome of sweetness; it merely happens to be the sweetest thing we happen to know of.

This argumentation also clearly instantiates the procedure of skeptical thought experimentation. And Xenophanes repeatedly employed this general technique to support his deeply skeptical position to the effect that:

> No man knows, or ever will know, the truth about the gods and about everything I speak of: for even if one chanced to say the complete truth, yet one knows it not. Seeming is wrought over all things.[41]

---

39 Kirk and Raven, *The Presocratic Philosophers*, p. 169, fragment 15; Clement, *Stromata*, (Berlin: Akademia Verlag, 1960), v, 109, 3.
40 Kirk and Raven, *The Presocratic Philosophers*, p. 179, fragment 38.
41 Frag. 34; Kirk and Raven, *The Presocratic Philosophers*, p. 179.

The very formulation of the position reflects the use of the thought experiment: "Suppose even that we asserted the full truth on some topic. The fact still remains that we would not be able to identify it as such." In this way, Xenophanes relied on thought experiments to establish the relativity of human knowledge, a device that was later to prove a major armament in the arsenal of the Skeptics.

Of all the Presocratics, however, it was Heraclitus of Ephesus (b. ca. 540 B.C.) to whom thought experimentation came the most naturally. In his thought, the projection of "strange" suppositions is a prominent precept of method:

> If one does not expect the unexpected, one will not make discoveries [of the truth], for it resists discovery and is paradoxical.[42]

Sometimes, Heraclitus' epigrams have the lucid pungency of proverbial wisdom: "[Offered the choice,] donkeys would choose straw rather than gold."[43] A nice thought experiment this—who, after all, ever did, or would, offer gold to a donkey!? Here, then, we have a Xenophanes-reminiscent argument for a Xenophanes-reminiscent relativism.

Frequently, however, we find Heraclitus proceeding to earn his nickname of "the obscure." The following thought experiment is an example: "If all things were turned to smoke, the nostrils would distinguish them."[44] It is not all that clear just what we are to make of this. But one construction is that here again we have a skeptical line of thought akin to the relativistic deliberations of Xenophanes: "Were all things smoky, the information we could obtain about them would be limited to what we can learn by smelling. Reality thus eludes the senses—and accordingly our knowledge as well. For our information about things is limited to their sensory aspect alone, and sense experience provides only information geared strictly and solely to the correlatively sensory aspect of things."

Heraclitus was also given to thought experimentation of the following essentially analogical format:
- Suppose someone did X.
- Then (one would say that) he is F (mad, bad, or the like).

---

[42] The fragments of Heraclitus are here numbered in the order: Diels/Bywater. I have generally adopted Bywater's translation as improved by John Burnet, *Early Greek Philosophy* (London, ⁴1930). But see also Geoffrey S. Kirk, *Heraclitus: The Cosmic Fragments* (Cambridge: Cambridge University Press, 1954). Frag. 18/7; Burnet, *Early Greek Philosophy*, p. 133; Kirk and Raven, *The Presocratic Philosophers*, p. 195.
[43] Frag. 9/51; Burnet, *Early Greek Philosophy*, p. 137.
[44] Frag. 7/37; Burnet, *Early Greek Philosophy*, p. 136.

2.10 A Historical Perspective on Thought Experiments and Unreal Possibilities — 43

- But doing *Y* is just like doing *X* in the *F*-relevant regards.
- Therefore (one should also say that) someone who does *Y* is *F*.

Examples of this line of reasoning are as follows:

> They vainly purify themselves by defiling themselves with blood, just as if one who had stepped into the mud were to wash with mud. Anyone who saw him doing this would deem him mad.[45]

> For if it were not to Dionysius that they make the procession and sing the phallic hymn, the deed would be most shameless...[46]

> And they pray to these statues as though one were to talk to horses, not realizing the true nature of gods or demi-gods.[47]

All of these passages exemplify the analogical use of thought experimentation described in the preceding paradigm. (We could call someone who tries to clear away mud with mud crazy; what then of those who try to clear away blood with blood; will we not have to call them crazy too?) This analogy-exploiting, critical use of thought experimentation is clearly something quite different from its explanatory use as exemplified in Thales.

Thought experimentation of this sort is evidently a useful tool for a thinker who maintains the Heraclitean thesis that:

> To God all things are fair and good and right, though men hold some things wrong and some right.[48]

And so, Heraclitus repeatedly used thought experiments to expose what he saw as deficiencies in contemporary religious practice, continuing the critique of early Greek religiosity launched by Xenophanes.

Heraclitus also employed thought experiments to argue that if reality differed in a certain respect, things could not be as they are in other, correlative respects:

---

[45] Frag. 5/129 and 130; Burnet, *Early Greek Philosophy*, p. 145; Kirk and Raven, *The Presocratic Philosophers*, p. 211.
[46] Frag. 15/127; Burnet, *Early Greek Philosophy*, p. 141; Kirk and Raven, *The Presocratic Philosophers*, p. 211.
[47] Frag. 5/126; Burnet, *Early Greek Philosophy*, p. 141; Kirk and Raven, *The Presocratic Philosophers*, p. 211.
[48] Frag. 102/61; Burnet, *Early Greek Philosophy*, p. 137.

> If the sun did not exist, it would (always) be night (despite all the other stars).[49]

Or again:

> The learning of many things teaches not understanding, else would it have taught Hesiod and Pythagoras, and again Xenophanes and Hekataios.[50]

We learn from Aristotle's *Eudemian Ethics* (H1, 1235a25) that, according to Heraclitus:

> Homer [*Iliad*, XVIII, 107] was wrong in saying "Would that strife might perish from among gods and men" for there would be no musical scale unless high and low existed, nor living creatures without male and female, which are opposites [and all things would be destroyed].[51]

With such deliberations about the consequences of supposing that there is no auditory high/low or no biological male/female, we have a straightforward instance of a refutatory (negatively probative) use of hypothetical reasoning. This method too was apparently a favorite of Heraclitus.

As these various illustrations indicate, the deliberate projection and exploitation of unreal possibilities was a prominent and productive instrumentality in the philosophy of the Presocratics. It is they who deserve the credit of first putting fictions to work in matters of serious inquiry and exploiting the idea of learning fact from fiction.[52]

---

49 Frag. 99/31; Burnet, *Early Greek Philosophy*, p. 135.
50 Frag. 401/16; Burnet, *Early Greek Philosophy*, p. 134
51 Frag. 22/43; Burnet, *Early Greek Philosophy*, p. 136; Kirk and Raven, *The Presocratic Philosophers*, p. 196.
52 For further aspects of the issue, see "Thought Experimentation in Presocratic Philosophy," in the author's *Baffling Phenomena* (Savage, MD: Rowman & Littlefield, 1991), pp. 143–155. On thought experimentation more generally, see Horowitz and Massey, *Thought Experiments in Science and Philosophy*. On thought experimentation in history, see Robert Cowley (ed.), *What If?* (New York: G. P. Putnam's Sons, 1999) and Niall Ferguson, *Virtual History* (New York: Basic Books, 1999).

3 Reality vs. Appearance

3.1 Reality vs. Appearance

The facts constitute reality. The characterization of something as *real* often serves simply to distinguish what is actual and authentic from that which is merely purported to be so. Reality then contrasts with such alternatives as:
- fiction: contrived or imaginary accounts
- fakery: imitations, spurious pretenses, illusions, "magic"/sleight of hand
- delusion: mirages, "voices"
- pretense: deceit, make-believe, seeming, merely apparent
- ersatz: synthetic, substitute
- simulacra: look-alikes (stuffed owls)

This sort of thing is not, however, the object of consideration here. There is also the sense of "real" as typical or paradigmatic—as with "a real hero" or even "a real beginner." This too is not our present concern.

In philosophical discussions, the salient contrast is that between the way things actually are and the way they merely seem to be. This too is not quite our present focus. For here we shall consider reality as something that presents itself as it actually and authentically is, be it a real truth or a real fact. In consequence, the fundamental distinction is not between the appearance available in our experience and that which is inaccessibly external to it, but rather between that which is correct within our experience and that which is somehow incorrect or misleading. It would thus be wrong-headed to think of reality as a distinct *sort of being* different from "the phenomenal realm" of what people take to be so. The crux is not the contrast between what is and what is thought to be, but rather between what is thought correctly and what is thought incorrectly and imperfectly.

In this context of consideration, reality just exactly is, and is nothing but, the condition of things that people purport when they avoid making mistakes and achieve the *adaequatio ad rem* that the medievals saw as the hallmark of truth. Properly conceived, reality is by its very nature accessible to inquiry, albeit to an inquiry which in practice will often get matters wrong. Reality, that is to say, is not something inherently extra-experiential: a mysterious something outside our cognitive reach. Instead, it encompasses that sector of experience which involves the true facts of the matter. After all, there is no reason why things cannot be what they appear in various respects, and in these respects appear as they actually are. Save in the world of the paranoid, things can be as they appear to be.

In distinguishing reality from *mere* appearance, what is fundamentally at issue is thus not an *ontological* distinction of different realms of being or thing-kinds, but an *epistemological* distinction between a correct and an incorrect view of things. Properly understood, the operative contrast is thus not that between reality and the phenomenon, but between reality (veridical and authentic phenomena included) and what is misleading or incorrect. For reality can make its appearance in different guises—sometimes correctly and sometimes not. Appearance is not something different in kind and nature from reality, it is how reality presents itself. And reality is not by nature something different from appearance: it sometimes—and one would hope often—actually is what it appears to be.

The fault line between the real and the apparent runs not only across the space of alternative possible *realities*, but also across the spectrum of envisioned *possibilities* as well. Certain real possibilities can be overlooked; certain impossibilities can be misjudged as available. Thus, suppose that a family owns a cat which family members indifferently call either Tom or Puss, whereas a guest thinks that there are two similar cats corresponding to these names. Then, Tom being in the house and Puss being in the yard figures in the guest's spectrum of envisioned possibilities, whereas reality's spectrum of possibility excludes this prospect.

Just as we must distinguish between actual and merely putative reality, so we must distinguish between actual and merely envisioned possibilities. It thus transpires that there are both ontologically authentic and ontologically inauthentic possibilities, and that the spectrum of real possibilities can differ from that of envisioned possibility.

An envisioned prospect can be classified as:
- actual (real)
- nonactual (unrealized)
  —authentic possibility
  —inauthentic (merely putative) possibility

In matters of uncertainly (of ignorance and unknowing) this difference between authentic and merely putative possibility can play a significant role. If we do not know how many cats there are in the family, then all sorts of possibilities will transpire in our imagination that just are not real possibilities.

Appearance can—and often does—have features that reality not only does not have but could not possibly have. For appearance can be vague, indefinite, indeterminate, blurry. But reality—and any of its alternatives—does not have these options. Unlike appearance it must be exact, precise, and definite in its pervasive and endlessly ramified detail. The letter on the optician's eye chart is something definite, even though its appearance is a blurry mess (an option which reality itself does not have). When we see things confusedly and fuzzily "as through a glass, darkly" we know we are dealing with *mere* appearance; authentic reality—reality proper—just could not be like that. Nor need reality *agree* with true belief in some literal sense of the term. For true belief can be disjunctive, while reality cannot manage that. It cannot hesitate between alternatives, but must "make up its mind." It is just as weird as it sounds to say that reality is by nature that which we know not of.

The salient idea of realism is that the existence and nature of the world are matters distinct from anyone's thinking about it: that—minds themselves and their works aside—the real world is what it is without any reference to our cognitive endeavors, and that the constituents of nature are themselves *impervious*, as it were, to the state of our knowledge or belief regarding them. As one expositor puts it: "Even if there were no human thought, even if there were no human beings, whatever there is other than human thought (and what depends on that, causally or logically) would still be just what it actually is."[53] Such a realism is predicated upon a commitment to the notion that human inquiry addresses itself to what really and truly is—the condition of things whose existence and character are altogether independent of our cognitive activities. Reality is not subordinate to the operations of the human mind; on the contrary, man's mind and its dealings are but a minuscule part of reality. The nature of things reaches beyond experience because the things that experience leads us to accept as real are invariably seen as having features that experience does not reveal. (The features that realia have outrun what we know of them.) Appearance is not something by nature different from reality; it can/will encompass that sector of reality which presents itself to us as it indeed is—albeit only in point since reals will, and invariably must, have features that experience does not make manifest.

---

53 William P. Alston, "Yes, Virginia, There is a Real World," *Proceedings and Addresses of the American Philosophical Association* 52 (1979), pp. 779–808 [see p. 779]. Compare: "[T]he world is composed of particulars [individual existing things or processes] which have *intrinsic characteristics*—i.e., properties they have or relationships they enter into with other particulars independently of how anybody characterizes, conceptualizes, or conceives of them." Frederick Suppe, "Facts and Empirical Truth," *Canadian Journal of Philosophy* 3 (1973), pp. 197–212 [see p. 200].

3.2 The Historical Perspective

The distinction between Reality and Appearance, between what things are and what they seem to be, has been at the forefront of philosophy from the very start. Heraclitus of Ephesus (b. ca. 540 B.C.) taught that people, "the many," fail to understand the reality of things, for "Nature loves to hide" and that "The learning of many things teaches not understanding."[54] For the ancient Greek atomists, the sensory observation yields no knowledge to the true make-up of things. In Plato's *Republic*, the Myth of the Cave carries the lesson that the senses disfigure the idea-shaped nature of the real. Skeptics, empiricists, and rationalists alike saw the deliverances of phenomenal experience as important to convey the nature of reality. With Kant, the phenomena give no insight into the realm condition of things in themselves. With science-minded positivists, our experience is unable to convey the true scheme of things. With Nietzsche, it does no more than provide convenient or comforting illusions. And so it goes. Much of the Western philosophical tradition erects a cognitively insurmountable barrier between Reality and Appearance.

Against this great body of opinion, the present discussion will argue that a basic fallacy has been all too often at work—a confusion or conflation of a cognitive dichotomy of true and false judgment with an ontological distinction between the genuine and the fraudulent. For what is lost sight of in much of the tradition is that even though the real is that which in reality and authenticity exists, there is no reason why things as they appear cannot actually have the features as they appear to have.

Regrettably, the contrast between appearance and reality is often identified —and thereby confused—with that between reality on the one side and *mistaken* or *misleading* appearance on the other. And this conflation will, effectively by definition, erect a Chinese wall between reality and appearance. And this, rather paranoid, view of the matter must be put aside from the outset. To reemphasize: the philosophically significant contrast is not that between the real and the apparent as such, but rather that between the real and the *merely* apparent.

---

[54] Fragments 10 and 16, John Burnet, *Early Greek Philosophy* (London, ⁴1930).

3.3 An Ontological Fallacy

Why are the appearances as they are? Simply because that's how reality has matters work out. We explain appearances in terms of reality and if reality were (sufficiently) different, then appearances would not be as they are.

But why is reality as it is? As long as we are dealing with this or that item within its scope, we have the opportunity of explaining it with reference to the rest. But why reality overall is as it is—that is in the lap of the gods!

"Appearance" as philosophers use the term encompasses not just how things manifest themselves in sensory observation, but also the much broader range of how we take matters to stand—how we accept them to be not just in sense observation but in conceptual thought as well. On this basis it would be gravely fallacious to take the step—as is often done—to map the real/unreal distinction and the real/apparent distinction. For this mixes the sheep and the goats in heaping vertical appearance together with mere (i.e., nonvertical) appearance, thereby subscribing to the paranoid delusion that things are never what they seem to be.

Reality is not a distinct realm of being standing apart and separate from the manifold of what we know in the realm of appearance. Those "appearances" will —insofar as correct—be appearances of *reality* that represent features thereof. And, accordingly, the contrast between Reality and Appearance is not one carried out in the ontological order of different sorts of things. The realm of appearance is homogeneous with that of reality insofar as those appearances are correct.

The fact of it is that things sometimes—perhaps even frequently—are substantially as they appear to be. Reality and its appearance just are not two separate realms: there is nothing to prevent matters actually being as they are perceived and/or thought to be.

Appearance can in principle be something self-contained and self-sufficient. When it appears to one that there is a pink elephant in your corner, there need not be a *something* in that corner which appears as an elephant to me. Appearances may not only be deceiving, but they may also be illusionary. In the sphere of appearance, things can go seriously awry. And yet while matters can go wrong here, they need not do so. Things can indeed be as they appear. Total paranoia is clearly unwarranted. There is no reason, that is, why appearance and reality cannot agree in this or that detail.

Could Reality possibly be just exactly as it appears? It certainly could in this or that detail. When Appearance put the cat on the mat, there is no reason why. Reality cannot also do so. But Reality could not be just as it appears overall and in total. For Appearance has imprecisions, vagueness, blank specks of ignorance.

Reality could not possibly be like that. There is always more to things than "meets the eye" of the appearances.

The crux of the matter is that things sometimes—perhaps even frequently—are exactly as they appear to be. For there is clearly nothing to prevent that things actually are as they are perceived and/or thought to be. In point of actual separation, the crucial contrast is that between appearance and reality.

A great deal of mischief has been done in philosophy by the idea of a "veil of appearance" based on the distinction of the real from the unreal. For this cannot be identified with the epistemically more natural distinction between:
- appearance = how things are thought to be, and
- reality = how things actually are.

It is critically important in the interests of clarity and agency not to conflate these two distinctions.

Kant maintained—very problematically indeed—that appearance and reality are different forms of being: the former, appearance, comprised of "mere phenomena" whose nature is irremediably mental, and the latter, reality, comprises of "things as they are in themselves" and thereby of a nature completely unknowable to us. He was convinced (for complex reasons) that something should not actually be as true thought about it represents it as being (which is, after all, what true thought is all about). But this view of the matter is deeply problematic. Reality and appearance are not two substantively different realms; they involve two different thought perspectives upon one selfsame realm—the realm of that which exists and thereby lays claim to authentic reality.

What happens all too commonly in this connection is that philosophers transmute such a *conceptual distinction* into a *substantial separation*. But it is a grave error to take the view that what is conceptually *distinct* is *ipso facto* also substantially *disjoint*. This idea is every bit as flawed as would be the idea that distinguishing between musicians and carpenters conceptually means that an item of the one type could not also belong to the other—that a carpenter could not possibly be a musician as well. In specific, it is emphatically not the case that knowledge of reality is in principle infeasible because reality is somehow a *Ding an sich*, hidden away behind the "veil of appearance." The fact of it is that much of reality stands in front of that "veil" by encompassing that part of appearance which happens to be correct.

And so, the salient lesson of acknowledging a potential discrepancy between Reality and Appearance is emphatically not that skepticism is true and that secure knowledge is unavailable. It is, rather, that a cogent skepticism is plausible only at the level of grandiosity in holding a secure knowledge *of the whole* to be unachievable—knowledge that is complete and correct in every detail. The facts that speak for skepticism are simply no impediment to achieving secure knowledge in limited and local matters.

3.4 The Impetus of Mind

To be sure, the linkage of reality to what true thought maintains seemingly still leaves open the question of: Insofar as thought agrees with reality, which is the dependent variable and which is the independent variable in this thought/reality coordination? Does reality depend on what is thought or does thought depend on reality? Are we to be realists and hold that reality is thought independent; it is as is independently of what people think? Or are we to be idealists and hold that reality is as is because thought correctly presents it so?

The long and short of it is that, as regards dependency, the relation of thought to reality is a two-way street. Thought depends *ontologically* upon reality, because thought proceeds as is because that's how reality works it out. And reality depends *epistemologically* on thought because the only pathway to reality that is open to cognizing beings is via their thought-mediated experience of it. The failure to give due heed to the distinction between an *ontological* and a *conceptual* dependency is yet another instance of a misunderstanding that has brought philosophical mischief in its wake.

And yet, the fact of it is that things sometimes—perhaps even frequently—are substantially as they appear to be. Reality and its appearance are not two separate realms: there is nothing to prevent matters actually being as they are perceived and/or thought to be. The paramount contrast is that between how things are *correctly* thought to be and how they are *erroneously* thought to be. And the salient distinction is accordingly not that between mere belief and actual fact, but that between belief that is true (correct) and that which is not—a distinction of status that involves no separation of kinds. When we accept a belief as true, we have no alternative but to hold that that is how reality actually stands.

Granted, reality need not be exactly as true thought has it. For true thought can be vague, inexact, even disjunctive. But reality must always lie at the basis as the truth-maker, the state of things that provides for the truth of true thinking. And there is more to it than even this. For it is also a matter of principle that: True claims about things can in principle characterize reality as it really is in some respect or aspect. This principle represents an indissoluble link between epistemology and ontology inherent in that medieval idea of truth as adequation to fact, the issue being one of conceptual relations and not of factual inquiry.[55]

Reality can stand by itself on a footing of its own. But appearance requires a mind—an intellect to which something appears. So, if life in the universe were extinguished so that there is no thought, would reality still remain? Yes—of course it would. After all, the thought correlativity of reality does not hinge on what thought *does* do, but on what it *could* do. The linkage of reality to thought is not categorical but conditional, not actualistic but potentialistic. (It is this circumstance that makes it possible to operate an idealistic realism.) Reality stands coordinate with the realm of true thought: things *really* are the way they are—or would be—*truly* thought to be. But the potentialistic nature of true thought indicates a richness that far exceeds our actual thought about it.[56]

If we did not have at our disposal the distinction between reality and its appearance, we would be saddled with a decidedly strange view of the nature of the real, and would have no way to effect a viable accommodation between subjective perception and the rational cogency of knowledge.

3.5 The Reality Postulate

Seeing that the existence of an objective domain of impersonally real existence is not a *product* of but a *precondition* for empirical inquiry, its acceptance has to be validated in the manner appropriate for postulates and prejudgments of any sort —namely in terms of its ultimate utility. Bearing this pragmatic perspective in mind, let us take a closer look at this issue of utility and ask: What can this postulation of a mind-independent reality actually do for us?

The answer is straightforward. The assumption of a mind-independent reality is essential to the whole of our standard conceptual scheme relating to inquiry and communications. Without it, both the actual conduct and the rational legitimation of our communicative and investigative (evidential) practice would be destroyed. Nothing that we do in this cognitive domain would make sense if we did not subscribe to the conception of a mind-independent reality.

To begin with, we indispensably require the notion of reality to operate the classical concept of truth as "agreement with reality" *(adaequatio ad rem)*. Once we abandon the concept of reality, the idea that in accepting a factual claim as true we become committed to how matters actually stand—"how it really is"—

---

55 Compare the author's *Metaphysics* (Amherst, NY: Prometheus, 2006), pp. 22–24.
56 On these issues, see also the author's *Metaphysics*, pp. 4–7.

would also go by the board. The very semantics of our discourse constrain its commitment to realism; we have no alternative but to regard as real those states of affairs claimed by the contentions we are prepared to accept. Once we put a contention forward by way of serious assertion, we must view as real the states of affairs it purports, and must see its claims as facts. We need the notion of reality to operate the conception of truth. A factual statement to the order of "There are pi mesons" is true if and only if the world is such that pi mesons exist within it. By virtue of their very nature as truths, true statements must state facts: they state what really is so, which is exactly what it is to "characterize reality." The conception of *truth* and of *reality* come together in the notion of *adaequatio ad rem*—the venerable principle that to speak truly is to say how matters stand in reality, in that things actually are as we have said them to be.

In the second place, the nihilistic denial that there is such a thing as reality would destroy once and for all the crucial Parmenidean divide between appearance and reality. And this would exact a fearful price from us: we would be reduced to talking only of what we (I, you, many of us) *think* to be so. The crucial contrast notion of the *real* truth would no longer be available: we would only be able to contrast our *putative* truths with those of others, but could no longer operate the classical distinction between the putative and the actual, between what people merely *think* to be so and what actually *is* so. We could not take the stance that, as the Aristotelian commentator Themistius put it, "that which exists does not conform to various opinions, but rather the correct opinions conform to that which exists."[57]

The third point is the issue of cognitive coordination. Communication and inquiry, as we actually carry them on, are predicated on the fundamental idea of a real world of objective things, existing and functioning "in themselves," without specific dependence on us and so equally accessible to others. Intersubjectively valid communication can only be based on common access to an objective order of things. The whole communicative project is predicated on a commitment to the idea that there is a realm of shared objects about which we as a community share questions and beliefs, and about which we ourselves as individuals presumably have only imperfect information that can be criticized and augmented by the efforts of others.

This points to a fourth important consideration. Only through reference to the real world as a *common object* and shared focus of our diverse and imperfect epistemic strivings are we able to effect communicative contact with one another.

---

[57] Moses Maimonides, *The Guide for the Perplexed*, tr. by Chaim Rabin (Indianapolis and Cambridge: Hackett), I, 71, 96a.

Inquiry and communication alike are geared to the conception of an objective world: a communally shared realm of things that exist strictly "on their own," comprising an enduring and independent realm within which—and, more importantly, with reference to which—inquiry proceeds. We could not proceed on the basis of the notion that inquiry estimates the character of the real if we were not prepared to presume or postulate a reality for these estimates to be estimates of. It would clearly be pointless to devise our characterizations of reality if we did not stand committed to the proposition that there is a reality to be characterized.

The fifth item is a recourse to mind-independent reality which makes possible a "realistic" view of our knowledge as potentially flawed. A rejection of this commitment to reality *an sich* (or to the actual truth about it) exacts an unacceptable price. For in abandoning this commitment we also lost those regulative contrasts that canalize and condition our view of the nature of inquiry (and indeed shape our conception of this process as it stands within the framework of our conceptual scheme). We could no longer assert: "What we have there is good enough as far as it goes, but it is presumably not 'the whole real truth' of the matter." The very idea of inquiry as we conceive it would have to be abandoned if the contract conceptions of "actual reality" and "the real truth" were no longer available. Without the conception of reality, we could not think of our knowledge in the fallibilistic mode we actually use—as having provisional, tentative, improvable features that constitute a crucial part of the conceptual scheme within whose orbit we operate our concept of inquiry.

Reality (on the traditional metaphysicians' construction of the concept) is the condition of things answering to "the real truth"; it is the realm of what really is as it really is. The pivotal contrast is between "mere appearance" and "reality as such," between "our picture of reality" and "reality itself," between what actually is and what we merely think (believe, suppose, etc.) to be. And our allegiance to the conception of reality, and to this contrast that pivots upon it, roots in the fallibilistic recognition that at the level of the detailed specifics of scientific theory, anything we presently hold to be the case may well turn out otherwise—indeed, certainly will do so if past experience gives any auguries for the future.

Our commitment to the mind-independent reality of "the real world" stands together with our acknowledgment that, in principle, any or all of our *present* scientific ideas as to how things work in the world, at *any* present, may well prove to be untenable. Our conviction in a reality that lies beyond our imperfect understanding of it (in all the various senses of "lying beyond") roots in our sense of the imperfections of our scientific world-picture—its tentativity and potential fallibility. In abandoning our commitment to a mind-independent reality, we would lose the impetus of inquiry.

Sixth and finally, we need the conception of reality in order to operate the causal model of inquiry about the real world. Our standard picture of man's place in the scheme of things is predicated on the fundamental idea that there is a real world (however imperfectly our inquiry may characterize it) whose causal operations produce *inter alia* causal impacts upon us, providing the basis of our world-picture. Reality is viewed as the causal source and basis of the appearances, the originator and determiner of the phenomena of our cognitively relevant experience. "The real world" is seen as causally operative both in serving as the external molder of thought and as constituting the ultimate arbiter of the adequacy of our theorizing. (Think here again of C. S. Peirce's "Harvard experiment.")

In summary, then, we need that postulate of an objective order of mind-independent reality for at least six important reasons:
1. to preserve the distinction between true and false with respect to factual matters and to operate the idea of truth as agreement with reality;
2. to preserve the distinction between appearance and reality, between our *picture* of reality and reality itself;
3. to serve as a basis for intersubjective communication:
4. to furnish the basis for a shared project of communal inquiry;
5. to provide for the fallibilistic view of human knowledge;
6. to sustain the causal mode of learning and inquiry and to serve as a basis for the objectivity of experience.

The conception of a mind-independent reality accordingly plays a central and indispensable role in our thinking about communication and cognition. In both areas alike we seek to offer answers to our questions about how matters stand in this "objective realm," and the contrast between "the real" and its "merely phenomenal" appearances is crucial here. Moreover, this is also seen as the target and *telos* of the truth-estimation process at issue in inquiry, providing for a common focus in communication and communal inquiry. The "real world" thus constitutes the "object" of our cognitive endeavors in both senses of this term—the *objective* at which they are directed and the *purpose* for which they are exerted. And reality is seen as pivotal here, affording the existential matrix in which we move and have our being, and whose impact upon us is the prime mover for our cognitive efforts. All of these facets of the concept of reality are integrated and unified in the classical doctrine of truth as it corresponds to fact *(adaequatio ad rem)*, a doctrine that only makes sense in the setting of a commitment to mind-independent reality.

Accordingly, the justification for this fundamental presupposition of objectivity is not *evidential* at all; postulates are not based on evidence. Rather, it is *functional*. We need this postulate to operate our conceptual scheme. The justification of this postulate accordingly lies in its utility. We could not form our existing conceptions of truth, fact, inquiry, and communication without presupposing the independent reality of an external world. We simply could not think of experience and inquiry as we do. (What we have here is a "transcendental argument" of sorts, from the character of our conceptual scheme to the acceptability of its inherent presuppositions.) The primary validation of that crucial objectivity postulate lies in its basic functional utility in relation to our cognitive aims.

We do—and must—adopt the standard policy that prevails with respect to all communicative discourse of letting the language we use, rather than whatever specific informative aims we may actually have in mind on particular occasions, be the decisive factor with regard to the things at issue in our discourse. For if we were to set up our own conception of things as somehow definitive and decisive, we would at once erect a barrier not only to further inquiry but also—no less importantly—to the prospect of successful communication with one another. Communication requires not only common *concepts* but also common *topics*, interpersonally shared items of discussion, a common world constituted by the self-subsistently real objects basic to shared experience.

The factor of objectivity reflects our basic commitment to a communally available world as the common property of communicators. Such a commitment involves more than merely *de facto* intersubjective agreement. Such agreement is a matter of *a posteriori* discovery, while our view of the nature of things puts "the real world" on a necessary and *a priori* basis. This stance roots in the fundamental convention of a shared social instance on communication. What links my discourse with that of my interlocutor is our common subscription to the governing presumption (a defensible presumption, to be sure) that we are both talking about the shared thing, our own possible misconceptions of it notwithstanding. This means that no matter how extensively we may change our minds about the *nature* of a thing or type of thing, we are still dealing with exactly the same thing or sort of thing. It assures reidentification across discordant theories and belief systems.

Our concept of a *real thing* is such that it provides a fixed point, a stable center around which communication revolves, an invariant focus of potentially diverse conceptions. What is to be determinative, decisive, definitive, etc., of the things at issue in my discourse is not my conception, or yours, or indeed anyone's conception at all. The conventionalized intention discussed means that a coordination of conceptions is not decisive for the possibility of communication. Your statements about a thing may well convey something to me even if my conception of it is altogether different from yours. To communicate we need not take ourselves to share views of the world, but only take the stance that we share the world being discussed. This commitment to an objective reality that underlies the data at hand is indispensably demanded by any step into the domain of the publicly accessible objects essential to communal inquiry and interpersonal communication about a shared world. We could not establish communicative contact about a common objective item of discussion if our discourse were geared to the substance of our own idiosyncratic ideas and conceptions.

And so, an important lesson emerges. The rationale of a commitment to ontological objectivity is, in the final analysis, functionally or pragmatically driven. Without a presuppositional commitment to objectivity with its acceptance of a real world independent of ourselves that we share in common, interpersonal communication would become impracticable. Objectivity is an integral part of the *sine qua non* presuppositional basis of the project of meaningful communication. To reemphasize, if our own subjective conceptions of things were to be determinative, informative communication about a world of shared objects and processes would be rendered unachievable.

3.6 Communicative Realism

Realism, then, is a position to which we are constrained not by the push of evidence but by the pull of purpose. Initially, at any rate, a commitment to realism is an *input* into our investigation of nature rather than an *output* thereof. Ultimately, however, it does not represent a discovered fact, but a methodological presupposition of our praxis of inquiry; its status is not constitutive (fact-descriptive) but regulative (praxis-facilitating). Realism is not a factual discovery, but a practical postulate justified by its utility or serviceability in the context of our aims and purposes, seeing that if we did not *take* our experience to serve as an indication of facts about an objective order, we would not be able to validate any objective claims whatsoever. (To be sure, what we can—and do—ultimately discover is that by taking this realistic stance we are able to develop a praxis of inquiry and communication that proves effective in the conduct of our affairs.)

The ontological thesis that there is a mind-independent physical reality to which our inquiries address themselves more or less adequately—and always imperfectly—is the key contention of realism. But on the telling of the presenting analysis, this basic thesis has the epistemic status of a presuppositional postulate that is initially validated by its pragmatic utility and ultimately retro-validated by the satisfactory results of its implementation (in both practical and theoretical respects). Our commitment to realism is, on this account, initially not a product of our *inquiries* about the world, but rather reflects a facet of how we *conceive* the world. The sort of realism contemplated here is accordingly one that pivots on the fact that we *think* of reals in a certain sort of way, and that in fact the very conception of the real is something we employ because doing so merits our ends and purposes.

Now, insofar as realism ultimately rests on a pragmatic basis, it is not based on considerations of independent substantiating evidence about how things actually stand in the world, but rather on considering, as a matter of practical reasoning, how we do (and must) think about the world within the context of the projects to which we stand committed. In this way, the commitment to a mind-independent reality plays an essentially utilitarian role as providing a functional requisite for our intellectual resources (specifically for our conceptual scheme in relation to communication and inquiry). Realism thus harks back to the salient contention of classical idealism that values and purposes play a pivotal role in our understanding of the nature of things. And we return also to the characteristic theme of idealism—the active role of the knower not only in the constituting but also in the constitution of what is known.

To be sure, this sort of idealism is not substantive but methodological. It is not a rejection of real objects that exist independently of mind and as such are causally responsible for our objective experience; quite the reverse, it is designed to facilitate their acceptance. But it insists that the justificatory *rationale* for this acceptance lies in a framework of mind-supplied purpose. For our commitment to a mind-independent reality is seen to arise not *from* experience but *for* it—for the sake of putting us into a position to exploit our experience as a basis for validating inquiry and communication with respect to the objectively real.

"Reality as such" is no doubt independent of our beliefs and desires, but what alone can concern us is reality as we view it. And the only view of reality that is available to us is one that is devised by us under the aegis of principles of acceptability that we subscribe to because doing so serves our purposes.

A position of this sort is in business as a realism all right. But seeing that it pivots on the character of our concepts and their *modus operandi*, it transpires that the business premises it occupies are actually mortgaged to idealism. The fact that objectivity is the fruit of communicative purpose allows idealism to infiltrate into the realist's domain.

And the idealism at issue cuts deeper yet. No doubt, we are firmly and irrevocably committed to the idea there is a physical realm out there which all scientific inquirers inhabit and examine alike. We hold to a single, uniform physical reality, insisting that all investigations exist within and investigate IT: this one single shared realism, this one single manifold of physical objects and laws. But this very idea of a single uniform domain of physical objects and laws represents just exactly that—*an idea of ours*. And the idea is itself a matter of how we find it convenient and efficient to think about things: it is no more—though also no less—than the projection of a theory devised to sort the needs and conveniences of our intellectual situation.

This approach endorses an object-level realism that rests on a presuppositional idealism at the justificatory intralevel. We arrive, paradoxical as it may seem, at a realism that is founded, initially at least, on a fundamentally idealistic basis—a realism whose ultimate *justificatory basis* is ideal.

4 Conceiving Facts

4.1 Conceivability

For the most part we do not make facts: generally, they are just "out there," beyond our reach and control. All that we can then do is to think about them. But alike in making and in thinking about them we must have a conception of the facts.

The human mind has two principal cognitive powers: to image possibilities and to adjudge realities, enabling it to deal with fact and fiction alike. In a way, possibility management is the more fundamental. After all, if it's not possible then it can't possibly be real, and if it's not conceivable by us then we can't possibly accept it as actual. (All this is not, however, to say that if we cannot conceive of it then it can't be actual—reality and possibility alike can hold very big surprises for us.)

Conceivability is a matter of the possibilities that people are in a position to contemplate given the concepts and beliefs at their disposal. It relates to both facts and fictions. A four-sided triangle is inconceivable, one that is small and red is not. The concepts and beliefs at our disposal set our conceptual horizons. They delimit the range of our cognitive domain beyond which there lies what is, for us, mere *terra incognita*.

Epistemologists have focused on our knowledge of the real and have pretty well left possibility to the logicians. But the logicians have left the epistemology of possibility to others: their concern has been with what actually *is* possible, and they have omitted concern for how we conduct the applicative business of learning and reasoning about it. The present discussion will offer some comments on this rather neglected theme.

Conceivability calls for being available as an object of meaningful thought. It is not a matter of imagining or picturing. One cannot picture or imagine a thousand-sided polygon but one can certainly conceive in describing it and supposing its possibility.

Some conceptions have to be formed systematically—they ramify out into related issues whose co-understanding they presuppose. To have a proper conception of a propeller, one needs some understanding of the technology of early airplanes; to have a proper conception of an electron, one needs some understanding of subatomic physics.

As construed here, conceivability is the prospect of entertaining something as a meaningful possibility. Two sorts of items can be inconceivable to a person: things and facts. A thing is effectively inconceivable to someone if its definitive features are wholly outside that person's experience. (A Polynesian cannot conceive of solid water (i.e., ice), Aristotle could not conceive of X-rays.) A fact is inconceivable to someone when they have totally unshakable belief in its contrary. (Pigs that can fly like bats or bees are inconceivable to most of us.) For individuals, the personally inconceivable is either (or both) foreign to established experience or contrary to absolutely certain conviction.

The truths we contemplate may well not actually *characterize* reality, but rather be related to its constitution in more complex and indirect ways. For example, we can have:
- negative truths ("No cats talk.")
- vague truths ("He looked thirtyish.")
- inexact truths ("It looks something like this.")
- approximate truth ("The table is roughly 32 inches wide.")
- indefinite truths ("She looked pleased.")
- possibilistic truths ("It might rain.")
- impressionistic truths ("They were lucky.")
- metaphorical truths ("It was a veritable bonanza.")

No doubt such truths will be so in virtue of what the facts are. But they certainly do not *characterize* the real facts. Thus, truths can be indefinite. But reality cannot; it must be concrete (rather than an abstract), definite (rather than vague, approximate, etc.), and positive (rather than negative), whereas truths need not be any of these. Thus, truths do not *correspond* to what the realities are, although their being truths is (loosely) dependent upon it. All truths have their "truth-makers" in reality—that is, there is (and must be) a "basis in concrete fact" for every truth, an aspect of reality in virtue of which that truth is true.

To *characterize* reality—to *"agree"* with it—would be to give an accurate representation of it that is correct and complete in all relevant detail. Thus, only a detailed (precise, exact, accurate) account of something can actually correspond to the reality of it. And this is something which our language-framed statements about the real—however true—almost invariably fail to achieve. An account that is vague, imprecise, approximate, fuzzy, or the like may well be *true* but nevertheless not be accurately consonant with it. The truth in general falls well short of the detailed accuracy that would be required here. No doubt the truth is *grounded* in reality, and concurs with it. But it certainly need not and often will not *correspond* to it.

Seeing that our true contentions regarding reality are generally indefinite (vague, ambiguous, metaphorical, etc.) whereas reality itself is always definite (precise, detailed, concrete), it follows that those truths of ours do not—cannot—give an adequate (faithful, accurate, precisely correct) account or representation of reality. It is a merciful fact of life in human communication that truth can be told without the determinative detail of precision, accuracy, and the like, required for an accurate representation of the facts. Reality's detail involves more than we can generally manage. We can achieve the truth and nothing but the truth, but the whole truth about something is always beyond our grasp.

There was a time when it was fashionable for English Hegelian philosophers such as Bernard Bosanquet to say that only the accurate truth is the real truth and that the real truth of things must be altogether exact and fully detailed. But this contention would involve us in critical errors of omission regarding reality. Thus, we would not be able to declare the truth that grass is green or the sky is blue. And moreover, we would lose the crucial principles that the logico-conceptual consequences of the truth must also be true, seeing that the inference from "There are 48 people in the room" to its vague logical consequence "There are several dozen people in the room" would now not qualify as correct, since the latter would not qualify as a truth. The truth is one thing, but the *precise* truth or the *exact* truth quite another.[58] Our truths need surely not convey the detailed nature of the realities that make them so. But in the end, we cannot come to cognitive grips with reality save via our true acceptance about it.

4.2 Inconceivability

Certain considerations may be inconceivable to someone owing to having mistaken ideas on the subject or because certain matters do not fall within the range of their experience. This sort of subjective (person-relative) inconceivability is not at issue here. Here, we are concerned only with inconceivability relative to meaningful conceptions and correct convictions, matters inconceivable on the basis of correct and adequate information.

And there is also the impersonal or generic conceivability characteristic of the typical and representative members of the group. Generic inconceivability is not a matter of what a particular individual can manage in thought but of what can be managed in rational thought as such. Items that are inconceivable include a greatest integer, a fastest motion, a largest circle—things whose very identification includes a contradiction in terms. But either way, personal or generic, conceivability requires experiential access and consonant belief.

---

58 For relevant material, see also the author's *Metaphysics* (Amherst, NY: Prometheus Books, 2006), pp. 101–104.

We must, however, distinguish between subjectively person-relative conceivability, which is a function of a particular individual's knowledge, and objective or culture-relative conceivability, which is a function of language and cognitive state of the art. Both alike set limits but these differ in that the former are personal and the latter societal. From the theoretical point of view, it is the latter that are paramount, and our focus will be on groups rather than individuals, and principles rather than people.

There are three principal levels of inconceivability/conceivability:
1. *Grammatical.* Meaningless gibberish: having not informative sense ("Twas brillig..."). Violation: Meaninglessness.
2. *Logico-Conceptual.* At odds with what is to be seen as absolutely necessary ("A day without hours; a four-sided triangle; a sphere without a center"). Violation: Incoherence.
3. *Factual.* Inconsistent with what is seen as a patent and necessary fact ("A talking tree; a brass banana"). Violation: Unacceptability.

Rather different modes of necessity/possibility are at issue with 2 and 3. Level 2 deals with absolute or logico-conceptual necessity/possibility ($\square$ and $\lozenge$). This is the way in which it is necessary for triangles to have vertices or a bird to have wings. By contrast, level 3 is the way in which it is necessary for animals to secure nourishment in order to survive or for fires to have oxygen in order to burn. These envision the sort of necessity involved in accommodating the workings of the actual world ($\boxdot$ and $\diamondsuit$). In this sense of the term, the basic laws of nature provide the basis for necessity.

One cannot, of course, give an illustrative example of something that is in principle inconceivable because presenting it defeats the very purpose.

And inconceivable theses cannot sensibly be maintained as informative truths, they can only be maintained, if at all, as suppositions or hypotheses. In failing to make tenable assertions and convey a meaningful message, they fail to fall under the descriptivity of correct/incorrect (and similarly probable, plausible, and the like). Its unintelligibility precludes it from qualifying for those evaluative assessments which—like the proceeding—are applicable only to propositions able to make a coherent claim of some sort. And only meaningful propositions (claims) can have a truth status—be it actually or even by assumption or supposition. Incomprehensible (and thereby meaningless) discourse cannot even be assured to be true or false. Its lack of truth status is unconditional and unavoidable.

In actual fact, claims to the realization of something inconceivable are always untenable and false. However, here as elsewhere error is possible. Someone ill-informed can certainty think (mistakenly) that something inconceivable is real. It is clear that something can be acceptable to one person and not to another. Thus, when one person is better informed than another they can differ in regard to conceivability—either way. If *x* does not realize that squaring the circle is impossible, he mistakenly conceives of someone (perhaps himself) having solved the problem. On the other hand, if *x* does not realize that black swans are possible, he may mistakenly regard the prospect of a black-swan dinner as inconceivable.

4.3 Meaninglessness

Logic deals with the truth relationships among propositions. But before there is truth, there must be meaning. And the *bête noir* in this regard is meaninglessness.

Meaninglessness is a malfunction of communication, something that results when our apparatus of communication does not manage to do its intended job.

There are several importantly distinct ways in which a statement can be meaningless, although all of them are alike in basing what is said on a presupposition that is simply false.

One mode of meaninglessness results from asserting absolute gibberish: "The number three ate yellow." We cannot even begin to make sense of this. This is *assertoric* meaninglessness, the failure to make any intelligible contention whatsoever. The mistaken presupposition here is that meaninglessness can be achieved simply by stringing words together grammatically. The senselessness of such gibberish that one can make neither heads nor tails of is the most drastic mode of meaningless. All of its other modes are at least minimally intelligible in that what is being said is sufficiently intelligible that one can comprehend the senselessness of it.

A prime form of such meaninglessness is *categorical* in nature and consists in ascribing to something of a certain type some feature that items of its category simply cannot have, as, for example, assigning a physical location to numbers (one cannot position three at the North Pole) or ascribing a color to obligations (one cannot have a yellow duty toward one's children).

A further form of meaninglessness is *conceptual* in making statements that conflict with the established meaning of words. Thus, consider such statements as "John's spouse is unmarried" or "Two's double is an odd number."

Then too, meaninglessness obtains when any attempt to class a statement either as true or false results in failure because a contradiction occurs either way. This is *alethic* meaninglessness, the failure to have any determinate truth status. The classically paradoxical self-contradictory thesis "This statement is false" is an example.

Yet another mode of meaninglessness is the *delusional*, which presupposes as existent something that just is not there. Examples are such statements as "The present king of France is bald" or "Noplace is the capital of Antarctica."

A further pathway to meaninglessness is by purporting the existence of something that not only does not but actually cannot exist. "The prime number between five and seven" or "The product of three multiplied by an even divisor of seven" are examples. This is *referential* meaninglessness, rooted in the, in principle, unavoidable nonexistence something that the statements purport to characterize.

Why is it that meaninglessness statements can and should be dismissed from serious consideration without much further ado? We do so for reasons of *cognitive economy*. We thereby spare ourselves from any further fruitless effort to deal with the matter.

Are self-contradictory statements meaningless? It all depends. Individually, self-contradictory statements are indeed meaningless. There is nothing we can do with such a statement as "The pair of them consisted of three items." But by way of contrast, consider the example of the three boxes I, II, III (Display 2).

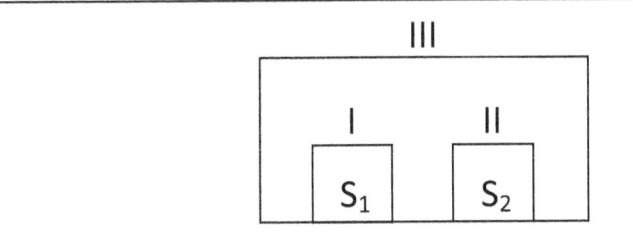

Display 2:

Now, let it be that that S_1 is:

The statement in Box II is true, but some statement in Box III is false.

Suppose S_1 is true. Then so (according to S_1 itself) is S_2. But with S_1 and S_2 both true, all the statements in Box III are true, so S_1 is false. Since S_1-true entails S_1-false, S_1 is self-contradictory and thus false.

The falsity of S_1 means that not-S_1 will be true. But by the content of S_1 we have:

$$\sim S_1 \text{ iff } \sim S_2 \vee [S_1 \& S_2]$$

Since $S_1 \& S_2$ is inescapably false by the reasoning indicated above, we have: $\sim S_1$ iff $\sim S_2$. So, the falsity of S_1 constrains that of S_2. That is, S_2 will be false *irrespective of what it is that S_2 asserts*. But this is absurd and we can make no stable sense of the situation.

It must be stressed that those individual sentences S_1 and S_2 are not meaningless. After all, their meaning is essential to the derivation of the paradox. Moreover, if you change one of them, the other can become perfectly meaningful. What is meaningless here is the whole complex—the entirety of what is being asserted. The difficulty of meaningful construal is collective not distributive. Individually regarded, the meaningfulness of those statements is incontestable.

A very special sort of supposed lack of "meaning" is at issue with the "empirical meaninglessness" purported by the logical positivists of the 1930s. For them, a proposition was "meaningless" in the sense of failing to admit of observational disinformation. In adopting this line, they thought they could demolish traditional metaphysics by dismissing it as meaningless nonsense. Unfortunately for this program, it came to light all too soon that a whole host of perfectly meaningful scientific statements would have to be classed as empirically meaningless, so that the baby was being thrown out along with the bath water. For it is clear that discursive verification will be unavailable with statements about the remote past or future, or such generalizations as "X will never happen" or "Caesar would have left the Rubicon uncrossed had he wanted to" and many other sorts of statements whose meaning is intelligible and whose truth is plausible.[59]

It is tempting to dismiss as meaningless those claims that we simply do not understand—to blame the message, as it were, for our own lack of comprehension. Many or most of us would not hesitate to adopt this line in relation to the explanation that Chinese adepts of acupuncture use in explaining their practice. And while such an argument may well be appropriate, one should nevertheless proceed with caution in these matters. For it is one of the most fundamental facts of epistemology that the proceedings of higher-level intellects are bound to seem like magic, to those who function at a lesser level of understanding, and that the discussions of technical experts seem gibberish to the uninitiated.

---

[59] See Carl G. Hempel, "Problems and Changes in the Empiricists Criterion of Meaning," *Révue Internationale de Philosophie* 4 (1950), pp. 41–63.

4.4 The Corrigibility of Conceptions

It must be stressed that these deliberations regarding cognitive inadequacy are less concerned with the correctness of our particular claims about real things than with our characterizing conceptions of them. And in this connection, it deserves stressing that there is a significant and substantial difference between a true or correct statement or contention, on the one hand, and a true or correct conception, on the other. To make a true contention about a thing, we merely need to get one particular fact about it straight. To have a true conception of the thing, on the other hand, we must get all of the important facts about it straight. And it is clear that this involves a certain normative element—namely what the "important" or "essential" facets of something are.

Anaximander of Miletus presumably made many correct contentions about the sun in the fifth century B.C.—for example, that its light is brighter than that of the moon. But Anaximander's conception of the sun (as the flaming spoke of a great wheel of fire encircling the earth) was totally wrong.

To assure the correctness of our conception of a thing, we would have to be sure—as we very seldom are—that nothing further can possibly come along to upset our view of just what its important features are and just what their character is. Thus, the qualifying conditions for true conceptions are far more demanding than those for true claims. With a correct contention about a thing, all is well if we get the single relevant aspect of it right, but with a correct conception of it, we must get the essentials right—we must have an overall picture that is basically correct. And this is something we generally cannot ascertain, if only because we cannot say with secure confidence what actually is really important or essential before the end of the proverbial day.

With conceptions—unlike propositions or contentions—incompleteness means incorrectness, or at any rate presumptive incorrectness. Having a correct or adequate conception of something as the object it is requires that we have all the important facts about it right. But since the prospect of discovering further important facts can never be eliminated, the possibility can never be eliminated that matters may so eventuate that we may ultimately (with the wisdom of hindsight) acknowledge the insufficiency or even inappropriateness of our earlier conceptions. A conception based on incomplete data must be assumed to be at least partially incorrect. If we can decipher only half an inscription, our conception of its overall content must be largely conjectural—and thus must be presumed to contain an admixture of error. When our information about something is incomplete, obtaining an overall picture of the thing at issue becomes a matter of theorizing, or guesswork, however sophisticatedly executed. And then we have no alternative but to suppose that this overall picture falls short of being wholly correct in various (unspecifiable) ways. With conceptions, falsity can thus emerge from errors of omission as well as those of commission, resulting from the circumstance that the information at our disposal is merely incomplete, rather than actually false (as would have to be the case with contentions).

To be sure, an inadequate or incomplete *description* of something is not thereby false—the statements we make about it may be perfectly true as far as they go. But an inadequate or incomplete *conception* of a thing is *ipso facto* one that we have no choice but to presume to be incorrect as well,[60] seeing that where there is incompleteness, we cannot justifiably take the stance that it relates only to inconsequential matters and touches nothing important. Accordingly, our conceptions of particular things are always to be viewed not just as cognitively *open-ended* but as *corrigible* as well.

We are led back to the thesis of the great idealist philosophers (Spinoza, Hegel, Bradley, Royce) that human knowledge inevitably falls short of "perfected science" (the Idea, the Absolute), and must be presumed deficient both in its completeness and its correctness.[61]

4.5 A "Logic" of Inconceivability

The notion of a "logic of inconceivability" would seem to be a contradiction in terms. For logic looks to what must (or cannot) be true if something related is accepted (or rejected) as such. It deals in relationships among claims in the face of their actual status as true or false—be it actual or assumptive. Any discussion which by virtue of inconceivability lacks a definite truth status falls outside logic as traditionally conceived.

There are, however, some cognate issues. To facilitate our deliberations we shall assume that our person variables x, y, z, etc. will range over limited—that is, finite—intelligences at the level of *Homo sapiens*. And we shall adopt the convention that:

> Cp abbreviates "p is conceivable," that is, it is possible for a human of ordinary intelligence to access the meaning of p; and Cxp abbreviates "p is conceivable to x."

---

[60] Compare Francis H. Bradley's thesis: "Error is truth, it is partial truth, that is false only because partial and left incomplete," *Appearance and Reality* (Oxford: Clarendon Press, 1893), p. 169.

[61] The author's *Empirical Inquiry* (Totowa, NJ: Rowman & Littlefield, 1982) discusses further relevant issues.

Given that *Cxp* abbreviates "*x*'s having a meaningful conception of *p*," we will have it that:

Cp = *p* is conceivable = $\Diamond(\exists x)Cxp$

And note that this neither states nor entails $(\exists x)\Diamond Cxp$. The conceivability at issue need not be realizable by some actual person. Also, when one can conceive of *p*, one can conceive of not-*p* as well, with the result that *Cxp* iff *Cx~p*. (And note, moreover, that by using $\Diamond$ rather than $\diamondsuit$ in equating *Cp* with $\Diamond(\exists x)Cxp$ we take purely theoretical rather than effectively practical conceivability into view.)

We now have it that:

If *p* then *Cp*, though not always conversely

And since we have:

$Cp \leftrightarrow \Diamond(\exists x)Cxp$

There now follows:

$\sim Cp \leftrightarrow \Box(\forall x)\sim Cxp$ and thereby also $\sim Cp \leftrightarrow \Box(\forall x)\sim Cx\sim p$

Accordingly, that which is inherently inconceivable must be so of necessity for anyone.

It transpires that any claims whose prerequisites or consequence are inconceivable will themselves qualify as such. Thus, $p \vdash q$ and *Cp*, then *C(q)*; and also if $p \vdash q$ and *Cq*, then *~Cq*. (Here $\vdash$ represents logico-conceptual entailment.) Moreover, impossible or impossibility-entailing claims are not conceivable:

If $p \vdash q$ & $\sim\Diamond q$, then $\sim Cxp$

These principles provide for the rudiments of a quasi-logic of conceivability.

4.6 Inconceivable Possibilities

But are there actually—or can there really be—such things as inconceivable objects, facts, or possibilities? Of course, one cannot provide examples. But it is clear on general principles that such items must exist. For we humans have to conduct our conceptualizing business by means of language. And as linguistic formulation is a recursive process—explanatory claims for a finite vocabulary via finite grammatical principles—one can have at most a denumerable number of describable experiences. But there is no good reason to think that items, facts, and possibilities are not similarly limited. So—as in Musical Chairs—when the music of language stops, there will yet remain unaccommodated possibilities. The range of what is theoretically conceivable outnumbers the reach of what can possibly be realized.

Actually conceiving of things is something personal and potentially idiosyncratic. But conceivability as such is something impersonal and objective inherent in the nature of the issues involved and the possibilities of conceptual operation. And even as a chasm may be bridgeable without ever being bridged, so an idea or circumstance may be conceivable without ever being conceived of. Conceivability is a matter of the possibilities of conceptualization: what actually happens within the contingent eventuations of the real world is irrelevant. What individuals can manage to conceive of in practice is a fraction of their range of experience. But what is conceivable in principle is something above and beyond the capabilities of individuals.

But would there actually be a bridgeable chasm if no bridge were ever built, and indeed if the very idea of a bridge were never even conceived of? The answer is, of course, affirmative. The domain of possibility—possibilities of bridging and conceiving included—is independent of and detached from what actually happens in the world. The bridges we build and the concepts we entertain are products of our doings. But the associated possibilities of things are independent of us. Of course, the contemplation and entertainment of these possibilities is a matter of reality and actualization. But not so with the possibilities themselves that are at issue. It is noteworthy and significant that we possess a faculty of imaginative thought that enables us to enter a realm of abstract possibilities whose being we do not produce and whose features we discover rather than create. Like the real world itself, the realm of possibility that lies open to our conception is not of our making, but is an independent manifold that we can contemplate but not produce. What we *do* conceive of is up to us, but what we *can* conceive of is not.

Appendix

An assertion may be made with or without affirmative intent. In the former (deliberately affirmative) case, the object is to endorse what the assertion maintains; in the second (merely deliberative) case, the object is only to pose the assertion as an item of consideration.

In the context of the present deliberations, the assertions represented by the variables p, q, r, etc. are also to encompass those made in the merely deliberative rather than substantively affirmative mode. An assertion so made is not being stated as a true affirmation but merely put forward for consideration. And since the range of our assertion variables p, q, r, etc. encompasses conceivable proposition in general, so that assertion comes to be coordinate with conceivability rather than actual truth. In the context of the present deliberations, we thus do not have the Tarski equivalence:

p iff $|p| = T$.

For this deliberative contention may turn out to be inconceivable and meaningless.

Any statement that has a definite truth value as T or F (rather than an indecisive *tertium datur*) must be conceivable, and conversely, any conceivable fact-claim must be alethically definite. Thus:

(1) Cp iff $(|p| = T \vee |p| = F)$

But suppose we were to adopt the Tarski Principle that:

p iff $|p| = T$ (and correspondingly $\sim p$ iff $|p| = F$)

Then of course, (1) will come to:

Cp iff $(p \vee \sim p)$

This would entail $(\forall p)Cp$. In view of our determination to accept even meaningless claims as objects of consideration, this result is unacceptable. Thus, the implementability of this result betokens a determination but it postulates that the present diagram be limited to conceivable propositions. In the context of the present deliberations, the Tarski Principle must be put into suspension.

5 Stating Facts: Formulating Facts in Language

5.1 Facts and Language

To think about facts, we have to formulate them in language. Only by projecting linguistic truths can we ever come to grips with facts. And this poses problems. For language imposes limits. It is developed recursively, and this limits quantity because *even in theory* only a countable number of items can ever be formulated in language. And here it is instructive to begin with the perspective of the great seventeenth-century polymath G. W. Leibniz (1646–1717), who deliberated the question of how much is in principle knowable—that is, *can be known*.

Leibniz took his inspiration from *The Sand Reckoner* of Archimedes, who in this study sought to establish the astronomically large number of sand grains that could be contained within the universe defined by the sphere of the fixed stars of Aristotelian cosmology—a number Archimedes effectively estimated at 10^{50}. Thus, even as Archimedes addressed the issue of the scope of *the physical universe*, so Leibniz sought to address the issue of the scope of *the universe of thought*.[62] For just this is what he proceeded to do in the fascinating 1693 tract *On the Horizon of Human Knowledge, De l'horizon de la doctrine humaine.*[63]

Here, Leibniz pursued this project along textual lines. He wrote:

> All items of human knowledge can be expressed by the letters of the alphabet...so that it follows that one can calculate the number of truths of which humans are capable and thus compute the size of a work that would contain all possible human knowledge, and which would contain all that could ever be known, written, or invented, and more besides. For it would contain not only the truths, but also all the falsehoods that men can assert, and meaningless expressions as well.[64]

---

[62] On Archimedes' estimate, see Archimedes, *The Works of Archimedes*, tr. by Thomas Heath (Cambridge: Cambridge University Press, 1897).

[63] See Gottfried Wilhelm Leibniz, *De l'horizon de la doctrine humaine*, ed. by Michael Fichant (Paris: Vrin, 1991). There is a partial translation of Leibniz's text in "Leibniz on the Limits of Human Knowledge" by Philip Beeley, *The Leibniz Review* 13 (December 2003), pp. 93–97. (Note that in old French "doctrine" means *knowledge*.) It is well known that Leibniz invented entire branches of science, among them differential and integral calculatus, the calculus of variations, topology (analysis situs), symbolic logic, and computers. But he deserves to be seen as a pioneer of epistemetrics as well. The relevant issues are analyzed in Nicholas Rescher, "Leibniz's Quantitative Epistemology," *Studia Leibnitiana* 36 (2004), pp. 210–230.

[64] Gottfried Wilhelm Leibniz, *De l'horizon de la doctrine humaine*, pp. 37–38. (My translation.)

Thus, if one could set an upper limit to the volume of printed matter that inquiring humans could possibly produce, then one could map out by combinatorial means the whole manifold of accessible verbal material—true, false, or gibberish—in just the manner that Leibniz contemplated.

5.2 Fact Outruns Language

Ours is a language-dependent intelligence. Granted, our perceptions and modes of experiential apprehension may involve ineffable components. But our understanding—our witting apprehension of fact (or putative fact)—is always language-embedded. And this leads to inevitable limitations. For our languages are effetely recursive exfoliations from a finite basis. Their productions never extend beyond the enumerable. But there is no reason to think that reality is subject to such limits—that its nature is digital instead of analogue. And when this concession is made, larger consequences come to the fore.

As regards the philosophy of science, one such consequence relates to physicalism. For physicalists hypothetically claim that a complete *physical* description is (or at least inferentially provides for) a complete description of it. And given their view of physics as essentially an axiomatic system, this discretizes and enumeralizes the facts about reality. But once one concedes (as it seems one must) that a complete axiomatization of the world's facts is impossible, then a physicalism of this type becomes untenable. Even as (courtesy of Kurt Gödel) we have it that mathematical truth extends beyond the reach of mathematical axiomatization, so it must be conceded that the realm of factual truth about reality extends beyond the reach of scientific axiomatization.

Again, linguistic philosophers also incline to identify facts and truths. They insist to hold not only that a true statement must state a fact, but that a fact has to be a stateable fact: in sum, they envision a one-to-one competence between truths and facts. But if—as seems to be the case—it is demonstrable that there are more facts than truths, then this sort of linguocentrism also become untenable. In sum, the circumstance that, as best we can judge, fact outruns language has significant philosophical implications.

There is good reason to think that language-based thought is insufficient for characterizing reality. When one construes the idea of an "alphabet" sufficiently broadly to include not only letters but symbols of various sorts, it still transpires that everything stateable in a language can be spelled out in print through the combination of some sequential register of symbols.[65] And with the conception of a "language" construed as calling for development in the usual recursive manner, the statements of a given language can inevitably be enumerated in a vast and indeed infinite—but nevertheless ultimately countable—listing.[66] Thus, since the world's languages will be, even if not finite in number, nevertheless at most enumerable, it follows that the set of all statements—including every proposition that can possibly be formulated—will be enumerably infinite.

Our resource for describing the world's concrete states of affairs by linguistic means is inherently limited in its reach within the confines of countability. For the limits of textuality impose quantitative restrictions upon propositionalized thought—albeit not limits of finitude. Accordingly, we arrive at the following contention:

>Thesis 1: *The Enumerability of Statements.* Statements—linguistically formulated propositions—are enumerable and thus (at most) denumerably infinite.

It serves the interests of clarity to distinguish between truths and facts at this stage. Truths are linguistically formulated facts—correct statements—which, as such, must be formulated in language (broadly understood to include symbol systems of various sorts). A "truth" is something that has to be framed in *linguistic/symbolic* terms—the representation of a fact through its statement in some language, so that any correct statement formulates a truth. A "fact," on the other hand, is not a linguistic entity at all, but an actual aspect of the world's state of affairs. A fact is thus a feature of reality.[67] Facts correspond to *potential* truths whose actualization as such waits upon their appropriate linguistic embodiment. Truths are statements and thereby language-bound, but facts outrun linguistic limits. Once stated, a fact yields a truth, but with facts there need in principle be no linguistic route to get from here to there.

Being inherently linguistic in character, truths are indissolubly bound to textuality, subject to our governing assumption that any language-framed declaration can be generated from a sequential string of symbols—i.e., that all spoken language can in principle be reduced to writing. Since they correlate to state-

---

[65] Compare Philip Hugly and Charles Sayward, "Can a Language Have Indenumerably Many Expressions?" *History and Philosophy of Logic* 4 (1983), pp. 112–126.

[66] This supposes an upper limit to the length of intelligible statements. And even if this restriction were waived, the number of statements will still be no more than *countably* finite.

[67] See footnote 9 of Chapter 2 above.

ments, it follows that truths cannot be more than countably infinite. We thus have:

> Thesis 2: *The Denumerability of Truth.* Being linguistic objects, truths are denumerably infinite.

With facts, however, we come to another matter altogether. It is a key facet of our epistemic stance towards the real world that its furnishings possess a refinement and diversity of detail that there is always more to be said than we have so far managed. In contrast to truths, facts are (presumably) too vast in quantity to be demonstrable. For facts are, in principle, inexhaustible. The facts regarding any particular actual existent run off into endlessly proliferating detail. In this way, even the facts about any actual physical object are theoretically inexhaustible: there is always something further to be said. Every part and parcel of reality has features beyond the range of our cognitive reach at any juncture whatsoever. After all, any such thing has dispositions that run off into uncountability.

And so we arrive at:

> Thesis 3: *The Inexhaustibility of Fact.* The manifold of fact is transdenumerably infinite.

The idea of a complete listing of *all* the facts—even an infinite list—is manifestly absurd. For consider the following statement: "The list F of stated facts fails to have this statement on it." But now suppose this statement to be on the list. Then it clearly does not state a fact, so that the list is after all not a list of facts (contrary to hypothesis). And so it must be left off the list. But then in consequence that list will not be complete since the statement is true. Facts, that is to say, can never be listed *in toto* because there will always be further facts—facts about the entire list itself—that a supposedly complete list could not manage to register. In the description of concrete particulars, we are caught up in an inexhaustible detail: there are always bound to be more descriptive facts about things than we are able to capture explicitly with our linguistic machinery. We are thus led to:

> Thesis 4: *There are quantitatively more facts than truths.* The domain of fact is ampler than that of truth, so that language cannot capture the entirety of fact.

With facts being too numerous for enumerabilty, there are more facts than language can manage to capture. We live in a world that is not digital but analogue and so the manifold of its states of affairs is simply too rich to be fully comprehended by our linguistically digital means.

We accordingly arrive at:

> Thesis 5: *The manifold of Truth as a Whole* is too vast to admit of ever being spelled out in detail in its totality.

The domain of fact inevitably transcends the limits of our capacity to *express* it, and *a fortiori* those of our capacity to canvass it in overt detail. When facts and language play their game of Musical Chairs, some facts are bound to be left in the lurch when the music of language stops.

The long and short of it is that the factual domain is so vast in its detail that our reliance on the symbolic mechanisms of language precludes wrapping our thought around the whole of it. The thesis that every fact has a linguistic formulation—$(\forall f)(\exists s)sFf$—cannot be maintained, simply and exactly because the range of the fact-variable is larger than that of the statement-variable.[68] There are, in sum, unstateable facts, though it is obviously impossible to give a substantively concrete example of this phenomenon.[69]

5.3 The Vastness of Fact

Twentieth-century philosophers of otherwise the most radically different orientation have agreed on privatizing the role of language. "The limits of my language set the limits of my world," *("Die Grenzen meiner Spache bedeuten die Grenzen meiner Welt,")* says the Wittgenstein of the *Tractatus*. "There is nothing outside text," *("Il n'y a pas de hors de texte,")* say the devotees of French deconstructionism. But already centuries earlier Leibniz had taken the measure of this sort of textualization.[70] He looked at it closely and saw that it could not be more wrong. The limits of language may be the limits to *my* world, but they are not the limits of *the* world.

---

[68] Note that if some fact cannot be formulated, then it follows that not every fact can be formulated. For a counter-instance is then provided by the mega-fact that encompasses all facts.
[69] The predicate "is an unstateable fact" is what I call *vagrant*: it has no identifiable address. On this issue, see my *Epistemic Logic* (Pittsburgh: University of Pittsburgh Press, 2005).
[70] On Leibniz's deliberations about the limits of language, see the author's "Leibniz's Quantitative Epistemology."

5.3 The Vastness of Fact

Reality bursts the confines of textualization.[71] And *that* this occurs must be accepted despite the inherent and unavoidable impossibility of ever indicating just *where* it does so. For, of course, we cannot possibly adduce any concrete example of an unstateable fact.

The cognitive beings with which we are concerned here are language-dependent finite intelligences. The information at their disposal by way of propositional knowledge that something or other is the case will—unlike how-to knowledge—have to be verbally formulated. And language, as emphasized above, stands coordinate with textuality in ways outdistanced by the facts themselves.

What are we to make of the numerical disparity between facts and truths, between what is knowable in itself and what we language-bound intelligences can possibly manage to know? Just what does this portend for our knowledge?

It means that our knowledge of fact is incomplete—and inevitably so!—because we cannot secure the means for its adequate presentation. Reality in all its blooming, buzzing complexity is too rich for faithful representation by the recursive and enumerable resources of our language. We do and must recognize the limitations of our cognition, acknowledging that we cannot justifiably equate reality with what can be known by us and expressed in language. And what transpires here for the situation of our sort of mind also obtains for any other sort of finite mind as well.

Does this state of affairs not mean that those unknown facts are unknowable? The answer is neither yes nor no. As already foreshadowed above, it all depends upon exactly how one is to construe this matter of "knowability." Using Kxf to abbreviate "the individual x knows the fact f," there will clearly be two rather different ways in which the existence of an unknowable fact can be claimed, namely:

$(\exists f)\Box(\forall x)\sim Kxf$ or equivalently $\sim(\forall f)\Diamond(\exists x)Kxf$

and:

$\Box(\exists f)(\forall x)\sim Kxf$ or equivalently $\sim\Diamond(\forall f)(\exists x)Kxf$

---

[71] The circumstance that not every *actual fact* can be articulated in a (true) statement shows *a fortiori* that not every *possible situation* can be characterized linguistically. If the domain of fact outruns the bounds of language articulation, then the manifold of possibility must certainly do so as well. We must accordingly acknowledge that not everything is sayable!

The first of these logically entails the second which is, inevitable in the circumstances, there being more facts than finite humans ever will or can know. But the first strong contention is clearly false. For as long as the nonexistence of God is not a *necessary* circumstance, there can be no fact that is of necessity unknown.

The difference in the quantifier placement in these two formulas is crucial when one contemplates the prospect of unlimited knowability—of the idea that all facts are knowable. (Think here again of children playing Musical Chairs—it is possible for *any* child to secure a seat even though it is not possible for *every* child to do so.) Thus, insofar as the issue is problematic, the idea of unknowable facts will have to pivot on the acceptability of the first thesis.

The situation as regards knowing facts is accordingly akin to that of counting integers in specifically the following manner:[72]

1. The manifold of integers is inexhaustible. We can never come to grips with all of them as specific individuals. Nevertheless—
2. Further progress is always possible: we can always go beyond whatever point we have so far managed to reach. In principle, we can always go beyond what has been attained. Nevertheless—
3. Moving forward gets ever more cumbersome. In moving onwards, we must be ever more prolix and make use of ever more elaborate symbol complexes. Greater demands in time, effort, and resources are inevitable here. Accordingly—
4. In actual practice, there will be only so much that we can effectively manage to do. The possibilities that obtain in principle can never be fully realized in practice. However—
5. Such limitations in no way hamper the prospect of establishing various correct generalizations about the manifold of integers in its abstract entirety.

And a parallel situation characterizes the cognitive condition of all finite intelligences whose cognitive operations have to proceed by a symbolic process that functions by language. Inductive inquiry, like counting, never achieves completeness. There is always more to be done: in both cases alike, we can always do better by doing more. But we can never manage to do it all.

---

[72] We here take "counting" to be a matter of indicating integers by name—e. g., as "thirteen" or "13"—rather than descriptively, as per "the first prime after eleven."

5.4 Facts Are Transdenumerable

The facts about anything whatsoever are beyond counting. There is no point in projecting an arithmetic of facts. There are certainly more ants than elephants in the world, but there are no more facts about the former than there are about the latter. Facts are, as it were, uncountable—literally beyond number.

This can be shown by adapting an argument due by Patrick Grim,[73] which can be framed essentially as follows. The domain of fact is too vast not only for enumerability but even for contemplation as an authentic *set* of any sort. For suppose:

(1) The totality of facts from a well-defined set F.
(2) We know from Georg Cantor's work that the cardinality of the power set (P) of F—the set of all its subsets—is greater than that of F:

$$\text{card }(F) < \text{card } P(F)$$

(3) But every member of $P(F)$ also corresponds to some unique member of F (for example, that it is the only $P(F)$ member that is identical with the one that it happened to be). Accordingly, the cardinality of $P(F)$ cannot be greater than that of F:

$$\text{card }(F) \geq \text{card } P(F)$$

The contradiction at work here constitutes a *reductio ad absurdum* of (1). The totality of facts does not constitute a well-defined set—it is, in effect, a manifold so vast as to preclude comprehension within the conceptual resources of standard set theory. And this consideration also puts it beyond the reach of language-formulatable truth.[74]

This conclusion can be also argued via the following considerations. Suppose that a certain:

---

[73] Patrick Grim, "There Is No Set of All Truths," *Analysis* 44 (1984), pp. 206–208.
[74] The preceding argumentation turns on the fact that while *every* subset of F (infinite subsets included) will be a member of $P(F)$, nevertheless not every such subset will analogously engender an F member. Thus, we cannot conjoin infinitely many sentences into yet another sentence nor infinitely many stories into yet another story, seeing that sentences and stories must be of finite scope. But an infinite complex of facts is still a fact and an infinite agglomeration of items yet another item. On this basis, it transpires that while sentences and stories will constitute sets, the manifold of facts and of items (things, objects) is outsize and represents something outside the range of sets as generally conceived on logico-mathematical principles.

$F: f_1, f_2, f_3, \ldots$

were to constitute a *complete* enumeration of all facts. And now consider the statement:

(Z) the list F of the form $f_1, f_2, f_3, \ldots$ is an all-inclusive listing of facts.

By hypothesis, this statement will present a fact. So, if F is indeed a complete listing of *all* facts, then there will be an integer k such that:

$Z = f_k$

Accordingly, Z itself will occupy the k-th place on the F listing, so that:

f_k = the list L takes the form $f_1, f_2, f_3, \ldots f_k, \ldots$

But this would require f_k to be an expanded version of itself, which is absurd. With the k-th position of the F listing *already* occupied by f_k we cannot also squeeze that complex f_k-involving thesis into it.

The point here is that any supposedly complete listing of facts $(f_1, f_2, f_3, \ldots)$ will itself exhibit, as a whole, certain features that none of its individual members can encompass. Once those individual entries are fixed and the series is defined, there will be further facts about that series as a whole that its members themselves cannot articulate.

Finally, the transdenumerability of fact can also be made via an analogue of the diagonal argument that is standardly used to show that no list of real numbers can manage to include all of them, thereby establishing the transdenumerability of the reals. Let us begin by imagining a supposedly complete inventory of *independent* facts, using logic to streamline the purportedly complete listing into a condition of greater informative tidiness through the elimination of inferential redundancies so that every item adds some information to what has gone before. The argument for the transdenumerability of fact can now be developed as follows. Let us suppose (for the sake of *reductio ad absurdum* argumentation) that the inventory:

$f_1, f_2, f_3, \ldots$

represents our (nonredundant but yet purportedly *complete*) listing of facts. Then, by the supposition of *factuality* we have (*i*)*fi*. And further by the supposition of *completeness* we have it that:

$(p)(p \to (i)[fi \to p])$

Moreover, by the aforementioned supposition of *non-redundancy*, each member of the sequence adds something quite new to what has gone before:

$(i)(j)[i < j \to \sim[(f1 \& f2 \& ... \& fi) \to fj)]$

Consider now the following course of reasoning:

(1) $(\forall i)fi$ — by "factuality"
(2) $(\forall j)f_j \to (\exists i)(f_i \to (\forall j)f_j)$ — from (1) by "completeness"
via the substitution of $(\forall j)f_j$ for p
(3) $(\exists i)(f_i \to (j) fj)$ — from (1), (2)

But (3) contradicts non-redundancy. This *reductio ad absurdum* of our hypothesis indicates that the facts about any sufficiently complex object will necessarily be too numerous for complete enumeration. In such circumstances, no purportedly comprehensive listing of truths can actually manage to encompass all facts because any such listing will itself bring more facts into being.

5.5 The Comprehensiveness and Integrity of Fact

Can anything be said with assured confidence about reality that is *counter-indicated* by its appearance as human inquiry presents it? Certainly nothing at the level of specific detail—of particular facts. But at the level of theoretical generalities, there is indeed something to be said.

Consistency. Whenever x is a real object of some kind and F is a fully specific property applicable to objects of this kind, then we never have it that X both has x and lacks it, so that never both Fx and not-Fx. (That both p and not-p cannot obtain conjointly is the Principle of Contradiction.) The definiteness of the predicates at issue is clearly a crucial requisite here. For if F shall be respect-differentiated, then it would apply to x in one respect and yet not in another (so that seemingly Fx and not-Fx) or else would fail to apply to x in one respect and yet also fail to apply to x in the other (so that seemingly neither Fx nor not-Fx).[75]

---

[75] This reasoning is set out clearly in Aristotle's *On Interpretation* (*De interpretatione*). See Ar-

Detail. There is going to be a range of descriptive detail to reality vaster than anything that our characterization of it could ever afford. Our putative knowledge of reality may be imprecise or indeterministic. Reality itself must be fully detailed.

Complexity. Each time we extend the information we have at hand with regard to the composition and operation of the real, we discover that there is more complexity than we had thought. Truth may or may not be stranger than fiction, but reality is bound to prove more complex than it appears in our cognitive.

Consistency. Our putative knowledge of reality may contain anomalies and even contradictions. But as F. H. Bradley insisted, this cannot be the case with reality itself.

Systematicity. Our putative knowledge of reality may overall prove to be discontent, disconnected, incoherent. But this would be (as with reality itself) where everything must dovetail smoothly into systemic coordination, unity, and coherence.

Coherence. Thus, suppose that we make only a very small alteration in the descriptive composition of the real, say, by adding one pebble to the river bank. But which pebble? Where are we to get it and what are we to put in its place? And where are we to put the air or the water that this new pebble displaces? And when we put that material in a new spot, just how are we to make room for it? And how are we to make room for the so-displaced material? Moreover, the region within six inches of the new pebble used to hold N pebbles. It now holds $N + 1$. Of which region are we to say that it holds $N - 1$? If it is that region yonder, then how did the pebble get here from there? By a miraculous instantaneous transport? By a little boy picking it up and throwing it? But then, which little boy? And how did he get there? And if he threw it, then what happened to the air that his throw displaced which would otherwise have gone undisturbed? Here problems arise without end.

Completeness. Above all, reality involucrates completeness. Whenever x is a real object of some kind and F is a fully specific property that is applicable to objects of this kind, then either x has F or x lacks it, so that always either Fx or not-Fx. (That either p or not-p should obtain is the Principle of Excluded Middle.) Here completeness means that if x is a specific and particular object of some sort and F is a definite and well-defined feature or property relevant to objects of the type to which x belongs, then either Fx or $\sim Fx$ (but not both) will ob-

---

istotle, *Categories and De Interpretatione: Translated with Notes and Glossary*, ed. by John L. Ackrill (Oxford: Clarendon Press, 1963).

tain. Both of these principles have figured prominently in philosophical deliberations since Aristotle's day.

Detail. Whenever x is an existing concrete object of some kind and F is an x-characterizing feature that admits of exactness and precision, then x has F in full and precise detail (Principle of Specificity). In its nature, reality has to be specifically this or that—and exactly so much of it. An apple tree cannot just have roughly or approximately 50 branches, it must have some particular number of them. A fly cannot simply have "a lot of eyes," it must have some definite quantity. A rock cannot just be "roughly a kilo in weight," it must be a definite weight of some sort. Reality itself must be one way or the other—and to just exactly so much of an extent. Its descriptive nature is not only determinate but *precisely* determinate. And its resulting scope means that it outruns the reach of language.

6 Knowledge of Fact

6.1 Cognition

We have no *cognitive* access to the facts apart from forming beliefs about them. In saying that reality is such and such—that a given state of affairs actually obtains—I will accomplish no more than to convey my conviction in the matter. No matter how hard I thump on the table when I maintain that p, I accomplish no more than would be accurately reported by saying, "Rescher holds p to be the case." Whether or not p actually is the case is virtually always a distinct and distinguishable issue. In affirming something to be a feature of reality, one accomplishes no more than to manifest that this is how the matter appears to be.

But one also accomplishes no less. The claim that one makes is not about appearance but about reality. After all, the claim "It appears to me that the cat is on the mat" is something quite different from—and far weaker than—the flat-out assertion that the cat is on the mat. For while factual claims may *manifest* how things appear to us, they are claims about reality and not just claims about appearance.

Thought and belief are inseparable from reality just exactly because true belief characterizes reality in that whenever our thought about things ("the appearances") actually is correct, then that is how the reality of it actually stands. The relevantly operative contrast is accordingly not that between what is and what is thought to be, but rather between what is correctly thought to be and what is not.

Some philosophers have proposed conceiving of reality as standing in contrast to what people think and thereby set reality apart from whatever people can conceive and know. But this makes no sense at all. To conceive of reality in a way that precludes as a matter of principle the prospect that people should come to know it is decidedly unreasonable. Reality is not to be construed as something inherently disjoint from the realm of the knowable.

6.2 Cognitive Principles

It is one thing, of course, to consider facts—to conceive of them as possibilities—but another to know them.

Accessible knowledge involves its holder in acceptance (endorsement, subscription, credence, belief, etc.). To accept a contention is to espouse and endorse it, to give it credence, to view it as an established fact, to take it to be able to serve as a (true) premiss in one's thinking and as a suitable basis for one's actions. And a person cannot be said to *know* that something is the case when this individual is not prepared to "accept" it in this sort of way. And accordingly, the claim "*x* knows that *p*" is only tenable when *x* holds *p* to be the case. It is senseless to say "*x* knows that *p*," but he does not really believe it or "*x* knows that *p*, but does not stand committed to accepting it."[76]

Accordingly, one cannot be said to know something if this is not true.[77] Let *Kxp* abbreviate "*x* knows that *p*." It then transpires that we have:

- *The Veracity Principle*

    If *Kxp*, then *p*

This relation between "*x* knows that *p*" and "*p* is true" is a necessary link that obtains *ex vi terminorum*. Knowledge must be veracious: the truth of *p* is a presupposition of its knowability; if *p* were not true, we would *(ex hypothesi)* have no alternative (as a matter of the "logic" of the conceptual situation) to withdraw the claim that somebody *knows p*.

Some writers see the linkage between knowledge and truth as a merely contingent one.[78] But such a view inflicts violence upon the concept of knowledge as it actually operates in our discourse. The locution "*x* knows that *p*, but it is not true that *p*" is senseless. One would have to say "*x thinks* he knows that *p*, but ..." When even *the mere possibility* of the falsity of something that one accepts comes to light, the knowledge claim must be withdrawn; it cannot be asserted flatly, but must be qualified in some such way as "While I don't actually *know* that *p*, I am virtually certain that it is so."

Knowledge veracity straightaway assures knowledge consistency. If someone knows something, then no one knows anything inconsistent with it.

- *The Knowledge-Coherence Principle*

    If *Kxp* and *Kyp* then *p* is compatible with *q*.

---

[76] Indeed, we cannot even say the more guarded "*x* thinks he knows that *p*, but does not accept it." On the other hand, knowledge-avoiding locutions like "*x* says that *p*, but he really knows better" are unproblematic.

[77] We are not concerned here with "the language as she is spoke," but with the *careful* usage of *conscientious* speakers—with what used to be called "correct" usage in the old normative days of grammatical theory.

[78] For example, David M. Armstrong, *Belief, Truth and Knowledge* (Cambridge: Cambridge University Press, 1973), p. 189.

Proof: If *Kxp*, then *p*, and if *Kxq*, then *q*. Hence, we have *p* & *q*, and so, since their conjunction is true, *p* and *q* cannot be incompatible.

Again, certain other "perfectly obvious" deductions from what is known must be assumed to be at the disposal of every (rational) knower. We thus have the principles that separately known items are cognitively conjunctive:

- *The Conjunctivity Principle*

Someone who knows both *p* and *q* separately, thereby also knows their conjunction:

If *Kxp* and *Kxq*, then *Kx(p* & *q)*—and conversely

A person who is unable to exploit his information by "putting two and two together" does not really have *knowledge* in the way that is at issue with specifically *inferential* knowledge. It seems only natural to suppose that any rational knower could put two and two together in this way.

To these principles of *inferential* knowledge, we can also adjoin the following:

- *The Knowledge-Reflexivity Principle*

Actually to know that someone knows something requires knowing this fact oneself.

If *KxKyp*, then *Kxp*; and indeed: if *Kx(∃y)Kyp*, then *Kxp*

Letting *i* be oneself so that *Kip* comes to "I know that *p*," we may note that The Knowledge-Reflexivity Principle entails:

If *KiKyp*, then *Kip*; and more generally: if *Kx(∃y)Kyp*, then *Kxp*

To claim to know that someone else knows something (i.e., some specific fact) is to assert this item for oneself. Put differently, one can only know with respect to the propositional knowledge of others that which one knows oneself.

However, it lies in the nature of things that there are—or can be—facts that *X* can know about *Y*, but *Y* cannot. Thus, *X* can know that *Y* has only opinions but no knowledge, but *Y* cannot.

Knowledge entails justification (warrant, grounding, evidence, or the like). One can maintain that someone knows something only if one is prepared to maintain that he has an adequate rational basis for accepting it. It is senseless to say things like "x knows that p, but has no adequate basis for its acceptance," or again "x knows that p, but has no sufficient grounding for it." To say that "x knows that p" is to say *(inter alia)* that x has *conclusive* warrant for claiming p, and, moreover, that x accepts p on the basis of the conclusive warrant he has for it (rather than on some other evidentially insufficient basis). It is senseless to say things like "x knows that p, but there is some room for doubt" or "x knows that p, but his grounds in the matter leave something to be desired."[79]

G. E. Moore pointed out long ago that it is anomalous to say "p but I don't believe it" or indeed even "p but I don't know it."[80] That this circumstance of what might be called "Moore's Thesis" be so is readily shown. For in maintaining a claim, one standardly purports to know it. Accordingly, one would not—should not—say p and $\sim Kip$ unless one were prepared to subscribe to:

$Ki(p$ & $\sim Kip)$ where i = oneself

But in view of Veracity and Conjunctivity, this straightaway yields:

Kip & $\sim Kip$

which is self-contradictory. (Observe, however, that "I suspect that p but do not fully believe it" (or "do not really know it") is in a different boat.)

It is also important to recognize that that which is known must be compatible with whatever else is actually known. No part of knowledge can constitute decisive counter-evidence against some other part. The whole "body of (genuine) knowledge" must be self-consistent. Accordingly, we shall have:

---

[79] It is worth distinguishing between objective grounding ("there are good grounds for accepting that p"), which reflects an altogether impersonal aspect of the epistemic situation, and subjective grounding ("x has good grounds for accepting that p"). For the person whose knowledge is incomplete may well have good grounds for accepting something whose grounding in itself (taken as a whole) is objectively insufficient. Thus, someone can have good grounds for p when (unbeknownst to him) decisive grounds for not-p in fact exist. However, with the conclusive grounding at issue in knowledge the distinction between the objective and the subjective disappears. One can only have *conclusive* grounds when whatever grounds that one has are in themselves conclusive.

[80] G. E. Moore, *Some Main Problems of Philosophy* (London: Allen and Unwin, 1953).

If Kxp & Kxq, then $\sim(p \vdash \sim q)$[81]

Given this circumstance, logic alone suffices to assure the implication:

If Kxp and $p \vdash q$, then $\sim Kx \sim q$

Accordingly, one decisive way of defeating a claim to knowledge is by establishing that its denial follows from something one knows.[82] But of course, not knowing something to be false (i.e., $\sim Kx \sim q$) is very different from—and much weaker than—knowing this item to be true (Kxq). And so—as was just noted in the preceding dismissal of "logical omniscience"—the just-indicated principle must *not* be strengthened to the objectionable:

If Kxp and $p \vdash q$, then Kxq

which has already been rejected above.

A further, particularly interesting, facet of knowledge discourse relates to *the automatic self-assumption of particularized knowledge attributions*. It makes no sense to say "You know that p, but I don't" or "x knows that p, but not I." In *conceding* an item of knowledge, one automatically *claims* it for oneself as well. To be sure, this holds only for "that..." knowledge, and not "how to" knowledge (even how to do something "purely intellectual," like "answering a certain question correctly"). It makes perfectly good sense to say that someone else knows how to do something one cannot do oneself. Again, abstract (i.e., unidentified) knowledge attributions will not be self-assumptive. One can quite appropriately say "x knows everything (or 'something interesting') about automobile engines, though I certainly do not." But particularized and identified "that..." knowledge claims are different in this regard. One cannot say "x knows that automobile engines use gasoline as fuel, but I myself do not know this." (To be sure, we certainly do *not* have the omniscience thesis:

If Kxp, then Kip (with i = I myself)

One's entitlement to claim Ksp follows from the entitlement to claim Kxp, but the content of the former claim does not follow from the content of the latter.)

---

[81] Actually, it is immaterial for these principles whether or not the same knower is at issue in the two cases. Not only must *a person's* knowledge be consistent, but the whole body of what is known (by someone or other) as well.

[82] This tactic is, of course, of no use to a skeptic.

Moreover, the ground rules of language-use being what they are, *mere assertion is in itself inherently knowledge-claiming*. One cannot say "*p* but I don't know that *p*." To be sure, one can introduce various qualifications like "I accept *p* although I don't actually know it to be true," But to affirm a thesis flatly (without qualification) is *eo ipso* to claim knowledge of it. (Again, what is at issue is certainly *not* captured by the—clearly unacceptable—thesis: If *p*, then *Kip*.)

Such "logical principles of epistemology" will, of course, hinge crucially on the exact construction that is to be placed on the conception of "knowledge." In particular, if it were not for the inferential availability character of this concept, the situation would be very different—and radically impoverished—in this regard.

One further point is worth noting. The statement "Possibly somebody knows *p*" (i.e., $\Diamond(\exists x)Kxp$) says something quite different from (and weaker than) "Somebody possibly knows *p*" (i.e., $(\exists x)\Diamond Kxp$). It is accordingly necessary to distinguish:

(1) Only if *p* is true will it be possible that somebody knows it:

If $\Diamond(\exists x)Kxp$, then *p*

from

(2) Only if *p* is true will there be someone who possibly knows it:

If $(\exists x)\Diamond Kxp$, then *p*

Because the modality in the antecedent of (1) precedes the qualification, the statement carries us beyond the bounds of the actual world into the realm of merely possible existence. But with the antecedent of (2) we remain within it: we discuss only what is possible for the membership of *this* world. Hence, (2) is a plausible thesis, while (1) is not.

Be this as it may, the cardinal point is that of clarifying the nature of knowledge. And in this regard, *putative* knowledge is a matter of someone's staking a claim to truth for which that individual (subjectively) deems himself to have adequate grounds, while *actual* knowledge by contrast is a matter of someone's correctly staking a claim to truth when that individual has (objectively) adequate grounds.

The various principles specified here all represent more or less straightforward facts about how the concept at issue in talk about actual knowledge actually functions. Any philosophical theory of knowledge must—to the peril of its own adequacy—be prepared to accommodate them.

But enough discussion of what knowledge is; let us now turn to the issue of how we obtain it.

6.3 Science and Reality

How is our scientific knowledge related to our everyday knowledge of things? What is the relationship between nature as science sees it and as it figures in the experience and discourse of everyday life?

Scientific realism is the doctrine that *science describes the real world:* that the world actually is as science takes it to be, and that its furnishings are as science envisages them to be.[83] If we want to know about the existence and the nature of heavy water or quarks, of man-eating mollusks or a luminiferous aether, we are referred to the natural sciences for the answers. On this realistic construction of scientific theorizing, the theoretical terms of natural science refer to real physical entities and describe their attributes and comportments. For example, the "electron spin" of atomic physics refers to a behavioral characteristic of a real, albeit unobservable, object—an electron. According to this currently fashionable theory, the declarations of science are—or will eventually become—factually true generalizations about the actual behavior of objects that exist in the world. Is this "convergent realism" a tenable position?

It is quite clear that it is not. There is clearly insufficient warrant for and little plausibility to the claim that the world indeed is as our science claims it to be —that we've got matters altogether right, so that *our* science is *correct* science and offers the definitive "last word" on the issues. We really cannot reasonably suppose that science as it now stands affords the real truth as regards its creatures of theory.

One of the clearest lessons of the history of science is that where scientific knowledge is concerned, further discovery does not just *supplement* but generally *emends* our prior information. Accordingly, we have little alternative but to take the humbling view that the incompleteness of our purported knowledge about the world entails its potential incorrectness as well. It is now a matter

---

[83] For discussions of scientific realism, see Wilfred Sellars, *Science Perception and Reality* (London: Humanities Press, 1963); Edward McKinnon (ed.), *The Problem of Scientific Realism* (New York: Appleton-Century-Crofts, 1972); Rom Harré, *Principles of Scientific Thinking* (Chicago: University of Chicago Press, 1970); and Frederick Suppe (ed.), *The Structure of Scientific Theories* (Urbana: University of Illinois Press, ²1977).

not simply of *gaps* in the structure of our knowledge, or errors of omission. There is no realistic alternative but to suppose that we face a situation of real *flaws* as well, of errors of commission. This aspect of the matter endows incompleteness with an import far graver than meets the eye on first view.

Realism equates the paraphernalia of natural science with the domain of what actually exists. But this equation would work only if science, as it stands, has actually "got it right." And this is something we are surely not inclined—and certainly not *entitled*—to claim. We must recognize that the deliverances of science are bound to a methodology of theoretical triangulations from the data which binds them inseparably to the "state of the art" of technological sophistication in data acquisition and handling.

The supposition that the theoretical commitments of our science actually describe the world is viable only if made *provisionally*, in the spirit of "doing the best we can now do, in the current state of the art" and giving our best estimate of the matter. The step of reification is always to be taken qualifiedly, subject to a mental reservation of presumptive revisability. We do and must recognize that we cannot blithely equate *our* theories with *the* truth. We do and must realize that the declarations of science are inherently fallible and that we can only "accept" them with a certain tentativeness, subject to a clear realization that they may need to be corrected or even abandoned.

These considerations must inevitably constrain and condition our attitude toward the natural mechanisms envisaged in the science of the day. We certainly do not—or should not—want to reify (hypostasize) the "theoretical entities" of current science, to say flatly and unqualifiedly that the contrivances of *our* present-day science correctly depict the furniture of the real world. We do not—or at any rate, given the realities of the case, should not—want to adopt categorically the ontological implications of scientific theorizing in just exactly the state-of-the-art configurations presently in hand. Scientific fallibilism precludes the claim that what we purport to be scientific knowledge is in fact *real* knowledge, and accordingly blocks the path to a scientific realism that maintains that the furnishings of the real world are exactly as our science states them to be. Scientific theorizing is always inconclusive.

The world *that we describe* is one thing, but the world *as we describe it* is another, and they would coincide only if our descriptions were totally correct —something that we are certainly not in a position to claim. The world as known is a thing of our contrivance and an artifact we devise on our own terms. Even if the "data" uniquely determined a corresponding picture of reality, and did not under-determine the theoretical constructions we base upon them (as they always do), the fact remains that altered circumstances lead to altered bodies of "data." Our recognition of the fact that the world-picture of science is ever-changing blocks our taking the view that it is ever *correct*.

Accordingly, we cannot say that the world *is* such that the paraphernalia of our science actually exist as such—that is, exactly as our science characterizes them. Given the necessity of recognizing the claims of our science to be tentative and provisional, one cannot justifiably take the stance that it depicts reality. At best, one can say that it affords an *estimate* of it, an estimate that will presumably stand in need of eventual revision and whose creatures of theory may in the final analysis not be real at all. This feature of science must crucially constrain our attitude toward its deliverances. Depiction is, in this regard, a matter of intent rather than one of accomplishment. Correctness in the characterization of nature is achieved not by *our* science but only by *perfected* or *ideal* science—only by that (ineradicably hypothetical!) state of science in which the cognitive goals of the scientific enterprise are fully and definitively realized. There is no plausible alternative to the view that reality is depicted by *ideal* (or perfected or "complete") science, and not by the real science of the day. But, of course, it is this latter science that is the only one we've actually got—now or ever.

A viable scientific realism must therefore turn not on what *our* science takes the world to be like but on what *ideal or perfected* science takes the world to be like. The thesis that "science describes the real world" must be looked upon as a matter of intent rather than as an accomplished fact, of aspiration rather than achievement, of the ideal rather than the real state of things. Scientific realism is a viable position only with respect to that idealized science which, as we fully realize, we do not now have—regardless of the "now" at issue. We cannot justifiably be scientific realists. Or rather, ironically, we can be so only in an idealistic manner—namely, with respect to an "ideal science" that we can never actually claim to possess.

The posture of scientific realism—at any rate, or a duly qualified sort—is nevertheless built into the very goal-structure of science. The characteristic task of science, the definitive mission of the enterprise, is to respond to our basic interest in getting the best answers we can to our questions about the world. On the traditional view of the matter, its question-resolving concern is the *raison d'être* of the project—to celebrate any final victories. It is thus useful to draw a clear distinction between a *realism of intent* and a *realism of achievement*. We are certainly not in a position to claim that science as we have it achieves a characterization of reality. Still, science remains unabashedly realistic in *intent* or *aspiration*.

Viewed as the doctrine that science *indeed describes* reality, it is decidedly premature, but viewed as the doctrine that science *seeks to describe* reality, it is virtually a truism. For there is no way of sidestepping the conditional thesis

6.3 Science and Reality

that if a scientific theory regarding heavy water or electrons or quarks or whatever is correct—if it were indeed to be true—*then* its subject materials would exist in the manner the theory envisages and would have the properties the theory attributes to them: the theory, that is, would afford descriptively correct information about the world.

However, this conditional relationship reflects what is, in the final analysis, less a profound fact about the nature of science than a near truism about the nature of truth as *adequation ad rem*. The fact remains that "our reality"—reality as we conceive it to be—goes no further than to represent our best estimate of what reality is like.

When we look to WHAT *science declares*, to the aggregate content and substance of its declarations, we see that these declarations are realistic in intent, that they *purport* to describe the world as it really is. But when we look to HOW *science makes its declarations* and note how tentatively and provisionally they are offered and accepted, we recognize that this realism is of an abridged and qualified sort—that we are not prepared to claim that this is how matters actually stand in the real world. At the level of generality and precision at issue in the themes of natural science, we are not now—or ever—entitled to lay claim to the scientific truth as such but only to the scientific truth as we and our contemporaries see it. Realism prevails with respect to the *language* of science (that is, the asserted content of its declarations); but it should be abandoned with respect to the *status* of science (that is, the ultimate tenability or correctness of these assertions). What science says is descriptively committal in making claims regarding "the real world," but the tone of voice in which it proffers these claims is (or should be) provisional and tentative.

The resultant position is one not of skepticism but of realism in two senses: (1) it is realistic about our capabilities of recognizing that here, as elsewhere, we are dealing with the efforts of an imperfect creature to do the best it can in the circumstances; and (2) it recognizes the mind-transcendent reality of a "real world" that our own best efforts in the cognitive sphere can only manage to domesticate rather imperfectly. We do, and always must, recognize that no matter how far we manage to extend the frontiers of natural science, there is more to be done. Within a setting of vast complexity, reality outruns our cognitive reach; there is more to this complex world of ours than that which lies—now or ever—within our ken.[84]

---

[84] Further discussion of some of this chapter's themes is presented in the author's *Limits of Science* (Pittsburgh: University of Pittsburgh Press, 2000).

6.4 The Potential Diversity of "Science"

Natural science is our means of access to knowledge regarding the real world's facts. To what extent does the involvement of our specifically human effort and action condition the character of our natural science? Does our science as a product reflect our particular *modus operandi?* It is instructive to consider this issue through the perspective of whether an astronomically remote civilization might be scientifically more advanced than ourselves. For the seemingly straightforward question about the possibility of scientifically more advanced aliens turns out, on closer inspection, to involve considerable complexity. And this complexity relates not only to the actual or possible facts of the situation, but also—and crucially—to theoretical questions about the very ideas or concepts that are at issue here.

To begin we must confront the problem of just what it is for there to be another science-possessing civilization. Note that this is a question that *we* are putting—a question posed in terms of the applicability of *our* term "science." It pivots on the issue of whether *we* would be prepared to call certain of *their* activities —once we came to understand them—as engaging in scientific inquiry, and whether we would be prepared to recognize the product of these activities as constituting a state of science—or a branch thereof.

A scientific civilization is not merely one that possesses intelligence and social organization, but one that puts these resources to work in a certain very particular sort of way. This consideration opens up the rather subtle issue of priority in regard to process vs. product. We must decide whether what counts for a civilization's "having a science" is primarily a matter of the substantive *content* of their doctrines (their belief structures and theory complexes) or it is primarily a matter of process, and thus of the aims and *purposes* with which their doctrines are formed.

As regards content, this turns on the issue of how similar their scientific beliefs are to ours. And a look at our own historical evolution indicates that this is clearly something on which we would be ill-advised to put much emphasis at the very outset. After all, the speculations of the nature theorists of Presocratic Greece, our ultimate ancestor in the scientific enterprise, bear precious little resemblance to our present-day sciences, nor does contemporary physics bear all that much doctrinal resemblance to that of Newton. So, it emerges as clearly more appropriate to give prime emphasis to matters of process and purpose.

Accordingly, the question of these aliens "having a science" is to be regarded as turning not on the extent to which their substantive *findings* resemble ours, but on the extent to which their purposive *project* resembles ours—of determining that we are engaged in the same sort of inquiry in terms of the sorts of issues being addressed and the ways in which they are going about addressing them. The issue accordingly is at bottom not one of the substantive similarity of their scientifically formed beliefs to ours, but one of the functional equivalency of the *projects* at issue in terms of the quintessential goals that define the scientific enterprise as what it is: explanation, prediction, and control over nature. It is this issue of teleology that ultimately defines what it is for those aliens to have a science.

This perspective enjoins the pivotal question: To what extent would the *functional equivalent* of natural science built up by the inquiring intelligences of an astronomically remote civilization be bound to resemble our science in substantive content-oriented regards? In considering this issue, one soon comes to realize that there is an enormous potential for diversity here.

To begin with, the *machinery of formulation* used by an alien civilization in expressing their science might be altogether different. In particular, their mathematics might be very unlike ours. Their "arithmetic" could be anumerical—purely comparative, for example, rather than quantitative. Especially if their environment were not amply endowed with solid objects or stable structures—if, for example, they were jellyfish-like creatures swimming about in a soupy sea—their "geometry" could be something rather strange, largely topological, say, and geared to structures rather than sizes or shapes. Digital thinking in all its forms might be undeveloped, while they might, like the ancient Greeks, have "Euclidean" geometry without analysis. And so, seeing that the mathematical mechanisms at their disposal could be very different from ours, it is clear that their description of nature in mathematical terms could also be very different (and not necessarily truer or falser, but just different.)

Secondly, the *orientation* of the science of an alien civilization might be very different. All their efforts might conceivably be directed at social intersections—to developing highly sophisticated analyses of intersecting agents and the economics of exchanges sociology, for example. Again, their approach to natural science might also be very different. Communicating by some sort of "telepathy" based upon variable odors or otherwise "exotic" signals, they might devise a complex theory of thought-wave transmittal through an ideaferous aether. Electromagnetic phenomena might lie altogether outside their ken; if their environment does not afford them lodestones and electrical storms, etc., the occasion to theorize about electromagnetic processes might never arise. The course of scientific development tends to flow in the channel of practical interests. A society of porpoises might lack crystallography but develop a very sophisticated hydrodynamics; one comprised of mole-like creatures might never dream of developing optics. The science of a different civilization would presumably be closely geared to the particular pattern of their interaction with nature as funneled through the particular course of their evolutionary adjustment to their specific environment.

Alien civilizations might scan nature very differently. The direct chemical analysis of environmental materials might prove highly useful to them, with bio-analytic techniques akin to our sense of taste and smell highly developed so as to provide the basis for a science of a very different sort. Acoustics might mean very little to them, while other sorts of pressure phenomena—say, the theory of turbulence in gases—might be the subject of intense and exhaustive investigation. Rather than sending signals by radio waves or heat radiation, they might propel gravity waves through space. After all, a comparison of the "science" of different civilizations here on earth suggests that it is not an outlandish hypothesis to suppose that the very *topics* of an alien science might differ radically from those of ours. In our own case, for example, the fact that we live on the surface of our planet (unlike whales or porpoises), the fact we have eyes (unlike worms or moles) and thus can *see* the heavens, the fact that we are so situated that the seasonal positions of heavenly bodies are intricately connected with our biological needs through the agricultural route to food supply, are all clearly connected with the development of astronomy. Accordingly, the constitution of the alien inquirers—physical, biological, and social—emerges as a crucial element here. It serves to determine the agenda of questions and the instrumentalities for their resolution—to fix what counts as interesting, important, relevant, significant. In determining what is seen as an appropriate question and what is judged as an admissible solution, the cognitive posture of the inquirers must be expected to play a crucial role in shaping and determining the course of scientific inquiry itself.

Thirdly, the *conceptualization* of an alien science might be very different. We must reckon with the theoretical possibility that a remote civilization might operate with a radically different system of concepts in its cognitive dealings with nature. To motivate this idea of a conceptually different science, it helps to cast the issue in temporal rather than spatial terms. The descriptive characterization of *alien* science is a project rather akin in its difficulty to that of describing our own *future* science. After all, it is effectively impossible to predict not only the answers but even the questions that lie on the agenda of *future* science, because these questions will grow out of the answers we obtain at yet unattained stages of the game. And the situation of an *alien* science could be much the same. As with the science of the remote future, the science of the remotely distant must be presumed to be of such a nature that we really could not achieve intellectual access to it on the basis of our own position in the cognitive scheme of things.

Just as the technology of another highly advanced civilization would most likely strike us as magic, so its science would most likely strike us as incomprehensible gibberish—until we had learned it "from the ground up." They might (just barely) be able to *teach* it to us, but they almost certainly could not *explain* it to us. After all, the most characteristic and significant sort of difference between variant conceptual schemes arises when one scheme is committed to something the other does not envisage at all—something that lies outside the conceptual range of the other. The "science" of different civilizations may well, like Galenic and Pasteurian medicine, in key respects simply *change the subject* so as no longer "to talk about the same things," but treat things (e.g., humors and bacteria, respectively) of which the other takes little or no cognizance at all. If, for example, certain intelligent aliens should prove that a diffuse and complex aggregate mass of units comprising wholes in ways that allow an overlap, then the role of social concepts might become so paramount that nature as a whole comes to be viewed in these terms. The results would be something very difficult for us to grasp, seeing that they are based on a mode of "shared experience" with which we have no contact.

It is only reasonable to presume that the conceptual character of the (functionally understood) "science" of an alien civilization is so radically different from ours in substantive regards as to orient their thought about "the nature of things" in altogether different directions. Their approach to classification and structurization, and their explanatory mechanisms, predictive concerns, and modes of control over nature, might all be very different. In all these regards they might have procedures and interests that depart significantly from our own.

Natural science—broadly construed as inquiry into the ways of nature—is something that is in principle almost infinitely plastic. Its development will trace out a historical course that is bound to be closely geared to the specific capacities, interests, environment, and opportunities of the creatures that develop it. We are deeply mistaken if we think of it as a process that must follow a route roughly parallel to ours and issue in a comparable product. It would be grossly unimaginative to think that either the journey or the destination must be the same—or even substantially similar.

6.5 The One World, One Science Argument

One recent writer raises the question of "What can we talk about with our remote friends?" and answers it with the remark: "We have a lot in common. We have mathematics in common, and physics, and astronomy."[85] This line of thought begs some very big questions.

Our alien colleagues would have to scan nature for regularities using (at any rate, to begin with) the sensors provided to them by their evolutionary heritage. And they will note, record, and transmit those regularities which they found to be intellectually interesting or pragmatically useful. Their inquiries will have to develop by theoretical triangulation that proceeds from the lines indicated by these resources. Now, this is clearly going to make for a course of development that closely gears their science to their particular situation—their biological endowment ("their sensors"), their cultural heritage ("what is interesting"), their environmental niche ("what is pragmatically useful"). Where these key parameters differ, there too we must expect that the course of scientific development will differ as well.

Admittedly, there is only one universe and its laws, as best we can tell, are everywhere the same. And so, if intelligent aliens investigate nature at all, they will investigate the same nature we ourselves do. But the sameness of the object of contemplation does nothing to guarantee the sameness of the ideas about it. It is all too familiar a fact that even where human (and thus *homogeneous*) observers are at issue, different constructions are often placed upon "the same" occurrences. Primitive peoples thought the sun to be a god and the most sophisticated among the ancient peoples thought it a large mass of fire. We think of it as a large thermonuclear reactor, and heaven only knows how our successors will think of it in the year 3000. As the course of human history clearly shows, there need be little uniformity in the conceptions held about one selfsame object by differently situated groups of thinkers.

It would certainly be naive to think that because one selfsame object is in question, its description must issue in the same result. This view ignores the crucial matter of one's intellectual orientation. One particular piece of driftwood is viewed very differently indeed by the botanist, the painter, the interior decorator, the chemist, the woodcarver, etc. The critical issue is that of the particular "aspect" of the item being focused upon as important or interesting. With science, as with any productive enterprise, it is not only the raw material but also the mode of productive processing that serves to determine the nature of the outcome. Minds with different sorts of concerns and interests and different backgrounds of information can deal with mutually common items in ways that

---

85 Edward Purcell, "Radioastronomy and Communication through Space," in: Alistair G. W. Cameron (ed.), *Interstellar Communication: A Collection of Reprints and Original Contributions* (New York and Amsterdam: W. A. Benjamin, 1963), pp. 121–143 [see p. 142].

yield wholly disjoint and disparate results, because altogether different features of the thing are being addressed. It is notorious that observers are "prisoners" (so to speak) of their cognitive preparation, interests, and predispositions—seeing only what their pre-established cognitive resources enable them to see and blind to that for which they are cognitively unprepared.

Accordingly, the sameness of nature and its laws by no means settles the issue of scientific uniformity. For a science is always the result of *inquiry* into some sector of nature and this is inevitably a matter of a *transaction* or *interaction* in which nature is but one party and the inquiring beings another. The result of such an interaction depends crucially on the contribution from both sides—from nature and from the intelligences that interact with it. A kind of "chemistry" is at issue, where nature provides only one input and the inquirers themselves provide another—one that can massively and dramatically affect the outcome in such a way that we cannot disentangle the respective contributions of the two parties.

Each inquiring civilization must be thought of as producing its own ever-changing cognitive product—all more or less adequate in their own ways—but with little if any actual overlap in conceptual content. Human organisms are essentially similar, but there is not much similarity between the medicine of the ancient Hindus and that of the ancient Greeks. There is every reason to think that the natural science of different astronomically remote civilizations should be highly diversified. Even as different creatures can have a vast variety of life-styles for adjustment within one selfsame physical environment like this earth, so they can have a vast variety of thought styles for cognitive adjustment within one selfsame world.

After all, throughout the earlier stages of man's intellectual history, different human civilizations have developed their "natural sciences" in a substantially different way. And the shift to an extraterrestrial perspective is bound to amplify such cultural differences. Perhaps reluctantly, we must face the fact that on a cosmic scale the "hard" physical sciences have something of the same cultural relativity to which we are accustomed with the material of the "softer" social sciences.

It seems reasonable to argue that: "Common problems constrain common solutions. Intelligent alien civilizations have in common with us the problem of cognitive accommodation to a shared world. Natural science as we know it is our solution to this problem. Ergo, it is likely to be theirs as well." But this tempting argument founders on its second premiss. Their problem is *not* common with ours because their situation must be presumed substantially different, seeing that they live in a significantly different environment and come equipped with significantly different resources. To presuppose a common problem is in fact to beg the question.

There is no quarrel here with "the principle of the uniformity of nature." But this principle merely tells us that when exactly the same question is put to nature, exactly the same answer will be forthcoming. However, the development of a science hinges crucially on this matter of questions—to the sorts of issues that are addressed and the sequential order in which they are posed. And here, the prospect of variation arises: We must expect alien beings to question nature in ways very different from our own. On the basis of an *interactionist* model, there is no reason to think that the sciences of different civilizations will exhibit anything more than the roughest sorts of family resemblance.

Our human science reflects not only our interests but also our capacities. It addresses a range of issues that are correlative with our specific modes of physical interaction with nature, the specific ways in which we monitor its processes. It is highly selective—the science of a being that secures its most crucial information through sight, monitoring developments along the spectrum of electromagnetic radiation, rather than, say, monitoring variations of pressure or temperature. A different sort of creature would have different interests and concerns. Ours is certainly not a phenomenalistic science geared to the feel of things or the taste of things. All the same, the science we have developed reflects our capacities and needs, our evolutionary heritage as a being inserted into the orbit or natural phenomena in a certain particular way.

The fact is that all such aspects as capacities, requirements, interests, and the course of development affect the shape and substance of the science and technology of any particular place and time. Unless we narrow our intellectual horizons in a parochially anthropomorphic way, we must be prepared to recognize the great likelihood that the "science" and "technology" of another civilization will be something *very* different from science and technology as we know it. We are led to view that our human sort of natural science may well be *sui generis*, adjusted to and coordinate with a being of our physical constitution, inserted into the orbit of the world's processes and history in our sort of way. It seems that in science, as in other areas of human endeavor, we are emplaced within the thought world where our biological, social, and intellectual heritage affords us.

6.6 A Quantitative Perspective

Let us attempt to give some quantitative structure to the preceding qualitative deliberations by bringing some rough order-of-magnitude estimates on the scene.

6.6 A Quantitative Perspective

First off, there is the problem of estimating H, the number of habitable planets in the universe. This assessment can be formed by means of the following quantities, themselves represented merely as order-of-magnitude specifications:

- n_1 = number of galaxies in the observable universe (10^{11})
- n_2 = average number of star systems per galaxy (10^{11})
- x_1 = fraction of star systems having suitably large and stable planets (1/10)
- n_3 = average number of such planets in the temperature zone of a suitably benign solar system, where it is neither too hot nor too cold for life (1)
- x_2 = fraction of temperature planets equipped with a surface chemistry capable of supporting life (1/10)

These figures—borrowed in the main from Dole and Sagan—can be subject to skepticism.[86] They, and those that are to follow, must be viewed realistically. They are not engraved in stone for all the ages, but represent conjectural "best estimates" in the present state of the art. The important point, as will emerge below, is that the overall tendency of our discussion is not acutely sensitive to precision in this respect. Accordingly, one should look on the calculations that are to follow as suggestive rather than in any sense conclusive. Their function is to indicate a general line of thought and not to establish a definitive conclusion.

Given the preceding estimates, the sought-for number of habitable planets will be the product of these quantities:

$$H = 10^{20}$$

This, of course, is a prodigiously large number, providing for some thousand million habitable planets per galaxy. Here, we confront a truly impressive magnitude. But it is only the start of the story.

A planet capable of supporting life might well have no life to support, let alone *intelligent* life. The point is that the physics, chemistry, and biology must all work out just right. The physical, chemical, and biological environments must all be duly auspicious and exactly the right course of triggering processes must unfold for the evolution of intelligence to run a successful course. Our next task is thus to estimate I, the number of planets on which intelligent life evolves.

---

86 See Stephen H. Dole, *Habitable Planets for Man* (New York: Blaisdell, 1964; New York: American Elsevier, ²1970) and also Carl Sagan, *Cosmos* (New York: Random House, 1980).

Let us proceed here via the following (again, admittedly rough and ready) quantities:

- r_1 = fraction of habitable planets on which life—that is, some sort of self-reproducing biological system—actually arises (1/100)
- r_2 = fraction of these on which highly complex life-forms evolve, possessed of something akin to a central nervous system and thus capable of complex (though yet instinctively programmed) behavior forms (1/100)
- r_3 = fraction of these on which intelligent and sociable beings evolve—beings who can acquire, process, and exchange factual information with relative sophistication—who can observe, remember, reason, and communicate (1/100)

As these fractions indicate, the evolutionary process that begins with the inauguration of life and moves on to the development of intelligence is certainly not an inexorable sequence, but one which could, given suitably inauspicious conditions, abort in a stabilization that freezes the whole course of development at some plateau along the way. Note that r_3 in particular involves problems. Conscious and indeed even intelligent creatures are readily conceivable who yet lack that orientation towards their environment needed to acquire, store, transmit, and process the factual information necessary to science. Where such conceptions as space, time, process, unit, function, and order are missing, it is difficult to see how anything deserving of the name "science" could exist. An intelligence unswervingly directed at the aesthetic appreciation of particular phenomena rather than their generally lawful structure is going to miss out on the scientific dimension.

And so, when we put the fractions of the preceding series to work, we arrive at:

$$I = 10^{14}$$

Unquestionably, this still indicates an impressively large number of intelligence-bearing planets. It would, in fact, yield a quota of some thousand per galaxy (a figure which, if correct, would cast a shadow over the prospect of us ever establishing contact with extraterrestrial intelligence, since it would indicate its nearest locale to be some 1,000 light-years away).

As regards this figure, one can say that it would certainly be possible to take a rosier view of the matter. One could suppose that nature has a penchant for life—that a kind of Bergsonian *élan vital* is operative, so that life springs forth wherever it can possibly get a foothold. Something of this attitude certainly underlies

J. P. T. Pearman's contention that the probability is 1 that life will develop on a planet with a suitable environment[87]—a stance in which most recent writers on the subject are concerned. One theorist cuts the Gordian Knot with a curious bit of reasoning:

> Biological evolution proceeds by the purely random process of mutation...Since the process is a random one, the laws of probability suggest that the time-scale of evolution on earth should resemble the average time-scale for the development of higher forms of life anywhere.[88]

However, this blatantly ignores the crucially differentiating role of initial conditions in determining the outcome of random processes. The terrain through which a random walk proceeds is going to make a lot of difference to its destination. The transition from habitability to habitation—from the possibility of life to its actuality—is surely not all that simple. Sir Arthur Eddington did well to remind us in this context of the prodigality of nature when he asked how many acorns are scattered for any one that grows into an oak.[89]

One could perhaps go on to suppose that nature incorporated a predisposition for intelligence—that there is a Teilhard-de-Chardin-reminiscent impetus towards *nous*, so that intelligence develops wherever there is life. Indeed, the suggestion is sometimes made in this vein that "the adaptive value of intelligence...is so great...that if it is genetically feasible, natural selection seems likely to bring it forth."[90] But this argument from utility to evolutionary probability clearly has its limitation. ("[T]here are no organisms on Earth which have developed tractor treads for locomotion, despite the usefulness of tractor treads in some environments."[91]) Moreover, this suggestion seems implausibly anthropocentric. To all appearances, the termite has a securer foothold on the evolutionary ladder than man; and the coelacanth can afford to smile when the survival advantages of intelligence are touted by a johnny-come-lately creature whose self-inflicted threats to long-term survival are a cause of general concern.

---

87 See p. 29 of Alistair G. W. Cameron (ed.), *Interstellar Communication: A Collection of Reprints and Original Contributions* (New York and Amsterdam: W. A. Benjamin, 1963).
88 Su-Shu Huang, "Life Outside the Solar System," *Scientific American* 202/4 (April 1960), p. 55.
89 See Sir Arthur Eddington, *The Nature of the Physical World* (New York: Macmillan; Cambridge: Cambridge University Press, 1928), p. 177.
90 Iossif S. Shklovskii and Carl Sagan, *Intelligent Life in the Universe* (San Francisco, London and Amsterdam: Holden-Day, 1966), p. 411.
91 Shklovskii and Sagan, *Intelligent Life in the Universe*, p. 359.

As J. P. T. Pearman has rightly noted, "the successful persistence of a multitude of simpler organisms from ancient times argues that intelligence may confer no unique benefits for survival in an environment similar to that of earth."[92] After all, it will prove survival-conducive mainly for a being of a particularly restless disposition, a creature like man, who refuses to settle down in a secured ecological niche, but shifts restlessly from environment to environment needing continually to readjust to self-imposed changes. The value of intelligence, one might say, is not absolute but remedial—as an aid to offsetting the problems of a particular sort of lifestyle. We would do well to think of the emergence of intelligence as a long series of fortuitous twists and turnings rather than an inexorable push towards a foreordained result. It would be glib in the extreme to assume that once life arises, its subsequent development would proceed in much the same way as here on earth.[93]

The indicated figures accordingly seem plausibly middle-roadish between undue pessimism and an intelligence-favoring optimism that seems unwarranted at this particular stage of the scientific game. Even so, it is clear that the proposed specification of I represents a strikingly substantial magnitude—one which contemplates many thousands of millions of planets equipped with intelligent creatures scattered throughout the universe.

Intelligence, however, is not yet the end of the line. (After all, dolphins and apes are presumably intelligent, but they do not have, and are unlikely to develop, a "science.") Many further steps are needed to estimate S, the number of planets throughout the universe in which scientific civilizations arise. The developmental path from intelligence to science is a road strewn with substantial obstacles. Here, matters must be propitious not just as regards the physics, chemistry, biochemistry, evolutionary biology and cognitive psychology of the situation. The social science requisites for the evolution of science as the cultural artifact of a multifocal civilization must also be met. Economic conditions, social organization, and cultural orientation must all be properly adjusted before the move from intelligence to science can be accomplished. For scientific inquiry to evolve and flourish, there must, in the first place, be cultural institutions whose development requires economic conditions and a favorable social organization. And terrestrial experience suggests that such conditions for the social evolution of a developed culture are by no means always present where intelligence is. We do well to recall that of the myriad human civilizations evolved here on earth, only one,

---

[92] Cameron, *Interstellar Communication*, p. 190.
[93] On this issue, see George G. Simpson, "The Nonprevalence of Humanoids," *Science* 143 (1964), pp. 769–775, Chapter 13 of *This View of Life: The World of an Evolutionist* (New York: Harcourt Brace, 1964).

the Mediterranean/European, managed to develop natural science in a form that is nowadays unproblematically recognizable as such by all advanced civilizations. The successful transit from intelligence to science is certainly not a sure thing. The crux lies in the fact that cognition is biologically rooted and that this will in the end enjoin a relativizing coordination with the perceptual resources of its developers.

Let us once more look at the matter quantitatively:

p_1 = probability that intelligent beings will (unlike dolphins) also possess developed manipulative abilities and will (unlike the higher apes) combine intelligence with manipulative ability so as to develop a technology that can be passed on as a social heritage across the generations (.01)

p_2 = probability that technologically competent intelligent beings will group themselves in organized societies of substantial complexity—a transition that stone-age man, for example, never managed to make (.1)

p_3 = probability that an organized society will not only acquire the means for transmitting across successive generations the political and pragmatic know-how indispensable to an "organized society" as such, but will also (unlike the ancient Egyptians) develop institutions of learning and culture for accumulating, refining, systematizing, and perpetuating factual information (.1)

p_4 = probability that society with cultural institutions will develop an unstable (i.e., continually developing and dynamic) technology—in a way the ancient Greeks and the old Chinese mandarins, for example, never did—so as to create a technologically progressive civilization (.01)

p_5 = probability that a technologically progressive civilization will develop and maintain an articulated "science" and concern itself with the theoretical study of nature at a level of high generality and precision (.1)

However firm the physical quantities with which we began, we are by now skating on very thin ice indeed. These latter issues of sociology and cognitive psychology can only be quantified in the most tentative and cautious way. But the one thing that is clear is that a good many conditions of this sort have to be met and that each involves a likelihood of relatively modest proportions.

The issue of technology reflected in p_1 and p_4 is particularly critical here. The urge to an ever-aggressive technological extension of self is certainly not felt by every intelligent life-form. It is a part of Western man's peculiar lifestyle to impatiently cultivate the active modification of nature in the pursuit of human convenience so as to create an artificial environment of ultra-low entropy. Even in human terms this is not a uniquely constrained solution to the problem of evolutionary adaptation. Many human societies seem to have remained perfectly content with the *status quo* for countless generations and very sophisticated cultural projects—literary criticism, for example—have developed in directions very different from the scientific. After all, a culture can easily settle comfortably into a frozen traditionary pattern with respect to technology. (If their attention span is long enough, our aliens might cultivate scholastic theology *ad indefinitum*.) Moreover, unless their oral lore is something very different from ours, it is hard to see how an alien civilization could develop science without writing — a skill which even many human communities did not manage to develop. The salient point is that for "science" to emerge in a distant planet it is not enough for there to be life and intelligence; there must also be culture and progressive technology and explanatory interest and theorizing competency.

The product of the preceding sequence of probability estimates is 10^{-7}. Multiplying this by I we would obtain the following expected-value estimate of the number of "science"-possessing planetary civilizations:

$$S = 10^7 = 10,000,000$$

This, of course, is still a large number, albeit now one that is rather modest on a cosmic scale, implying a chance of only some .01% that a given galaxy actually provides the home for a "science." (Note too that we ignore the temporal dimension—the scientific civilizations at issue may have been destroyed long ago, or perhaps simply have lost interest in doing science.) A more conservative appraisal of the sociological parameters has thus led us to a figure that is more modest by many orders of magnitude than the estimate by Shklovskii and Sagan (op. cit.) that some $10^{5\pm1}$ scientifically sophisticated civilizations exist in our galaxy alone. Nevertheless, even this modest ten million is still a sizable number.

6.7 Comparability and Judgments of Relative Advancement or Backwardness

Let us now come to grips with the crux of our present concerns: the issue of scientific advancement. Earlier, we defined "science" in terms of a rather generic sort of *functional* equivalency. The question, however, from which we began was not whether a remote civilization has a "science" of some sort, but whether it is *scientifically more advanced* than ours. But if another science is to represent an advance over ours, we must clearly construe it as *our sort* of science in much more particularized and substantive terms. And given the *immense* diversity to be expected among the various modes of "science" and "technology," the number of extraterrestrial civilizations possessing a science and technology that is duly consonant and contiguous with ours—and in particular, heavily geared towards the mathematical laws of the electromagnetic spectrum—must be judged to be very small indeed.

We have come to recognize that sciences can vary (1) in their formal mechanisms of *formulation*—their "mathematics," (2) in their *conceptualization*, that is, in the kinds of explanatory and descriptive concepts they bring to bear, and (3) in their *orientation* towards the manifold pressures of nature, reflecting the varying "interest" directions of their developers. While "science" as such is clearly not anthropocentric, science *as we have it*—the only "science" that we ourselves know—is a specifically human artifact that must be expected to reflect in significant degree the particular characteristics of its makers. Consequently, the prospect that an alien "science"-possessing civilization has a *science* that we would acknowledge (if sufficiently informed) as representing the same general line of inquiry as that in which we ourselves are engaged seems extremely implausible. The possibility that *their* science and technology is "sufficiently similar" in orientation and character to substantively proximate to *ours* must be viewed as extremely remote. We clearly cannot estimate this as representing something other than a very long shot indeed—certainly no better than one in many thousands.

Just such comparability with "our sort of science" is, however, the indispensable precondition for judgments of relative advancement or backwardness *vis-à-vis* ourselves. The idea of their being scientifically "more advanced" is predicated on the uniformity of the enterprises—doing better and more effectively the kinds of things that *we* want science and technology to do. Any talk of advancement and progress is predicated on the sameness of the direction of movement: only if others are traveling along the same route as we, can they be said to be ahead or behind us. The issue of relative advancement is linked inseparably to the idea of doing the same sort of thing better or more fully. And this falls apart when "this sort of thing" is not substantially the same. One can say that a child's expository writing is more primitive than an adult's, or that the novice's performance at arithmetic or piano playing is less developed than that of the expert. But we can scarcely say that Chinese cookery is more or less advanced than Roman, or Greek pottery than Renaissance glassblowing. The salient point for present purposes is simply that where the enterprises are sufficiently diverse, the ideas of comparative advancement and progress are inapplicable for lack of a *sine qua non* condition.

Claiming scientific superiority is not as simple as may seem at first sight. To begin with, it would not automatically emerge from the capacity to make many splendidly successful predictions. For this could be the result of precognition or empathetic attunement to nature or such-like. Again, what is wanted is not just a matter of *correct*, but of cognitively underwritten, and thus *science-guided* prediction—predictions guided by insight based on understanding and not mere lucky guesswork. And that's just exactly what is to be proved.

It clearly is not enough for establishing their being scientifically more advanced than ourselves that the aliens should perform "technological wonders"—that they should be able to do all sorts of things we would like to do but cannot. After all, bees can do that. The technology at issue must clearly be the product of intelligent contrivance rather than evolutionary trial and error. What is needed for advancement is that their performatory wonders issue from superior theoretical knowledge—i.e., from superior science. And then we are back in the circle.

Nor would the matter be settled by the consideration that an extraterrestrial species might be more "intelligent" than us in having a greater capacity for the timely and comprehensive monitoring and processing of information. After all, whale or porpoises, with their larger brains, may (for all we know) have to manipulate relatively larger quantities of sheer data than ourselves to maintain effective adaptation within the highly changeable environment. What clearly counts for scientific knowledge is not the *quantity* of intelligence in sheer volumetric terms but its *quality* in substantive, issue-oriented terms. Information handling does not assure scientific development. Libraries of information (or misinformation) can be generated about trivia or dedicated to matters very different from science as we know it.

It is perhaps too tempting for humans to reckon cognitive superiority by the law of the jungle—judging as superior those who do or would come out on top in outright conflict. But surely the Mongols were not possessors of a civilization superior to that of the New Eastern cultures they overran. Again, we earthlings might easily be eliminated by not very knowledgeable creatures able to produce at will, perhaps by using natural secretions—a biological or chemical agent capable of killing us off.

The key point, then, is that if they are to effect an *advance* on our science, they must both (1) be engaged in doing roughly our sort of thing in roughly our sort of way, and (2) do it significantly better. In speaking of the "science" of another civilization as "more advanced" than our own, we contemplate the prospect that they have developed *science* (*our* sort of science—"science" as we know it) further than we have ourselves. And this is implausible. Even assuming that "they" develop a "science" at all—that is, a *functional equivalent* of our science—it seems unduly parochial to suppose that they are at work constructing *our* sort of science in substantive, content-oriented terms. Diverse life-modes have diverse interests; diverse interests engender diverse technologies; diverse technologies make for diverse modes of science. And where the parties concerned are going in different directions, it makes no sense to say that one is ahead of or behind the other.

If a civilization of intelligent aliens develops a science at all, it seems plausible to expect that they will develop it in another direction altogether and produce something that we, if we could come to understand it at all, would regard as simply detached in a content orientation—though perhaps not in intent—from the scientific enterprise as we ourselves cultivate it. (Think of the attitude of orthodox sciences to "exotic" phenomena like hypnotism, or acupuncture, let alone to parapsychology.)

The crucial consideration is that there is just not a single-track itinerary of scientific/technological development that different civilizations travel in common with mere differences in speed or in staying power (notwithstanding the penchant of astrophysics for the neat plotting of numerical "degrees of development" against time in the evolution of planetary civilizations. In cognition and even in "scientific" evolution we are not dealing with a single-track railway, but with a complex network leading to many mutually remote destinations. Even as cosmic evolution involves a red shift that carries different star systems ever farther from each other in space, so cognitive evolution may well involve a red shift that carries different civilizations even farther from each other into mutually remote thought-worlds.

The prospect that an alien civilization is going about the job of doing *our* science—a "science" that reflects the sorts of interests and involvement that *we* have in nature—better than we do ourselves must accordingly be adjudged as extremely far-fetched. Specifically, two conditions would have to be met for the science of an intelligent civilization to be in a position to count as comparable to ours:

1. that, given that they have a "science" and a developing "technology," they have managed to couple the two and have proceeded to develop (unlike the ancient Greeks, Chinese, and Byzantines) a *science-guided* technology (Probability p_6);
2. that their science-guided technology is oriented sufficiently closely towards issues regarding natural processes as those of our science-guided technology that a comparison can reasonably be made between them (Probability p_7).

To judge by terrestrial experience, it seems rather optimistic to estimate p_6 to be even so large as one in a thousand (with $p_6 = .001$). And p_7 must also be adjudged as quite small. As we have seen, science-guided technology could be oriented in very different directions. The potential diversity of different modes of "science" is enormous, so that there is little choice but to see p_7 as an eventuation whose chances are no better than, say, one in ten thousand (so $p_7 = .0001$). If our alien scientists are differently constructed (if they are silicon-based creatures, for example), or if their natural environment is very different, their practical interests and its accordant technology will be oriented in very different directions from ours. For example, their technology might be wholly independent of "hardware," oriented not towards physical machinery, but towards the software of mind-state manipulation, telepathy, hypnotism, autosuggestion, or the like. (Ray Bradbury's Martians destroy an expedition from Earth armed with atomic weapons by thought control.) And we must not keep our imagination on a short leash in this regard. Given the diversity of different modes of "science" and the enormous spectrum of possible issues and purposes in principle available to extraterrestrial aliens, the prospect must be recognized that the direction of their science-guided technology might be vastly different from ours.

Accordingly, we have it that:

$$p_6 \times p_7 = 10^{-7}$$

Now, the product of this quantity with the previously estimated quantity S, the number of civilizations that possess a technologized science as we comprehend it, is clearly not going to be very substantial—it is, in fact, going to be strikingly close to 1.

If "being there" in scientific regards means having *our* sort of scientifically guided technology and our sort of technologically channeled science, then it does not seem all that far-fetched to suppose that as regards science as we have it, *we might be there alone*—even in a universe amply furnished with other intelligent civilizations. The prospect that somebody else could do "our sort of thing" in the scientific sphere better than we can do it ourselves seems very remote.

6.8 Cosmic Limitations

The overall structure of our analysis thus emerges in the picture of Display 3. Its figures interestingly embody the familiar situation that as one moves along a nested hierarchy of increasing complexity, one encounters a greater scope for diversity—that the further layers of system complexity provide for an ever-widening spectrum of possible state and conditions. (The more elementary that system, and narrower its correlative range of alternatives, the more complex, the wider.) If each unit ("letter," "cell," "atom") can be configurated in ten ways, then each ordered group of ten such units ("word," "organ," "molecule") can be configurated in 10^{10} ways, and each complex of ten such groups ("sentences," "organisms," "objects") in $(10^{10})^{10} = 10^{100}$ ways. Thus, even if only a small fraction of what is realizable in theory is realizable in nature, any increase in organizational complexity will nevertheless be accompanied by an enormous amplification of possibilities.

To be sure, the numerical particulars that constitute the quantitative thread of the discussion cannot be given much credence. But their general tendency nevertheless conveys an important lesson. For people frequently seem inclined to reason as follows:

> There are, after all, an immense number of planetary objects running about in the heavens. And proper humility requires us to recognize that there is nothing at all that special about the Earth. If it can evolve life and intelligence and civilization and science, then so can other planets. And given that there are so many other runners in the race, we must assume that—even though we cannot see them in the cosmic darkness—some of them have got ahead of us in the race.

Planets of sufficient size for potential habitation		10^{22}
fraction thereof affording:	temperate location for life	10^{-1}
	chemistry for life-support	10^{-1}
	biochemistry for the actual emergence of life	10^{-2}
	biology and psychology for the evolution of intelligence	10^{-4}
	sociology for developing a culture with a "technology" and a "science"	10^{-7}
	epistemology for developing science as we know it	10^{-7}

Display 3: Conditions for the Development of Science

As one recent writer formulates this familiar argumentation, "Since man's existence on the Earth occupies but an instant in cosmic time, surely intelligent life has progressed far beyond our level on some of these 100,000,000 (habitable) planets (in our galaxy)."[94] But such plausible-sounding argumentation overlooks the numerical complexities. Even though there are an immense number of solar systems, and thus a staggering number of planets (some 10^{22} by our estimate), nevertheless, a substantial number of conditions must be met for "science" (as we understand it) to arise. The astrophysical, physical, chemical, biological, psychological, sociological, and epistemological parameters must all be in prop-

---

94 Cameron, *Interstellar Communication*, p. 75.

er adjustment. There must be habitability, and life, and intelligence, and culture, and technology, and a "science" coupled to technology, and an appropriate subject-matter orientation of this intellectual product, etc.—a great many turnings must go right en route to science of a quality comparable to ours. Each step along the way is one of finite (and often smallish) probability. And to reach the final destination, all these probabilities must be multiplied together, yielding a quantity that might be very small indeed. Even if there were only twelve turning points along this developmental route, each involving a chance of successful eventuation that is, on average, no worse than a one-in-a-hundred, the chance of an overall success would be immensely small, corresponding to an aggregate success-probability of merely 10^{-24}.

It is tempting to say "The Universe is a big place; surely we must expect that what happens in one locality will be repeated someplace else." But this overlooks the issue of probability. Admittedly, cosmic locales are very numerous. But probabilities can get to be very small: no matter how massive N may be, there is that diminutive $1/N$ that can countervail against it.

The workings of evolution—be it of life, intelligence, culture, technology, or science—are always the product of a great number of individually unlikely events. Things can eventuate very differently at many junctures. The unfolding of developments involves putting to nature a series of questions whose successive resolution produces a process reminiscent of the game "Twenty Questions," sweeping over a possibility spectrum of awesomely large proportions. The result eventually reached lies along a route that traces our one particular contingent path within a space of alternatives that provides for an ever-divergent fanning out of alternative as each step opens up yet further possibilities. And evolutionary process is a very iffy proposition—a complex labyrinth where a great many twists and turns in the road must be taken right for matters to end up as they do.

Of course, it all looks easy with the wisdom of hindsight. If things had not turned out appropriately at every stage, we would not be here to tell the tale. The many contingencies on the long route of cosmic, galactic, solar-systemic, biochemical, biological, social, cultural, and cognitive evolution have all turned out satisfactorily—the innumerable obstacles have all been surmounted. In retrospect, it all looks easy and inevitable. The innumerable possibilities of variation along the way are easily kept out of sight and out of mind. The wisdom of hindsight makes it all look very easy. It is so easy, so tempting to say that a planet on which there is life will, of course, evolve a species with the technical capacity for interstellar communication.[95] It is tempting, but it is also nonsense.

---

95 Compare Cameron, *Interstellar Communication*, p. 312.

6.8 Cosmic Limitations — 113

The ancient Greek atomists' theory of possibility affords an interesting object lesson in this connection. Adopting a Euclideanly infinitistic view of space, the atomist taught that every (suitably general) possibility is realized in fact someplace or other. Confronting the question of "Why do dogs not have horns: just why is the theoretical possibility that dogs be horned not actually realized?" the atomists replied that it indeed is realized but just elsewhere—*in another region of space*. Somewhere within infinite space there is another world just like ours in every respect save one, that its dogs have horns. For the circumstance that dogs lack horns is simply a parochial idiosyncrasy of the particular local world in which we interlocutors happen to find ourselves. Reality accommodates all possibilities of worlds alternative to this one through spatial distribution: as the atomists saw it, *all* alternative possibilities are in fact actualized in the various subworlds embraced within one spatially infinite superworld.

This theory of virtually open-ended possibilities was shut off by the closed cosmos of the Aristotelian world-picture, which dominated European cosmological thought for almost two millennia. The break-up of the Aristotelian model in the Renaissance and its replacement by the "Newtonian" model is one of the great turning points of the intellectual tradition of the West—elegantly portrayed in Alexandre Koyré's book of the splendid title "From the Closed World to the Infinite Universe" (New York, 1957). Strangely enough, the refinitization of the universe effected by Einstein's general relativity in one of its principal interpretations produced scarcely a ripple in philosophical or theoretical circles, despite the immense stir caused by other aspects of the Einstein revolution. (Einsteinian space-time is, after all, even more radically finitistic than the Aristotelian world-picture, which left open at any rate the prospect of an infinite future, with respect to time.)

To be sure, it might well seem that the finitude in question is not terribly significant because the distances and times involved in modern cosmology are so enormous. But this view is rather naive. The difference between the finite and the infinite is as big as differences can get to be. And it represents a difference that is—in this present context—of the most far-reaching significance. For this means that we have no alternative to supposing that a highly improbable set of eventuations is not going to be realized in very many places, and that something sufficiently improbable may well not be realized at all. The decisive *philosophical* importance of the Einsteinian finitization of space-time is that it means that an eventuation that is sufficiently improbable may well not be realized at all. A finite universe must "make up its mind" about its contents in a far more radical sense than an infinite one. And this is particularly manifest in the context of low-probability possibilities. In a finite world—unlike an infinite one—we cannot avoid supposing that a prospect that is sufficiently unlikely is simply not going to be realized at all, that in piling improbability on improbability we eventually outrun the reach of the actual. It is, accordingly, quite conceivable that our science represents a solution of the problem of cognitive accommodation that is terrestrially locale-specific.

Here lies a deep question: Is the mission of intelligence uniform or diversified? Two fundamentally opposed philosophical positions are possible with respect to cognitive evolution in its cosmic perspective. One is a uniformitarian *monism* which sees the universal mission of intelligence in terms of a certain shared destination, a common cosmic "position of reason as such." The other is a particularistic *pluralism* which allows each solar civilization to forge its own characteristic cognitive destiny, and sees the mission of intelligence as such in terms of spanning a wide spectrum of alternatives and realizing a vastly diversified variety of possibilities, with each thought-form realizing its own peculiar destiny in separation from all the rest. The conflict between these doctrines must, in the final analysis, be settled not by armchair speculation for general principles, but by rational triangulation from the empirical data. That said, it must be observed that the whole tendency of these present deliberation is towards the pluralistic side.

In many minds, there is, no doubt, a certain charm to the idea of companionship. It would be comforting to think that however estranged we are in other ways, those alien minds and ourselves share *science* at any rate—that we are fellow travelers on a common journey of inquiry. Mythology and scientific speculation alike manifest our yearning for companionship and contact. (Pascal was not the only one frightened by the eternal silence of infinite spaces.) It would be pleasant to think ourselves not only colleagues but junior collaborators whom other, wiser minds might be able to help along the way. Even as many in sixteenth-century Europe looked to those strange, pure men of the Indies (East or West) who might serve as moral exemplars for sinful European man, so we are tempted to look to alien inquirers who surpass us in scientific wisdom and might assist us in overcoming our cognitive deficiencies. The idea is appealing, but it is also, alas, very unrealistic.

In the late-1600s Christiaan Huygens wrote:

> For 'tis a very ridiculous opinion that the common people have got among them, that it is impossible a rational Soul should dwell in any other shape than ours... This can proceed from nothing but the Weakness, Ignorance, and Prejudice of Men, as well as the humane Figure being the handsomest and most excellent of all others, when indeed it's nothing but

> a being accustomed to that figure that makes me think so, and a conceit... that no shape or color can be so good as our own.⁹⁶

What is said here about people's tendency to emplace all rational minds into a physical structure akin to their own familiar one is paralleled by a tendency to emplace all rational knowledge into a cognitive structure akin to their own familiar one.

With respect to biological evolution, it seems perfectly sensible to reason as follows:

> What can we say about the forms of life evolving on these other worlds?... [I]t is clear that subsequent evolution by natural selection would lead to an immense variety of organisms; compared to them, all organisms on Earth, from molds to men, are very close relations.⁹⁷

It is plausible that much the same situation should obtain with respect to cognitive evolution: that the "sciences" produced by different civilizations here on earth—the ancient Chinese, Indians, and Greeks, for example—should exhibit immensely greater points of similarity than obtains between our present-day science and anything devised by astronomically remote civilizations. And where movement in altogether different directions is at issue, the idea of a comparison in terms of "advance" or "backwardness" would simply be inapplicable.

The present deliberations accordingly convey two principal lessons. The first is that the prospect that some astronomically remote civilization is "scientifically more advanced" than ourselves—that somebody else is doing "our sort of science" *better* than us ourselves—requires in the first instance that they be doing our sort of science at all. And this deeply anthropomorphic supposition is extremely unlikely.

Moreover, a second main lesson follows from the consideration that natural science *as we know it* is to all visible intents and purposes a characteristically human enterprise—a circumstance that endows science with an inexorably economic dimension. For this means that the sorts of results of scientific inquiry that we are able to achieve will hinge crucially on *the way* in which we deploy resources in cultivating our scientific work as well as on *the extent* to which

---

96 Christiaan Huygens, *Cosmotheoros: The Celestial Worlds Discovered—New Conjectures Concerning the Planetary Worlds, Their Inhabitants and Productions* (London, 1698; reprinted London: F. Cass & Co., 1968), p. 359.
97 Shklovskii and Sagan, *Intelligent Life in the Universe*, p. 350.

we do so. Accordingly, our science and the knowledge it conveys is bound to be limited by the simple fact of being ours.[98]

6.9 Hidden Depths: The Impetus to Realism

The fact that we do and should always think of real things as having hidden depths inaccessible to us finite knowers—that they are always cognitively opaque to us to some extent—has important ramifications that reach to the very heart of the theory of communication.

Any particular thing—the moon, for example—is such that two related but critically different versions can be contemplated:

(1) the moon, the actual moon as it "really" is

and

(2) the moon as somebody (you or I or the Babylonians) conceives of it.

The crucial fact to note in this connection is that it is virtually always the former item—the thing itself—that we *intend* to communicate or think (self-communicate) about, the thing *as it is*, and not the thing *as somebody conceives of it*. Yet we cannot but recognize the justice of Kant's teaching that the "I think" (I maintain, assert, etc.) is an ever-present implicit accompaniment of every claim or contention that we make. This factor of attributability dogs our every assertion and opens up the unavoidable prospect of "getting it wrong."

However, this fundamental objectivity intent—the determination to discuss "the moon itself" (the real moon) regardless of how untenable one's own *ideas* about it may eventually prove to be—is a basic precondition of the very possibility of communication. It is crucial to the communicative enterprise to take the egocentrism-avoiding stance of an epistemological Copernicanism that rejects all claims to a privileged status for *our own* conception of things. Such a conviction roots in the fact that we are prepared to "discount any misconceptions" (our own included) about things over a very wide range indeed—that we are committed to the stance that factual disagreements as to the character of things are communicatively irrelevant within enormously broad limits.

---

98 This chapter draws upon the author's essay "Extraterrestrial Science," *Philosophia Naturalis* 21 (1984), pp. 400–424.

6.9 Hidden Depths: The Impetus to Realism

We are able to say something about the (real) Sphinx thanks to our subscription to a fundamental communicative convention or "social contract" to the effect that we *intend* ("mean") to talk about it—the very thing itself as it "really" is —our own private conception of it notwithstanding. We arrive at the standard policy that prevails with respect to all communicative discourse of letting "the language we use," rather than whatever specific informative aims we may actually "have in mind" on particular occasions, be the decisive factor with regard to the things at issue in our discourse. When I speak about the Sphinx—even though I do so on the basis of my own conception of what is involved here—I will nevertheless be taken to be discussing "the *real* Sphinx" by virtue of the basic conventionalized intention at issue with regard to the operation of referring terms.

Communication requires not only common *concepts* but common *topics*— shared items of discussion, a common world of self-subsistently real *"an sich"* objects basic to shared experience. The factor of objectivity reflects our basic commitment of a shared world as the common property of communicators. Such a commitment involves more than merely *de facto* intersubjective agreement. For such agreement is a matter of *a posteriori* discovery, while our view of the nature of things puts "the real world" on a necessary and *a priori* basis. This stance roots in the fundamental convention of a socially shared insistence on communicating—the commitment to an objective world of real things affording the crucially requisite common focus needed for any genuine communication.

Any pretensions to the predominance, let alone the correctness, of our own potentially idiosyncratic conceptions about things must be put aside in the context of communication. The fundamental intention to deal with the objective order of this "real world" is crucial. If our assertoric commitments did not transcend the information we ourselves have on hand, we would never be able to "get in touch" with others about a shared objective world. No claim is made for the *primacy* of our conceptions, or for the *correctness* of our conceptions, or even for the mere *agreement* of our conceptions with those of others. The fundamental intention to discuss "the thing itself" predominates and overrides any mere dealing with the thing as we ourselves conceive of it.

To be sure, someone might object:

> But surely we can get by on the basis of personal conceptions alone, without invoking the notion of "a thing itself." My conception of a thing is something I can convey to you, given enough time. Cannot communication proceed by correlating and matching personal conceptions, without appeal to the intermediation of "the thing itself"?

But think here of the concrete practicalities. What is "enough time"? When is the match "sufficient" to underwrite outright identification? The cash value of our commitment to the thing itself is that it enables us to make this identification straight away by imputation, by fiat on the basis of modest indicators, rather than on the basis of an appeal to the inductive weight of a body of evidence that is always bound to be problematic. Communication is something *we set out* to do, not something we ultimately discern, with the wisdom of eventual hindsight, to have accomplished retrospectively.

The objectifying imputation at issue here lies at the very heart of our cognitive stance that we live and operate in a world of real and objective things. This commitment to the idea of a shared real world is crucial for communication. Its status is *a priori*: its existence is not something we learn of through experience. As Kant clearly saw, objective experience is possible only if the existence of such a real, objective world is *presupposed* at the onset rather than seen as a matter of *ex post facto* discovery about the nature of things.

The information that we may have about a thing—be it real or presumptive information—is always just that, viz. information that WE lay claim to. We cannot but recognize that it is person-relative and in general person-differentiated. Our attempts at communication and inquiry are thus undergirded by an information-transcending stance—the stance that we communally inhabit a shared world of objectively existing things, a world of "real things" among which we live and into which we inquire but about which we do, and must presume ourselves to, have only imperfect information at any and every particular stage of the cognitive venture. This is not something we learn. The "facts of experience" can never reveal it to us. It is something we postulate or presuppose to be able to put experience to cognitive use. Its epistemic status is not that of an empirical discovery, but that of a presupposition that is a product of a transcendental argument for the very possibility of communication or inquiry as we standardly conceive of them.

And so, what is at issue here is not a matter of *discovery*, but one of *imputation*. The element of community, of identity of focus is not a matter of *ex post facto* learning from experience, but of an *a priori* predetermination inherent in our approach to language-use. We do not *infer* things as being real and objective from our phenomenal data, but establish our perception as an authentic perception OF genuine objects through the fact that these objects are given—or rather, *taken*—as real and objectively existing things from the first.[99] Objectivity is not

---

99 The point is Kantian in its orientation. Kant holds that we cannot experientially learn through our perceptions about the objectivity of outer things, because we can only recognize our perceptions as perceptions (i.e., representations of outer things) if these outer things are

deduced but imputed. We do, no doubt, *purport* our conceptions to be objectively correct, but whether this is indeed so is something we cannot tell with assurance until "all the returns are in"—that is, never. This fact renders it critically important *that* (and understandable *why*) conceptions are communicatively irrelevant. Our discourse *reflects* our conceptions and perhaps *conveys* them, but it is not in general substantively *about* them but rather about the things in which they actually or supposedly bear.

We thus reach an important conjuncture of ideas. The ontological independence of things—their objectivity and the autonomy of the machinations of the mind—is a crucial aspect of realism. And the fact that it lies at the very core of our conception of a real thing that such items project beyond the cognitive reach of mind betokens a conceptual scheme fundamentally committed to objectivity. The only plausible sort of ontology is one that contemplates a realm of reality that outruns the range of knowledge (and indeed even of language), adopting the stance that character goes beyond the limits of characterization. It is a salient aspect of the mind-independent status of the objectively real that the features of something real always transcend what we know about it. Indeed, yet further or different facts concerning a real thing can always come to light, and all that we *do* say about it does not exhaust all that *can and should* be said about it. In this light, objectivity is crucial to realism and the cognitive inexhaustibility of things is a certain token of their objectivity.

As these deliberations indicate, authentic realism can only exist in a state of tension. The only reality worth having is one that is in some degree knowable. But it is the very limitation of our knowledge—our recognition that there is more to reality than what we do and can know or ever conjecture about it— that speaks for the mind-independence of the real. It is important to stress against the skeptic that the human mind is sufficiently well attuned to reality that some knowledge of it is possible. But it is no less important to join with realists in stressing the independent character of reality, acknowledging that reality has a depth and complexity of make-up that outruns the reach of the cognitive efforts of the mind.

---

given as such from the first (rather than being learned or inferred). As Kant summarizes his "Refutation of Idealism": "Idealism assumed that the only immediate experience is inner experience, and that from it we can only *infer* outer things—and this, moreover, only in an untrustworthy manner... But on the above proof it has been shown that outer experience is really immediate..." (Immanuel Kant, *Critique of Pure Reason*, tr. by Norman Kemp Smith [New York: Random House, 1958], B276.)

7 The Ramifications of Ignorance

7.1 Modes of Error: Ignorance

Our attempts to get at the facts often misfire. And this deficiency often roots in cognitive ignorance arising from lack of a knowledge of fact. Error is a matter of commission; with error we have the facts wrong. Ignorance, by contrast, is a matter of omission: with ignorance we do not have the facts, period. Thus, by and large, error is worse than ignorance. As Thomas Jefferson wrote: "Ignorance is preferable to error; and he is less removed from the truth who believes nothing, than he who believes what is wrong."[100] In a way, this is true enough. Ignorance leaves us without guidance; error sends us off in the wrong direction. And frequently, we are better off staying put.

However, the reality of it is that ignorance ("errors of omission") often leads to outright error ("errors of commission"). Of course, ignorance is not an all-or-nothing matter; it is only too often a thing of aspects and facets. "Give me a five-letter word for *visitor* beginning with G," asks the crossword puzzle solver. Granted, he does not know the word. But he has narrowed things down quite a bit.

The clearest index of ignorance is the inability to answer meaningful questions in a way that manages to convince people—ourselves included. For if a question indeed is authentically meaningful, then it will have an answer, and if we are unable to resolve that question, then we are—through this very fact—ignorant of what the answer is. The inability to identify the answer convincingly is the clearest possible indication that we do not know it.

Often, we do not simply respond to ignorance by leaving a mere blank. We have a natural and perfectly reasonable inclination to fill in those gaps in the easiest, most natural, and sometimes even most attractive way. Who has not been startled by the actual deeds that filled the gap left open by a political candidate's vacuous campaign? Jumping to conclusions over a chasm of ignorance is a natural human tendency from which few of us are exempt.

The price of ignorance in general is incapacity. The person who does not know where to find food cannot eat. The person who does not know the combination cannot open the lock. The person who does not know how to start the engine cannot drive the car. Even as knowledge is power, so ignorance is impotence. This is a key motivator for hoarding information and keeping secrets.

---

[100] Thomas Jefferson, *Notes on the State of Virginia* (New York and London: Penguin, 1999), p. 35.

7.1 Modes of Error: Ignorance — 121

Ignorance encompasses a vast and varied terrain. All sorts of information is simply not available. Many aspects of reality vanish leaving no trace behind—the array of yesterday's clouds, for example. And much about the thought life of others is inscrutable to us, unless they tell us—and do so honestly. (What was on Napoleon's mind on the long journey to St. Helena?) But while such things are difficult—perhaps even impossible—to find out about them is not in principle unknowable. (We could have photographed yesterday's clouds—though we didn't. Napoleon could have poured out his mind into a journal—though he didn't.) Nobody knows the day on which the last of the Neanderthals died or what was on Washington's mind when crossing the Delaware. But it is in theory possible that the requisite information should come to light—there is nothing inherently unattainable about it. The issue of contingent ignorance—of what people are too lazy or too incompetent to find out about—does not hold much interest for cognitive theory. What matters from the theoretical point of view is those aspects of ignorance that betoken inherent limits to human knowledge.

The ignorance of people can only be compared in this, that, or the other respect. To amalgamate ignorance overall would involve comparing apples and oranges. There is no way to measure ignorance. Perhaps information can be measured textually by comparing the space that needs to be dedicated to its storage—the size of library holdings or the computer bits involved. But ignorance is immeasurable: we cannot know the lineaments of the unknown.

If we adopt the distinction between *substantive* knowledge about the factual matters of some domain and *metaknowledge* about our knowledge itself, then it is going to transpire that, even in domains where (as per the skeptic's contention) substantive knowledge is not to be had, nevertheless the prospect of metaknowledge remains open and indeed is bound to be non-empty in view of what is, by hypothesis, the fact of our knowing substantive knowledge to be unavailable. And so, to acknowledge pervasive ignorance is not to endorse skepticism. After all, to claim to know that there is nothing that one knows is a paradox. On the other hand, the claim that there are some things that we do not know affords us as secure a piece of knowledge as there is.

It is important to heed the distinction between facts that nobody *does actually* know and facts that nobody *can possibly* know—between merely unknown facts and inherently unknowable ones.[101] Of some things we are (and

---

[101] The difference between unknown and unknowable facts is most clearly expressed in symbolic terms. A fact is unknowable when:
$\sim\Diamond(\exists x)Kxf$ or equivalently $\Box(\forall x)\sim Kxf$

must remain) ignorant because of the world's contingent arrangements. Of others our ignorance lies in the conceptual structure of the situation with regard to the item at issue. The really interesting issue, accordingly, relates not to that which *is not* known to some or even to all of us. The examples one can offer of the former are too many and of the latter too few. Instead, the really interesting question relates to that which cannot be known at all. From the theoretical point of view, this represents the most interesting form of ignorance.

One of the most obvious sources of ignorance is sheer volume of available factual information. There is so much out there to be known that any given individual cannot ever begin to make more than an insignificant fraction of it. The vastness of any given person's ignorance is unfathomable. Isaac Newton wrote of himself as "a boy standing on the seashore...whilst the great ocean of truth lay all underscored before me." This holds in spades for the rest of us. And ironically, the more one leans, the vaster our scope of ignorance is destined to become.

But are there actually any unknowable truths—cases in which there indeed are actual facts of the matter of such a sort that no one can possibly get to know them?

7.2 Ignorance About Our Own Ignorance Is Fundamental

The very idea of cognitive limits has a paradoxical air. It suggests that we claim knowledge about something outside knowledge. But (to hark back to Hegel) with respect to the realm of knowledge, we are not in a position to draw a line between what lies inside and what lies outside—seeing that *ex hypothesi* we have no cognitive access to the latter. One cannot contemplate the relative extent of knowledge or ignorance about reality except by basing it on some picture of reality that is already in hand—that is, unless one is prepared to take at face value the deliverances of existing knowledge.

And it is even difficult to obtain a taxonomy of ignorance. For the realm of ignorance is every bit as vast, complex, and many faceted as that of knowledge itself. Whatever someone can know, they can also be ignorant about—arguably with a handful of Cartesian exceptions such as the fact that knowers are pretty much bound *ex officio* to realize that they themselves exist and can think.

By contrast, a fact is merely unknown but not unknowable when:
$\sim(\exists x)Kxf$ & $\Diamond$ or equivalently $(\forall x)\sim Kxf$ & $\Diamond(\exists x)Kxf$

7.2 Ignorance About Our Own Ignorance Is Fundamental

Now, one key consideration here is that while one can know indefinitely *that* one is ignorant of something—that there are facts one does not know—one cannot know specifically *what* it is that one is ignorant of, i.e., what the facts at issue are. One of the most critical but yet problematic areas of inquiry relates to knowledge regarding our own cognitive shortcomings. It is next to impossible to get a clear fix on our own ignorance, because in order to know that there is a certain fact that we do not know, we would have to know the item at issue to be a fact, and just this is, by hypothesis, something we do not know.[1]

And so, "being a fact I do not know" is a noninstantiable predicate as far as I am concerned. (You, of course, could proceed to instantiate it.) But "being a fact that *nobody* knows" is flat-out noninstantiable—so that we have here a typical vagrant predicate.

But it lies in the nature of things that one's ignorance about facts is something regarding which one can have only generic and not specific knowledge. I can know about my ignorance only abstractly at the level of indefiniteness (*sub ratione generalitatis*), but I cannot know it in concrete detail. I can meaningfully hold that two plus two being four is a *claim* (or a *purported* fact) that I do not know to be the case, but cannot meaningfully maintain that two plus two being four is an *actual* fact that I do not know to be the case. In sum, I can have general but not specific knowledge about my ignorance, although my knowledge about *your* ignorance will be unproblematic in this regard.[102]

And so, if indeed there is always a fact which a given individual does not know, then there will be a fact that nobody knows. For if F_1 is a fact that X_1 does not know, and F_2 is a fact that X_2 does not know, then there will be a fact, namely F_1-and-F_2 which neither X_1 nor X_2 manage to know. And this cognitive route to unknown facts will extend across the entire landscape of existing individuals. There will, accordingly, have to be unknowns—facts that are not known to anyone at all.

To be sure, all we claim to know is *that* there are such facts. But *what* they are is itself one of those matters of unknowability. Obviously, we cannot give an illustrative example of an unknown fact, seeing that this requires knowing the item to be a fact, contrary to hypothesis.[103] One can, in principle, illustrate igno-

---

102 Accordingly, there is no problem about "t_0 is a truth *you* don't know," although I could not then go on to claim modestly that "You know everything that I do." For the contentions $\sim Kyt_0$ and $(\forall t)(Kit \supset Kyt)$ combine to yield $\sim Kit_0$ which conflicts with the claim Kit_0 that I stake in claiming t_0 as a truth.

103 If I am to claim that f is a fact that nobody knows, then I affirm:

(1) $Ki(f\ \&\ \sim(\exists x)Kxf)$

since $Kx(p\ \&\ q)$ entails $Kxp\ \&\ Kxq$, (1) entails:

rance by adding questions no one can answer, but indicating the detail of facts that nobody knows is totally impracticable for us.

The actual situation is not that of a crossword puzzle—or of geographic exploration—where the size of the *terra incognita* can be somehow measured in advance of securing the details that are going to be filled in. We can form no sensible estimate of the imponderable domain of what can be known but is not. To be sure, we can manage to compare what one person or group knows with what some other person or group knows. But mapping the realm of what is knowable as such is something that inevitably reaches beyond our powers. And for this reason, any question about the cognitive completeness of our present knowledge is and will remain inexorably unresolvable.

That our knowledge is sufficient for our immediate purposes—specifically, by enabling us to answer the questions we then and there have before us—is something that is in principle readily determinable. But that it is *theoretically* adequate to answer not just our present questions but those that will grow out of them in the future is something we can never manage to establish. For it is clear that the sensible management of ignorance is something that requires us to operate in the realm of practical considerations exactly because the knowledge required for theoretical adequacy on this subject is—by hypothesis—not at our disposal. We have no cogently rational alternative to proceed, here as elsewhere, subject to the basic pragmatic principle of having to accept the best that we can do as good enough.

It is accordingly needful to distinguish between contingent and necessary ignorance. The former is the result of the way in which things work in the world—time covers its tracks, the future does not foreshadow its doings, chaos precludes prediction, that sort of thing. By contrast, necessary ignorance relates to situations where claiming knowledge leads to self-introduction. "I know that I am ignorant to the fact that," or "f is a fact I will never come to realize" would be paradigm illustrations, there being truths of this format I cannot possibly come to realize.

---

(2) Kif & $\sim Ki\sim(\exists x)Kxy$

But since Kxp entails P, (2) entails:

(3) Kif & $\sim(\exists x)Kxf$

And this thesis is self-contradictory. I can unproblematically claim that there are unknown facts, but cannot possibly adduce a specific example of one. The best one can ever do to be specific here is to give examples of unanswerable questions.

7.3 Some Prime Sources of Ignorance

The Unavailable Future

Perhaps the clearest and most decisive impediments to knowledge are our *conceptual* limitations. It was not for lack of intelligence of brain power that Caesar could not have known that his sword contained tungsten, but the very idea was not as yet available because tungsten just did not figure on the conceptual agenda of the time. We cannot gain cognitive access to a fact whose conceptualization outruns the available ideational resources. Those facts whose conceptualization awaits the innovations of an as-yet unrealized fabric are inevitably unknowable by the individuals of the present.

The Statistical Fog

Consider the inauguration of public safety measures. A speed limit is set, a traffic light installed, an inoculation campaign developed. There is no question that many lives are saved. But whose? Many among us would not be here if these steps had not been taken. Yet who are they? We know there are some who were saved by the measure but there is no way of telling who they are: this is something that nobody knows or indeed can know.[104] There are bound to be individuals of whom it is true that their life was saved, and so there is a fact of the matter here: "X's life was saved" will—and will have to be—true for certain values of X, for certain individuals. But there is no possible way for us ever to identify such an individual. The fact at issue is an inherently unknowable fact. It is hidden away undetectably in a statistical fog.

Statistics can tell us how many suicides there will be next year. But who will they be? We have no way of finding out. Such facts about the world are concealed in a statistical fog. We know some of the generalization of the matter, but cannot possibly come to grips with the specifics.

The circumstance reflects the crucial difference between the cognitively infinite $K(\exists x)Sx$ and the cognitively specific $(\exists x)KSx$. We know that there many people whose life has been saved by certain preventive measures. But there is no one at all of whom we know that *their* life was saved—such as speed limits or drivers'

---

[104] Symbolically, we have $K(\exists x)Sx$ but emphatically not $(\exists x)KSx$. That quantifier placement makes all the difference.

education classes. The issue of which specifics lives were saved represents a paradigmatic instance of an unknowable fact.

The Stochastic Universe of Chance

A coin is to be tossed. We know full well *that* it will come up heads or tails. But we do—and can—have no idea as to which it will be. This too is a salient substance of inevitable ignorance. Here, we deal with items that are hidden out of our sight by the stochastic character of natural causality. Thus, given an atom of a heavy and unstable transuranic element, we can predict *that* it will decay but not when. How long it will last is a matter of inevitable ignorance.

The Ravages of Time

The world's causal processes so unfold as to erase all traces of various realities that have been. The sand dunes of the past leave no detectable traces in the desert of the present. The writing on the page is lost irretrievably when the paper is burned and its ashes scattered. The swans of yesteryear are undetectable in the waters of the present. And so, even as much of the future is as-yet invisible, so much of the past has become as-of-now unvisited.

The Ways of The World

The examples of unknowability that we have been considering—those rooted in undetectability, unpredictability, and irrecoverability—are all in their way inevitable given the nomic structure of natural process. Each of them hinges on the way in which things work in the world. They are necessary alright but only *physically* necessary. In this regard, they stand in contrast with our ignorance regarding matters that we could readily find out about.

7.4 Culpable vs. Venial Ignorance: Invincible vs. Vincible Ignorance

Does ignorance have an ethical or moral dimension? Is it something blameworthy or are the ignorant more to be pitied than censured? It all depends. For there is culpable ignorance and excusable ignorance. Excusable ignorance prevails in circumstances where there is a plausible excuse for the individual's being ignorant—an excuse which renders it "only natural" that someone might be ignorant in the circumstances. Culpable ignorance, by contrast, is inexcusable—ignorance where we have every right and reason to expect that there should not be any. But ignorance about the extent of our own ignorance is for the most part excusable on grounds of inevitability. One surely cannot be blamed for a failure to know things one never had an. (It would be absurd to reproach the travel agent who booked passengers on the Titanic.) On the contrary!

Is ignorance as such a sin? Yes and no. Sometimes, to be sure, breaches of ignorance are problematic. There are, after all, things one ought not to know—other people's personal secrets, for example. Certain kinds of confidential or proprietary information belongs to others. Lifting the veil of ignorance from information that, properly speaking, should be concealed behind can be inappropriate. There is certainly no general obligation to accumulate information at large and unrestrictedly. On the other hand, there is a body of information—generally characterized as "common sense"—which everyone is expected to know (for example, that long-term immersion in water causes people to drown). And besides this come all those categories of information that people are expected to know *ex officio* by virtue of their role or status as parents, as physicians, as algebra teachers, or whatever.

Culpable ignorance obtains when the requisite information is available but insufficient, incompetent, or inadequate efforts are made to obtain it. While this sort of thing is perhaps the most frequent and widespread sort of ignorance, it is however of less theoretical interest than its contrary: venial or excusable ignorance. For the latter obtains in all of those situations where ignorance is inevitable because the requisite information regarding the fact is unavailable thanks to the general principles of the situation. It is this business of in-principle-unattainable information that is at center-stage throughout the present book.

Ignorance deserves censure only when it is culpably willful. Venial ignorance is in general remediable by adequate effort. Then, as the saying has it: "You can fix ignorance" (though it shrewdly goes on to say "but you can't fix stupidity"). But often as not, ignorance is a perfectly appropriate defense against reproach: he simply had no way of knowing. Clearly, it will only be those cases in which culpable ignorance leads to untoward consequences where moral reproach would be in order.

One of the great defects of cognitive skepticism is that it annihilates the very idea of culpable ignorance. For if (per impossible) the skeptic were right and we can know nothing whatsoever, then, of course, ignorance of any and all sorts would at once be inevitable. Where no one can know anything, no one is open to reproach for a lack of knowledge.

That certain sorts of knowledge can be expected of, and must be at least provisionally attributed to, variously situated people is simply a matter of social common sense.

To be sure, besides informative ignorance there is also practical or performative ignorance: lack of know-how rather than lack of know-that. Even the best informed among us may well not know how to steer a supertanker or how to shear a sheep. And those sorts of possible ignorance will, of course, be culpable in an individual who is supposed to know by virtue of his office or position—except perhaps in those cases where such a function is reprehensible in itself. (One would not want to recriminate his incompetence against the professional burglar or assassin, unlike the incompetent sea-captain or hangman).

Then too there is the distinction between vincible and invincible ignorance. Vincible ignorance is that which an individual can overcome with an expenditure of a reasonable amount of effort and application, and invincible ignorance, by contrast, is that which would be overcome only with a substantial effort if at all. If something significant is at stake—either *prudentially* in affecting a person's well-being or *morally* in affecting the well-being of others—we would expect people to devote duly proportionate efforts to remove vincible ignorance and would fault them (prudentially or morally) for not doing so. The distinction at issue accordingly has a significant ethical bearing.

The overall situation can be dependent as per Display 4. It should be noted that invincible ignorance is always *ipso facto* venial: invincibility excuses—no culpability attaches to that which is inevitable and cannot be helped. But what of that which can be helped but only by extraordinary effort—ignorance that can indeed be removed, but requires laborious inquiry or elaborate reasoning? St. Thomas Aquinas holds that this too diminishes culpability to a nullity.

There are four key sources of inevitable ignorance: unavailable factuality, statistical immorality, stochastic variability, and chaotic unpredictability. Accordingly, there are large areas of unknowing where the ignorance at issue is in no way culpable but rather inherent in the very nature of the realities within which the cognitive efforts of *Homo sapiens* have to unfold.

7.5 Presumption as Gap-Filler for Ignorance

Someone who has dropped from sight for seven years is presumed dead. Nature abhors a vacuum. So does the human mind. We try not to let the gaps in our knowledge be mere empty blanks, but fill them in with speculation and suppositions. The cognitive instrument that does the work here is presumption, which often serves as placeholders for knowledge. For the reality of it is that we operate with a source of standard perceptions of presumption—of how to proceed in the absence of evidence to the contrary. These prominently include such presumptions as those of conformity, normalcy, and symmetry, all of which envision having the things we do not know accord harmoniously with those that we do. (Nobody expected the other side of the moon to offer much beyond a variety of craters.)[105]

	There is an information lack that:	
	One can remove	*One cannot remove*
One ought to remove	Culpable ignorance	[Case excluded]
One need not remove	Venial ignorance	Invincible (and thereby venial) ignorance

Note: Venial ignorance is always vincible; the inevitable (invariable) is never culpable (blameworthy); invincibility is an effective excuse.

Display 4: Types of Ignorance

Ignorance is thus subject to a wide variety of presumptions. First stands the universal that the people we encounter do actually know the things that any normal intelligent person would be expected to know: that people need air to breath, that stabbing people causes pain and does harm, etc. Other presumptions govern matters that people would be expected to know *ex officio*—as doctors, plumbers, babysitters, etc. Barring blue-ribbon excuses (going mad, sustaining brain damage, etc.), ignorance that rises counter to such presumptions is culpable: someone who exhibits ignorance here ought not to do so and is thereby guilty of a virtually ethical transgression. By contrast, ignorance is venial—understandable and excusable—when it exists in circumstances where there is no good reason why there should be any knowledge to the contrary. All of these things that people cannot possibly be expected to know—and above all, those they cannot possibly know—afford instances of venial ignorance.

We standardly operate on the presumption of an absence of culpable ignorance—that people know the sorts of things which, in the circumstances, they ordinarily would and certainly should be aware of. For practical purposes we

---

[105] For further details regarding presumptions, see the author's book of this title (Cambridge: Cambridge University Press, 2006).

can convert the dictum that "Ignorance of the law is no excuse" into an expanded counterpart: "Ignorance of readily available fact has no excuse."

7.6 The Extent of Ignorance

Some writers analogize the cognitive exploration of the realm of fact to the geographic exploration of the earth. But this analogy is profoundly misleading. For the earth has a finite and measurable surface, and so even when some part of it is unexplored *terra incognita*, its magnitude and limits can be assessed in advance. Nothing of the kind obtains in the cognitive domain. The ratio and relationship of known truth to knowable fact is subject to no fixed and determinable proportion. Geographic exploration can expect eventual completeness, cognitive exploration cannot.

What is the extent of our ignorance? Just how vast is the domain of what we do not know?

When confronted with these questions there lies before us the temptation of the analogy of global exploration with its property between "the known world" on the one hand, and the unexplained *terra incognita* on the other. Now, once it was grasped that the earth can be viewed as what is, at least roughly, a large sphere, it becomes possible to estimate its surface area and thereby to establish a proportion between the area of what has been explored and the unexamined remainder. But this picture of geographic knowledge is clearly missing in the case of knowledge at large. There just is no *a priori* way of measuring the size of the domain of *possible* knowledge to state it to the domain of *available* knowledge. The idea of establishing a proportion here founders on the total infeasibility of making a here-and-now assessment of the extent of our ignorance.

Notwithstanding the dictum that "Ignorance is bliss,"[106] most would agree that it is, in fact, something of a misfortune. True, for the most part ignorance is unfortunate and regrettable. But not always! There is some modicum of justice to the saying that "Ignorance is bliss." For human life being what it is would bring a full quota of misfortunes to oneself and those one holds dear. And prior knowledge of such developments would greatly augment their distressing impact. The joys of the present would be overshadowed by the anticipations of misfortunes to come. And in other cases where precognition indicates not mishaps as such but merely increased risks, we would often undergo needless

---

106 Thomas Gray, "Ode on a Prospect of Eton College" (London: R. Dodsley, 1747), ll. 98–99.

worry about misfortunes that may very possibly never arrive. Thus, it very much depends whether ignorance is something fortunate or unfortunate. That a terrorist does not know how to make a bomb is fortunate; that he knows where to obtain the necessary materials is not. The status of knowledge in point of positivity/negativity depends not so much on the information as such but on what is done with it.[107]

---

[107] The author's *Epistemic Logic* (Pittsburgh: University of Pittsburgh Press, 2005) also deals with some of themes relevant to this chapter's deliberations.

8 Access to Fact
(The Rational Intelligibility of Nature)

8.1 On The Claims of Majority Judgment

It is widely accepted that majority judgment deserves if not outright acceptance then at least an acknowledgment of plausibility and provisional credibility. St. Augustine was not alone in his conviction that general acceptance merits credence. *(Securues iudicat omnia terrarum.)*

But why should it be that majoritarian judgment has something of a *correctness tropism* towards the right answer? Why should it be that in such matters "the middle way" tends to get it right and with issues of belief, something of a "majority rules" principle is at work?

A significant finding in this regard relates to the experiment of having people guess the number of beans in a jar. With a substantial number of people involved, the performance of the group as a whole—determined simply by the average—is remarkably accurate. And the like also holds in a variety of similar cases; for example, Francis Galton's classic account of cattlemen estimating the weight of an ox.[108]

The reason why that accounts for such judgmental majoritarianism lies in the fundamentality of the human situation. For we humans are creatures that act on the basis of thought. Other sorts of creatures may make their evolutionary way in the world by swiftness (as with antelopes) or fecundity (as with turtles). But our evolutionary survival advantage lies in the use of intelligence. It is by the access and use of information that we ensure the survival of self and species.

For a creature that makes its way along the corridor of time by means of thought—that guides its actions on the basis of beliefs regarding the constitution of reality—there has to be an at least rough and statistical adequation between belief and fact. And such an "on the whole" and "by and large" adequacy means that reasonable correctness will emerge on the whole in the long run. In short, that averaging out properly over multitudes can be a critical aspect of survivability.

We need and have a cognitive capacity that enables us to achieve adequacy if not always and everywhere then at least generally and by and large. Were it not

---

108 On these matters, see the vivid reportage in James Surowiecki, *The Wisdom of Crowds* (New York: Anchor Books, 2005).

so, then we simply would not be here—at any rate not under the aegis of evolutionary principles.

Accuracy in quantitative judgment is surely an evolutionary advantage in many respects—for example, in relation to judging the size of a hostile band, the adequacy of a supply of food or water, the magnitude of an abstract to be surmounted, the distance a weapon must be projected to strike its target, and numberless such matters. Evolution is bound to foster traits and processes that have a survival advantage. And this is bound to happen at the biological, social, and even (to some extent) personal levels.

Of course, such evolutionary considerations do not support the idea of omniscience—we simply do not always get it right. But it will have to be and apparently is that we will generally by and large do so, and if not perfectly, then in adequate degree.

Granted, majorities are not always right and worthy of trust—what recourse of ours ever is? But experience soon teaches about those issues where majority judgment proves unreliable. In matters remote from evolutionary advantage, the "wisdom of crowds" vanishes—for example, in matters of investment with its not infrequent market "bubbles." (Sometimes these lessons are not rapidly drawn—witness the longer timespan before index funds achieved acceptance in investment circles.) In the end, majoritarianism can specify on its own behalf.

And at this point the issue becomes a matter of the mathematical statistics of estimation.

The reality of it is that majoritarian credibility is only to be expected when dealing with individuals who (individually) have some randomly distributed tendency towards getting the matter right.

In matters where individuals are advantaged by getting it right, then the scatter diagram for performance over a large population is bound to be a bell-shaped curve climaxing at the correct value. (And the greater the accuracy choices of those individuals, the steeper the form of the bell.)

To be sure, in such matters the competencies affiliated to accuracy are never absolute and fail-proof. At best and most they are tendential. They manifest themselves over a multitude of cases and over the spread of time ("the long run"). Only by averaging things out over multi-historical cases can accuracy come to the fore. Adequacy in point of accuracy and relatability becomes a statistical phenomenon subject to "the laws of large numbers."

As long as over-estimation and under-estimation are equal-opportunity errors, the outliers will balance off against each other in a sufficiently large sample and the centrists will cluster around the true value. The majoritarian clustering of diverse cases provides an index for credibility. The reliability of multilateral guesswork inheres in a balance of error.

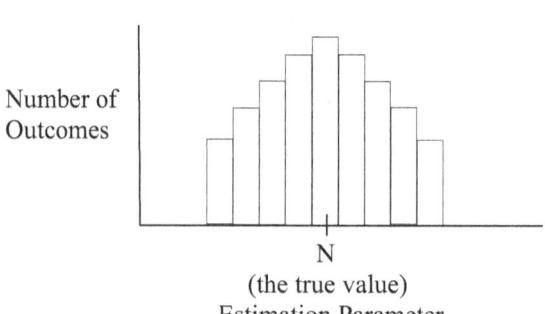

Display 5: The Normal Distribution of Outcomes

As a "Monte Carlo" procedure of repeated trials could soon bring to the fore, the frequency tabulation of outcomes will have the bell curve in the "normal distribution" indicated in Display 5.[109]

Thus, in matters of evolutionary advantageous judgment we would (and should) expect majoritarian competency in that the aggregate judgment of the group is likely to target matters right.

To be sure, this cannot be the whole evolutionary story. Evolutionary development cannot proceed from settled fixities alone. There must be changes and innovations as well—departure from the established ways of things that conform to the thoughts and practices of the majority. There must be eccentricity and innovation as well. New procedures must arrive to offer themselves to the test of experimental experience.

For evolutionary selection to proceed there must be cycles of innovation and selection. The inertia of majorities must receive occasional shocks. Established practices must suffer occasional destabilization.

And so, while the claims of the majority are paramount in general and "as a rule," they are not invariably fail-proof. The very evolutionary considerations that account for their appropriateness in general and on the whole also indicate that there are bound to be occasional exceptions.

In matters of belief and practice—of inquiry and action—the majority never occupies the entire terrain and "has everything all on its side." There are always

---

[109] For detail see C. Robert and G. Castella, *Monte Carlo Statistical Methods*, 2nd ed. (New York: Springer, 2004).

nonconformists—eccentrics, innovators, outliers—prepared to contend what they see as the mistaken "tyranny of the majority." The just claims of the majority rest on the fact that for the most part the position of those nonconforming eccentrics is "just crazy" and that the majority position is usually both better and better justified.

All the same, "usually" is not "invariably." Variation is the driving force for developmental progress and the evolutionary fact of it is that sometimes—just occasionally—those universal eccentrics prove to be appropriate and advantageous. (Variation, after all, is the driving force of evolution.)

The irony, of course, is that in matters of cognitive and procedural development, the difference between mere unconformity and craziness is seldom if ever apparent *at the time*. Survivalist merit is something that comes to view only "with the wisdom of hindsight."

And herein lies the irony of it as far as majoritarianism is concerned. We realize full well that the established position is imperfect and is not going to be "the last word." We know that readjustments will be possible. But at the time we have no idea where the actuality of it lies—which of those competing alternatives can and should prevail.

The claim of majoritarianism lies in the fact that it represents the bird in hand at a juncture when we simply cannot tell which bird in the bush it is that sings a more melodious song.

But in the end, it is perhaps only fitting that the validating rationale of majoritarianism itself proves to be only majoritarian.

8.2 Explaining the Possibility of Natural Science

How is natural science—and, in particular, *physics*—possible at all? How is it that we insignificant humans, inhabitants of a minor satellite of a minor star in one of the world's myriad galaxies, can manage to unlock nature's secrets and gain access to her laws? And how can our mathematics—seemingly a free creative invention of the human imagination—be used to characterize the workings of nature with such uncanny effectiveness and accuracy? Why is it that the majestic lawful order of nature is intelligible to us humans in our man-devised conceptual terms?

This issue remained unproblematic as long as people thought of the world as the product of the creative activity of mathematizing intelligence—as the work of a creator who proceeds on mathematical principles (*more mathematico*, in Spinoza's expression) in designing nature. For then one could take the line that God endows nature with a mathematically intelligible order and mind with a duly consonant mathematizing intelligence. There is thus no problem about how the two get together—God simply arranged it that way. But, of course, if *this* is to be the canonical rationale for the mind's grasp on nature's laws, then in foregoing explanatory recourse to God, we also—to all appearances—lose our grip on the intelligibility of nature.

Some of the deepest intellects of the day accordingly think that this possibility is gone forever, confidently affirming that there just is no way to solve this puzzle of nature's being intelligible in a mathematically lawful manner. In his classic treatise, Erwin Schrödinger characterizes the circumstance that man can discover the laws of nature as "a miracle that may well be beyond human understanding."[110] Eugene Wigner asserts that "the enormous usefulness of mathematics in the natural sciences is something bordering on the mysterious, and there is no rational explanation for it,"[111] and he goes on to wax surprisingly lyrical in maintaining that:

> The miracle of the appropriateness of the language of mathematics for the formulation of the laws of physics is a wonderful gift which we neither understand nor deserve.[112]

Even Albert Einstein stood in awe before this problem. In a letter written in 1952 to an old friend of his Berne days, Maurice Solovine, he wrote:

> You find it curious that I regard the intelligibility of the world (in the measure that we are authorized to speak of such an intelligibility) as a miracle or an eternal mystery. Well, *a priori* one should expect that the world can be rendered lawful only to the extent that we intervene with our ordering intelligence... [But] the kind of order, on the contrary, created, for example, by Newton's theory of gravitation, is of an altogether different character. Even if the axioms of the theory are set by men, the success of such an endeavor presupposes in the objective world a high degree of order that we were *a priori* in no way authorized to expect. This is the "miracle" that is strengthened more and more with the development of our knowledge... The curious thing is that we have to rest content with recognizing the "miracle" without having a legitimate way of going beyond it...[113]

According to all these eminent physicists, we are confronted with a profound mystery. As they see it, we have to acknowledge *that* nature is intelligible, but have no prospect of understanding *why* this is so. The problem of nature's intel-

---

110 Erwin Schrödinger, *What is Life?* (Cambridge: Cambridge University Press, 1945), p. 31.
111 Eugene P. Wigner, "The Unreasonable Effectiveness of Mathematics in the Natural Sciences," *Communications on Pure and Applied Mathematics* 13 (1960), pp. 1–14 [see p. 2].
112 Wigner, "The Unreasonable Effectiveness," p. 14.
113 Albert Einstein, *Lettres à Maurice Solovine* (Paris: Gauthier-Villars, 1956), pp. 114–115. (My translation.)

ligibility by means of our mathematical resources is seen as intractable, unresolvable, hopeless. All three of these distinguished Nobel Laureates in physics unblushingly employ the word "miracle" in this connection.

Perhaps, however, the very question is illegitimate and should not be raised at all. Perhaps the issue of nature's intelligibility is not just *intractable*, but actually *inappropriate* and improperly based on a false presupposition. For to ask for an explanation of *why* scientific inquiry is successful presupposes that there indeed *is* an explanatory rationale for this fact. But if this circumstance is something fortuitous and accidental, then of course no such rationale will exist at all. Just this position is advocated by various philosophers—for example, by Karl Popper, who wrote:

> [Traditional treatments of induction] all assume not only that our quest for [scientific] knowledge has been successful, but also that we should be able to explain why it is successful. However, even on the assumption (which I share) that our quest for knowledge has been very successful so far, and that we now know something of our universe, this success becomes [i.e., remains] miraculously improbable, and therefore inexplicable; for an appeal to an endless series of improbable accidents is not an explanation. (The best we can do, I suppose, is to investigate the almost incredible evolutionary history of these accidents...)[114]

Mary Hesse, too, thinks that it is inappropriate to ask for an explanation of the success of science "because science might, after all, be a miracle."[115]

And so, on this grand question of how the success of natural science is possible at all, some of the shrewdest scientific intellects of the day avow themselves baffled and unhesitatingly enshroud the issue in mystery or miracle. On this sort of view, the question of the intelligibility of nature becomes an illegitimate pseudo-problem—a forbidden fruit at which sensible minds should not presume to nibble. We must simply rest content with the fact itself acknowledging that any attempt to explain it is foredoomed to failure because of the inappropriateness of the very project.

Surely, however, such an approach has very questionable merit. Eminent authorities to the contrary notwithstanding, the question of nature's intelligibility via quantifying science is not only interesting and important, but is also surely one which we should, in principle, hope and expect to answer in a more or less sensible way. Clearly, this important issue needs and deserves a strong dose of demystification.

---

[114] Karl R. Popper, *Objective Knowledge* (Oxford: Clarendon Press, 1972), p. 28.
[115] Mary Hesse, *Revolutions and Reconstructions in the Philosophy of Science* (Bloomington, IN: University of Indiana Press, 1980), p. 154.

How is it that we can make effective use of mathematical machinery to characterize the *modus operandi* of nature? The pure logical theorist seems to have a ready answer. He says: "Mathematics *must* characterize reality. Mathematical propositions are purely *abstract* truths whose validation turns on conceptual issues alone. Accordingly, they hold of *this* world because they hold of *every possible* world."

But this response misses the point of present concerns. Admittedly, the truths of *pure* mathematics obtain in and of every possible world. But they do so only in virtue of the fact that they are strictly hypothetical and descriptively empty—wholly uncommitted regarding the substantive issues of the world's operations. Their very conceptual status means that the theses of pure mathematics are beside the point of our present purposes. It is not the *a priori* truth of pure mathematics that concerns us, its ability to afford truths of reason. Rather, what is at issue is the *empirical applicability* of mathematics, its pivotal role in framing the *a posteriori* contingent truths of lawful fact that render nature's ways amenable to reason.

After all, the circumstance that pure mathematics holds true in a world does not mean that this world's *laws* have to be characterizable in relatively straightforward mathematical terms. It does not mean that nature's operations have to be congenial to mathematics and graspable in terms of simple, neat, elegant, and rationally accessible formulas. In short, it does not mean that the world must be mathematically tractable and "mathematophile" in admitting to the sort of concise descriptive treatment it receives in mathematical physics.

How, then, are we to account for the fact that the world appears to us to be so eminently intelligible in the mathematical terms of our natural science?

The answer to this question of the cognitive accessibility of nature to mathematizing intelligence has to lie in a somewhat complex two-sided story in which both sides, intelligence and nature, must be expected to have a part. After all, when two things fit together, each must accommodate the other. Let us trace out this line of thought—one step at a time.

8.3 "Our" Side

Our human side of this bilateral story is relatively straightforward. After all, *Homo sapiens* is an integral part of nature. We are connected into nature's scheme of things as an intrinsic component thereof—courtesy of the processes of evolution. Our experience is thus inevitably an experience *of nature*. (That, after all, is what "experience" is—our intelligence-mediated reaction to the world's stimulating impacts upon us.) So, the kind of mathematics—the kind of theory of periodicity and structure—that we devise in the light of this experience is the kind that is in principle applicable to nature as we can experience it. As C. S. Peirce insisted, evolutionary pressures conform our intellectual processes to the *modus operandi* of nature. For nature not only *teaches* us (when we choose to study it) but also *forms* us (whether or not we choose to study it). And it proceeds in doing the latter in a way that is not, and cannot be, without implications for the former.

Our mathematics is destined to be attuned to nature because it is a natural product itself as a thought instrument of ours: it fits nature because it reflects the way we ourselves are emplaced within nature as integral constituents thereof. Our intellectual mechanisms—mathematics included—fit nature because they are themselves a product of nature's operations, as mediated through the cognitive processes of an intelligent creature that uses its intelligence to guide its interaction with a nature into which it is itself fitted in a particular sort of way.

The very selfsame forces that are at work in shaping the physical world are also at work in shaping our bodies and brains and in providing the stimuli that impinge on our senses and minds. It is these interactions between thought and world that condition our sense of order and beauty—of regularity, symmetry, economy, elegance. Evolutionary pressure coordinates the mind with its environment. Even as we are destined to find healthy foods palatable and reproductively advantageous activities pleasant, so nature's inherent order and structure are bound to prove congenial to our mathematical sense of elegance and beauty.

The modes of order that attract the attention of mathematical theorists interested in structures—and that underlie their ideas of beautiful theories—are thus, unsurprisingly, also at work in the nature within which these conceptualizations arise. The mathematical mechanisms we employ for understanding the standard features of things themselves reflect the structure of our *experience*. For others the processes that underlie their mathematizing might be very different indeed.

Admittedly, mathematics is not a natural science but a matter of theorizing about hypothetical possibilities. Nevertheless, these are possibilities as conceived by beings who do their possibility-conceiving with a nature-evolved and nature-implanted mind. It is thus not surprising that the sort of mathematics we contrive is the sort of mathematics we find applicable to the conceptualization of nature. After all, the intellectual mechanisms we devise in coming to grips with the world—in transmuting sensory interaction with nature into intelligible experience—have themselves the aspect (among many others) of being nature's contrivances in adjusting to its ways of holding creatures at its mercy.

It is no more a miracle that the human mind can understand the world through its intellectual resources than that the human eye can see it through its physiological resources. The critical step is to recognize that the question of

"Why do our conceptual methods and mechanisms fit 'the real world' with which we interact intellectually?" is to be answered in basically the same way as the question "Why do our bodily processes and mechanisms fit the world with which we interact physically?" In neither case can we proceed on the basis of purely theoretical grounds of general principle. Both issues alike are to be resolved in essentially evolutionary terms. It is no more surprising that our minds can grasp nature's ways than it is surprising that our eyes can accommodate nature's rays or our own stomachs can hold nature's food. As we have noted from the outset, evolutionary pressure can take credit for the lot: they are part and parcel of what is mandated by attainment to our niche in nature's scheme of things. There is nothing "miraculous" or "lucky" in our possession of efficient cognitive faculties and processes—effective "hardware" and "software" for productive inquiry. If we did not, we just would not be here as inquiring creatures emplaced in nature thanks to evolutionary processes.

Nevertheless, it could perhaps be the case that we succeed in mathematizing nature only as regards the immediate local microenvironment that defines our particular limited ecological niche. The possibility still remains open that we secure a cognitive hold on only a small and peripheral part of a large and impenetrable whole. And so, man's own one-sided contribution to the matter of nature's intelligibility cannot be the *whole* story regarding the success of science. For even if we do reasonably well in regard to our own immediate evolutionary requirements, this might still be very inadequate in the larger scheme of things. Nature's receptiveness to our cognitive efforts remains to be accounted for—the fact that nature is *substantially* amenable to reason and not just *somewhat* (and perhaps only very marginally) so.

To clarify this issue, we must therefore move on to consider nature's contribution to the bilateral mind/nature relationship.

8.4 Nature's Side in Evolutionary Perspective

What needs to be explained for present purposes is not just why mathematics is merely of *some* utility in understanding the world, but why it is actually of *very substantial* utility in that its employment can provide intelligent inquirers with an impressively adequate and accurate grasp of nature's ways. We must thus probe more deeply into the issue of nature's amenability to inquiry and its accessibility to the probes of intelligence.

To be sure, the effective applicability of mathematics to the description of nature is in no small part due to the fact that we actually devise our mathematics to fit nature through the mediation of experience. But how can one get beyond this to establish that nature simply *"must"* have a fairly straightforward law structure? Are there any fundamental reasons why the world that we investigate by the use of our mathematically informed intelligence should operate on relatively simple principles that are readily amenable to mathematical characterization?

There are indeed. For a world in which intelligence emerges by anything like standard *evolutionary* processes has to be pervaded by regularities and periodicities in the organism–nature interaction that produces and perpetuates organic species. And this means that nature must be cooperative in a certain very particular way: it must be stable, regular, and structured enough for there to be appropriate responses to natural events that can be "learned" by creatures. If such "appropriate responses" are to develop, nature must provide suitable stimuli in a duly structured way. An organically viable environment—to say nothing of a *knowable* one—must incorporate experiential structures. There must be regular patterns of occurrence in nature that even simple single-celled creatures can embody in their make-up and reflect in their *modus operandi*. Even the humblest organisms, snails, say, and even algae, must so operate that certain *types of stimuli* (patterns of recurrently discernible impacts) call forth appropriately corresponding *types of response*—that such organisms can "detect" a structured pattern in their natural environment and react to it in a way that proves to their advantage in evolutionary terms. Even its simplest creatures can maintain themselves in existence only by swimming in a sea of detectable regularities of a sort that will be readily accessible to intelligence. Their world must encapsulate straightforwardly "learnable" patterns and periodicities of occurrence in its operations—relatively simple laws, in other words.

If an inquiring being—positioned by evolution within nature and forming its mathematized conceptions and beliefs about this nature on the basis of physical interaction with it—is to achieve a reasonably appropriate grasp of its workings, then nature too must "do its part" in being duly cooperative. Given the antecedent supposition, nature must, obviously, permit the evolution of inquiring beings. And to do this, it must present them with an environment that affords sufficiently stable patterns to make coherent "experience" possible, enabling them to derive appropriate *information* from those structured interactions that prevail in nature at large. Nature's own contribution to solving the problem of its mathematical intelligibility must accordingly be the possession of a relatively simple and uniform law structure—one that deploys so uncomplicated a set of regularities that even a community of inquirers possessed of only rather moderate capabilities can be expected to achieve a fairly good grasp of the processes at work in their environment.

Accordingly, a world in which intelligence can develop by evolutionary processes also *must*—on this very basis—be a world amenable to understanding in mathematical terms.[116] It must be a world whose cognizing beings will find much grist to their mill in endeavoring to "understand" the world. Galileo hit close to the mark long ago when he wrote in his *Dialogues* that: "Nature initially arranged things her *own* way and subsequently so constructed the human intellect as to be able to understand her."[117] And, of course, nature's construction of a mathematizing mind has proceeded by evolutionary processes.

The development of *life* and thereafter of *intelligence* in the world may or may not be inevitable; the emergence of intelligent creatures on the world's stage may or may not be surprising in itself and as such. But once they are there, and once we realize that they got there thanks to evolutionary processes, it can no longer be seen as surprising that their efforts at characterizing the world in mathematical terms should be substantially successful. *A world in which intelligent creatures emerge through the operation of evolutionary processes must be an intelligible world.*

On this line of deliberation, then, nature admits of mathematical depiction not just because it has laws—is a *cosmos*—but because as an evolution-permitting world it must have many *relatively simple* laws. And those relatively simple laws must be there because if they were not, then nature just would not afford the sort of environment requisite for the evolutionary development of intelligent life. An intelligence-containing world whose intelligent beings came by this capacity through evolutionary means must be substantially intelligible in mathematical terms.[118]

The apparent success of human mathematics in characterizing nature is thus in no way amazing. It may or may not call for wonder that intelligent creatures should evolve at all. But thereupon, once they have safely arrived on the scene through evolutionary means, it is only natural and to be expected that they should be able to achieve success in the project of understanding nature in

---

116 Conversations with Gerald Massey have helped in clarifying this part of the argument.
117 Galileo Galilei, *Dialogo sopra i due massimi sistemi del mondo*, in: *Le Opere di Galileo Galilei*, vol. 7 (Florence, 1897), p. 298. (My translation.) (I owe this reference to Jürgen Mittelstrass.) Kepler wrote, "Thus God himself was too kind to remain idle, and began to play the game of signatures, signing his likeness into the world. I therefore venture to think that all nature and all the graceful sky are symbolized in the art of geometry." (Quoted in Freeman Dyson, "Mathematics in the Physical Sciences," in: Committee on Support of Research in the Mathematical Sciences (ed.), *The Mathematical Sciences* [Cambridge, MA: MIT Press, 1969], pp. 82–105 [see p. 99].)
118 To say that such a world must be *understandable* in such terms is not, of course, to say anything about how far intelligent beings will actually succeed in understanding it.

mathematical terms. A mathematizing intelligence *arrived at through evolution* must for this very reason prove to be substantially successful in achieving adequation to the world's ways.

The strictly hypothetical and conditional character of this general line of reasoning must be recognized. It does not maintain that by virtue of some sort of transcendental necessity the world has to be simple enough for its mode of operation to admit of elegant mathematical representation. Rather, what it maintains is the purely conditional thesis that *if* intelligent creatures are going to emerge in the world by evolutionary processes, *then* the world must be mathematophile, with various of its processes amenable to mathematical representation.

It must be stressed, however, that this merely conditional fact is quite sufficient for present purposes. For the question we face is why we intelligent creatures present on the world's stage should be able to understand its operations in terms of our mathematics. The conditional story at issue fully suffices to accomplish this particular job.

One brief digression to avert a possible misunderstanding is in order. Nothing whatever in the present argumentation can properly be construed to claim that the development of mathematics is an evolutionary requirement or desideratum as such—that creatures are somehow impelled to develop mathematics because it advantages them in the struggle for existence. (This idea would be a foolish anachronism, since evolution produced man long before man produced mathematics.) To say that *intelligence*, the precondition of mathematics, is of evolutionary advantage, is not to claim that this is the case with mathematics itself. All that is being maintained is: (1) that intelligence is (in certain circumstances) of evolutionary advantage, (2) that any sufficiently intelligent creature *can* develop a mathematics (a theory of structure), and (3) that any sufficiently intelligent creature must be able to develop an *effectively applicable* "mathematics" in any world able to give rise to it through evolutionary means.

8.5 Synthesis

The preceding deliberations maintain that the overall question of the intelligibility of nature has two sides:
1. Why is mind so well attuned to nature?
2. Why is nature so well attuned to mind?

And it is further maintained that the answers to these questions are not all that complicated—at least at the level of schematic essentials. The crux is simply this:

Mind must be attuned to nature since intelligence is a generalized guide to conduct that has evolved as a natural product of nature's operations. And nature must be substantially accessible to mind if intelligence manages to evolve within nature by a specifically evolutionary route.

For nature to be intelligible, then, there must be an alignment that requires cooperation on both sides. The analogy of cryptanalysis is suggestive. If A is to break B's code, there must be due reciprocal alignment. If A's methods are too crude, too hit and miss, he can get nowhere. But even if A is quite intelligent and resourceful, his efforts cannot succeed if B's procedures are simply beyond his powers. (The cryptanalysts of the seventeenth century, clever though they were, could get absolutely nowhere in applying their investigative instrumentalities to a high-level naval code of World War II vintage.) Analogously, if mind and nature were too far out of alignment—if mind were too "unintelligent" for the complexities of nature, or nature too complex for the capacities of mind—the two just couldn't get into step. It would be like trying to rewrite Shakespeare in a pidgin English with a 500-word vocabulary, or like trying to monitor the workings of a system with ten degrees of freedom by using a cognitive mechanism capable of keeping track of only four of them. If something like this were the case, mind could not accomplish its evolutionary mission. It would then be better to adopt an alignment process that doesn't take the cognitive route to the guidance of action. Just as any creature that evolves in nature must find due physical accommodation within it (a due harmonization of its bodily operations with its physical environs), so any mind that evolves in nature must find due intellectual accommodation within it (a due harmonization of its intellectual operations with its structural environs). In consequence, there must be a due equilibration between the mind's mathematizing operations and the world's mathematical structure.

The solution to our problem thus roots in the combination of two considerations: (1) a world that admits of the evolutionary emergence of intelligence must be sufficiently regular and simple—i.e., must be mathematophile, and (2) a sufficiently powerful intelligence must be able effectively to comprehend in mathematical terms any world in which it gains its foothold by evolutionary means. The possibility of a mathematical science of nature is accordingly to be explained by the fact that, in the light of evolution, intelligence and intelligibility must stand in mutual coordination.

Two points are accordingly paramount here:
1. Once intelligent creatures evolve, their cognitive efforts are bound to have some degree of adequacy because evolutionary pressures align them with nature's ways.

2. It should not be surprising that this alignment can eventually produce a substantially effective mathematical physics, because the structure of the operations of a nature that engenders intelligence by an evolutionary route is bound to be relatively accessible to this intelligence.

No doubt, this somewhat schematic account requires much amplification and concretization. A long and complex tale must be told about physical and cognitive evolution to fill in the details needed to put such an account into a properly compelling form. But there is surely good reason to hope and expect that a tale of this sort can ultimately be told.

And this is the pivotal point. Even if one has doubts about the particular outlines of the evolutionary story we have sketched, it must be acknowledged that *some such story* can provide a perfectly workable answer to the question of why nature's ways are intelligible to us humans in terms of our mathematical instrumentalities. The mere fact that such an account is in principle possible shows that the issue need not be painted in the black-on-black of impenetrable mystery.

There may indeed be mysteries in this general area. (Questions like "Why should it be that *life* evolves in the world?" and—even more fundamentally—"Why should it be that the world exists at all?" may plausibly be proposed as candidates.) But be that as it may, the presently deliberated issue of why nature's facts are intelligent to us, and why this intelligibility should incorporate a mathematically articulable physics, does not qualify as all that mysterious, let alone miraculous.

There is simply no need to join Einstein, Schrödinger, and Co. in regarding the intelligibility of nature as a miracle or mystery that passes all human understanding. If we are willing to learn from science itself how nature operates and how man goes about conducting his inquiries into its workings, then we should be increasingly able to remove the shadow of incomprehension from the problem of how it is that a being of *this* particular sort, probing an environment of *that* particular type and doing so by means of *those* particular evolutionarily developed cognitive and physical instrumentalities, manages to arrive at a relatively workable account of how things work in the world. We should eventually be able to see it as only plausible and to be expected that inquiring beings should emerge in nature and get themselves into a position to make a relatively good job of coming to comprehend it. We can thus *look to science itself* for the materials that enable us to understand how natural science is possible. And there is no good reason to expect that it will let us down in this regard.

Admittedly, any such scientifically informed account of science's ability to understand the world is in a way circular. It explains the possibility of our knowledge of nature on the basis of what we know of nature's ways. Its explanatory strategy uses the deliverances of natural science retrospectively to provide an account of how an effective natural science is possible. Such a procedure is *not*, however, a matter of vitiating circularity, but one of the healthy and virtuous self-sufficiency of our knowledge that is in fact an essential part of its claims to adequacy.[119] Any scientific world-picture that does not provide materials for explaining the success of science itself would thereby manifest a failing in its grasp of the phenomena of nature that betokens its own inadequacy.

8.6 Implications

But does such a scientific explanation of the success of science not explain too much? Will its account of the pervasiveness of mathematical exactness in science not lead to the (obviously problematic) consequence that "science gets it right"—a result that would fly in the face of our historical experience of science's fallibilism?

By no means! It is fortunate (and evolutionarily most relevant) that we are so positioned within nature that many "wrong" paths lead to the "right" destination—that flawed means often lead us to cognitively satisfactory ends. If nature were a combination lock where we simply "had to get it right"—and *exactly* right—to achieve success in implementing our beliefs, then we just wouldn't be here. Evolution accordingly does not provide an argument that speaks unequivocally for the adequacy of our cognitive efforts. On the contrary, properly construed, it is an indicator of our capacity to err and "get away with it." Admittedly, applicative success calls for *some* alignment of thought-governed action with "the real *nature* of things"—but only enough to get by without incurring overly serious penalties in failure.

The success of science should be understood somewhat on an analogy with the success of the thirsty man who drank white grape juice, mistaking it for lemonade. It is not that he was roughly right—that such grape juice is "approximately" lemonade. It's just that his beliefs were not wrong in ways that lead us to his being baffled in his present purposes—that such defects as they have do not matter for the issues currently in hand. The reality of it is that we simply cannot, in the circumstances, help laboring under the impression that our science is highly successful, even though subsequent experience repeatedly disillusions us in this regard. It follows that intelligence and the "science" it devises must pay off in

---

[119] Just this approach is the salient feature of the Quinean program of "epistemology naturalized."

terms of applicative success—irrespective of whether it manages to get things substantially right or not. It is not that there are no mistakes, but that the mistakes at issue lie below the radar screen of current detectability.

We thus arrive at the picture of nature as an error-tolerant system. For consider the hypothetical situation of a species of behaviorally belief-guided creatures living in an environment that invariably exacts a great penalty for "getting it wrong." Whenever the creature makes the smallest mistake—the least little cognitive misstep—bang, it's dead! Our hypothesis is not viable: any such creature would long ago have become extinct. It could not even manage to survive and reproduce long enough to learn about its environment by trial and error. If the world is to be a home for intelligent beings who develop in it through evolution, then it has to be benign—it has to be error-tolerant. If *seeming* success in intellectually governed operations could not attend even substantially erroneous beliefs, then we cognizing beings who have to learn by experience—by trial and error—just couldn't have made our way along the corridor of time. For if nature were *not* error-forgiving, then a process of evolutionary trial and error could not work in matters of cognition, and intelligent organisms could not emerge at all.[120]

Accordingly, the applicative success of our science is not to be explained on the basis of its actually getting at the real truth, but rather in terms of its being the work of a cognitive being who operates within an error-tolerant environment —a world-setting where applicative success may attend even theories that are substantially "off the mark." The applicative efficacy of science undoubtedly requires *some* degree of alignment between our world-picture and the world's actual arrangements—but only just enough to yield the particular successes at issue. No claims to finality or perfection can therefore be substantiated for our science as it stands here and now.

Evolution indeed serves as the guarantor of the reciprocal attunement of mind and nature envisioned by classical idealism. But it by no means requires that this attunement be of a very high grade by any absolute standard. It is one thing to be right and another to be so badly wrong that one is baffled by one's purposes. And this sort of functional adequacy is something very different from truth. Such a perspective indicates that the success of the applications of our current science does not betoken its actual truth, but merely means that those ways (whatever they be) in which it fails to be true are immaterial to the achievement of success—that in

---

[120] It is this unavoidable error-tolerant aspect of nature that blocks any prospect of a naive "it works, therefore it's true" pragmatism at the level of *theses*. To be sure, as regards large-scale *methods* providing action-guiding theses, the situation is different. Here, "it works *systematically*, therefore it is cogent (as a cognitive method—i.e., its deliverances are rationally credible)" is something else again. (See the author's *Methodological Pragmatism* [Oxford: Basil Blackwell, 1977].)

the context of the particular applications at issue, its inadequacies and incorrectnesses lie beneath the penalty threshold of failure. This critical fact that evolution requires an error-tolerant environment means that we can explain the impressive successes of mathematizing natural science without needing to stake untenable claims as to its definitive correctness.

* * *

Such evolutionary ruminations indicate that the *capacity* to develop an effective natural science, and also the *motivation* to pursue this cognitive project of inquiry, form a natural part of humanity's evolutionary developed natural heritage. But, at the same time, they suggest that the scope, scale, and nature of such a science is bound to be essentially conditioned by the cognitive resources and interests that we humans bring to bear on its development. The conceptual mechanisms we deploy in studying the world's facts are instrumentalities of our own devising. But the responsibility for their efficacy lies with nature rather than ourselves.[121]

8.7 Coda

Eminent authorities have repeatedly characterized it as a miracle that nature's facts are intelligible to us humans. But this ability of mind to come to terms with nature is a two-sided one. On our side, it roots in the fact that we ourselves are a part of nature, a species evolved as intelligent beings within its ambit. And, on nature's side, it lies in its affording a setting within which the evolution of intelligent beings is possible. Thus, while nature's nature may itself be a mystery, the circumstance that intelligent beings have evolved within it is something only natural and to be expected. On the other hand, such argumentation would certainly not support the unrealistic conclusion that our understanding of nature is somehow complete or perfect.

---

[121] Further deliberations regarding some of this chapter's themes are presented in the author's *Scientific Realism* (Dordrecht: D. Reidel, 1987).

9 Our Limited Knowledge of Fact

9.1 Cognitive Incapacity

What confronts us is, in effect, a sort of Cognitive Heracliteanism. Heraclitus said that as the world is ever changing we cannot step into the same river twice. And also its epistemic counterpart: the world of knowledge is ever changing. In the course of cognitive progress, we do not—cannot—confront the same question agenda twice.

Thus, one way in which the question-resolving capacity of our knowledge can be limited is by way of the mode of the situation described in the following thesis:

> *Weak Limitation (The Permanence of Unsolved Questions).* There are *always*, at every temporal stage,[122] questions to which no answer is in hand. At every juncture of cognitive history there exist then-unanswerable questions for whose resolution then-current science is inadequate (yet which may well be answerable at some later date).

Now, if Immanuel Kant was right, and every state of knowledge generates further new and yet unanswered questions, then we will clearly never reach a position where all questions are resolved. Thus, given Kant's Principle of Question Propagation, such a condition of weak limitation inexorably characterizes our knowledge seeing that of the permanence of unsolved questions is at once assured.

However, while Kant's principle assures us *that* new questions will emerge from the answers we presently give to our questions, it provides no detailed information about *what* these questions will be—nor about *when* they will arise. Accordingly, we realize at the level of nonspecific generality that *various questions will arise tomorrow that we cannot as yet identify today.* But since one cannot possibly *identify* the question that will arise tomorrow, it follows that one cannot possibly say whether all of the questions that will arise belong to the family of those for which one can provide satisfactory answers.

But now consider the proposition:

(P) A new question that I cannot answer within one year will arise tomorrow.

---

[122] Or perhaps alternatively: always after a certain time—at every stage subsequent to a certain juncture.

This thesis—somewhat reminiscent of a halting problem in computation theory—is clearly a proposition whose truth I am unable to determine one way or the other. Accordingly, the question "Is (P) true or not?" is to all intents and purposes an undecidable question: it is as firm a fact as can be that I am unable to determine the truth status of (P) one way or the other. Therefore, we now have before us a specific example—viz. "Is (P) true?"—that instances a concrete and perfectly meaningful question I cannot answer. But, of course, all this only bears on the issue of what I myself can or cannot do and does not address that of what can or cannot be done within the unbounded community of inquirers at large—now or ever. To address this issue, we must dig deeper.

9.2 Insolubilia Then and Now

A medieval insolubilium was represented by a question that cannot be answered satisfactorily one way or another because every possible answer is unavailable on grounds of *a logical insufficiency of inherent coherence*. Such an insolubilium poses a paradox. By contrast, a modern insolubilium poses a puzzle. It is represented by a question that cannot be answered satisfactorily one way or another because every possible answer is unavailable on grounds of *an evidential insufficiency of accessible information*.

An example of the former (medieval) sort of logical insolubilium is posed by the self-referential statement: "This sentence is false." Is this statement true or not? Whatever answer we give, be it yes or no, we are in deep trouble either way.[123]

But what about factual insolubilia of the modern type—informatively unanswerable questions?

Consider some possible examples of this phenomenon. In 1880 the German physiologist, philosopher, and historian of science Emil du Bois-Reymond published a widely discussed lecture of *The Seven Riddles of the Universe (Die sieben*

---

[123] *Socrates dicens, se ispum dicere falsum, nihil dicit.* (Carl Prantl, *Geschichte der Logik im Abendlande*, vol. 4 [Leipzig: S. Hirzel, 1955], p. 139 n569.) It became a commonly endorsed doctrine in late-medieval times that paradoxical statements are not preset propositions and for this reason cannot be classed as true or false. (See E. Jennifer Ashworth, *Language and Logic in the Post-Medieval Period* [Dordrecht: Reidel, 1974], p. 115 for later endorsements of this approach.) Thus, later writers dismissed insolubles as not being propositions at all, but "imperfect assertions" *(orationes imperfectae)*. (See Ashworth, *Language and Logic*, p. 116.)

Welträtsel),[124] in which he maintained that some of the most fundamental problems regarding the workings of the world were irresolvable. Du Bois-Reymond was a rigorous mechanist. On his view, nonmechanical modes of inquiry cannot produce adequate results, and the limit of our secure knowledge of the world is confined to the range where purely mechanical principles can be applied. As for all else, we not only *do not* have but *cannot* in principle obtain reliable knowledge. Under the slogan *ignoramus et ignorabimus* ("we *do not* know and *shall never* know"), du Bois-Reymond maintained a skeptically agnostic position with respect to basic issues in physics (the nature of matter and of force, and the ultimate source of motion) and psychology (the origin of sensation and of consciousness). These issues are simply *insolubilia* which transcend man's scientific capabilities. Certain fundamental biological problems he regarded as unsolved, but perhaps in principle soluble (though very difficult): the origin of life, the adaptiveness of organisms, and the development of language and reason. And as regards the seventh riddle—the problem of freedom of the will—he was undecided.

The position of du Bois-Reymond was swiftly and sharply contested by the zoologist Ernest Haeckel in the book *Die Welträtsel* published in 1889,[125] which soon attained a great popularity. Far from being intractable or even insoluble—so Haeckel maintained—the riddles of du Bois-Reymond had all virtually been solved. Dismissing the problem of free will as a pseudo-problem—since free will "is a pure dogma [which] rests on mere illusion and in reality does not exist at all"—Haeckel turned with relish to the remaining riddles. Problems of the origin of life, of sensation, and of consciousness, Haeckel regarded as solved—or solvable—by appeal to the theory of evolution. Questions of the nature of matter and force, he regarded as solved by modern physics except for one residue: the problem (perhaps less scientific than metaphysical) of the ultimate origin of matter and its laws. This "problem of substance" was the only remaining riddle recognized by Haeckel, and it was not really a problem of sci-

---

124 This work was published together with a famous prior (1872) lecture *On the Limits of Scientific Knowledge* as *Ueber Die Grenzen des Naturerkennens: Die Sieben Welträtsel—Zwei Vorträge* (11th ed., Leipzig: Veit, 1916). The earlier lecture has appeared in English tr. "The Limits of Our Knowledge of Nature," *Popular Scientific Monthly* 5 (1874), pp. 17–32. For Reymond cf. Ernest Cassirer, *Determinism and Indeterminism in Modern Physics: Historical and Systematic Studies of the Problems of Causality* (New Haven: Yale University Press, 1956), Part 1.
125 Bonn, 1889. Tr. by Joseph McCabe as *The Riddle of the Universe—at the Close of the Nineteenth Century* (New York and London, 1901). On Haeckel, see the article by Rollo Handy in Paul Edwards (ed.), *The Encyclopedia of Philosophy*, vol. 3 (New York: Macmillan, 1967), pp. 399–402.

ence: in discovering the "fundamental law of the conservation of matter and force," science had done pretty much what it could do with respect to this problem—the rest that remained was metaphysics with which the scientist had no proper concern. Haeckel summarized his position as follows:

> The number of world-riddles has been continually diminishing in the course of the nineteenth century through the aforesaid progress of a true knowledge of nature. Only one comprehensive riddle of the universe now remains—the problem of substance... [But now] we have the great, comprehensive "law of substance", the fundamental law of the constancy of matter and force. The fact that substance is everywhere subject to eternal movement and transformation gives it the character also of the universal law of evolution. As this supreme law has been firmly established, and all others are subordinate to it, we arrive at a conviction of the universal unity of nature and the eternal validity of its laws. From the gloomy *problem* of substance we have evolved the clear *law* of substance.[126]

The basic structure of Haeckel's teaching is clear: science is rapidly nearing a state where all the big problems have been solved. What remains unresolved is not so much a *scientific* problem as a *metaphysical* one. In science itself, the big battle is virtually at an end, and the work that remains to be done is pretty much a matter of mopping-up operations.

But is this rather optimistic position tenable? Can we really dismiss the prospect of factual insolubilia? Let us explore this issue more closely.

9.3 Cognitive Limits

The situation as regards the knowledge of facts is akin to that of the counting of integers, specifically in the following respects:[127]
1. The manifold of integers is inexhaustible. We can never come to grips with all of them as particular individuals. Nevertheless—
2. Further progress is always possible: we can always go beyond whatever point we have so far managed to reach. In principle, we can always go beyond what has been attained. Nevertheless—
3. Moving forward gets ever more cumbersome. In moving onwards, we must be ever more prolix and make use of ever more elaborate symbol complexes. Greater demands in time, effort, and resources are inevitable here. Accordingly—

---

126 Haeckel, *The Riddle of the Universe*, pp. 365–366.
127 We here take "counting" to be a matter of indicating integers by name—e.g., as "thirteen" or "13"—rather than descriptively, as per "the first prime after eleven."

4. In actual practice there will be only so much that we can effectively manage to do. The possibilities that obtain in principle can never be fully realized in practice. However—
5. Such limitations in no way hamper the prospects of establishing various correct generalizations about the manifold of integers in its abstract entirety.

A substantially parallel situation characterizes the cognitive condition of all finite intelligences whose cognitive operations have to proceed by a symbolic process that functions by language. Inductive inquiry, like counting, never achieves completeness. There is always more to be done: in both cases alike, we can always do better by doing more. But we can never do it all.

But, of course, even though there are—or may well be—*unknowable facts* (in the indicated sense of this term), they can never be identified as such, seeing that to identify a fact *as such*, namely *as a fact*, is effectively to claim knowledge of it. It is, accordingly, in principle impossible for us ever to give an example of one.

First, the good news. Generalizations can, of course, refer to *everything*. Bishop Butler's "Everything is what it is and not another thing" holds with unrestricted universality.

And fortunately, a case-by-case determination is not generally needed to validate generalizations. We can establish claims about groups larger than we can ever hope to inventory. Recourse to arbitrary instances, the process of indirect proof by *reductio ad absurdum*, and induction (mathematical and scientific) all afford procedures for achieving generality beyond the range of an exhaustive case-by-case check.

But will this *always* be so? Or are there also general truths whose determination would require the exhaustive surveying of all specific instances of a totality too large for our range of vision?

At this point, our cognitive finitude becomes a crucial consideration. The difference between a finite knower and an infinite knower is of fundamental importance and requires closer elucidation. For an "infinite knower" need not and should not be construed as an *omniscient* knower—one from whom nothing knowable is concealed (and so who knows, for example, who will be elected U. S. President in the year 2200). Rather, what is at issue is a knower who can manage to know in individualized detail an infinite number of independent facts. Such a knower might, for example, be able to answer such a question as: "Will the decimal expansion of π at some point have a million 1s?" (And, of course, the circumstance that an infinite knower can know *some* infinite set of independent facts does not mean that he can know *every* such set.)

Finite knowers can, of course, know universal truths. After all, we must acknowledge the prospect of inductive knowledge of general laws; we will have it that a knower can unproblematically know—for example—that "All dogs eat meat."[128] But what finite knowers *cannot* manage is to know this sort of thing *in detail* rather than at the level of generality. They cannot know specifically of each and every *u* in that potentially infinite range that *Fu* obtains—that is, while they can know collectively *that all individuals have F*, they cannot know distributively *of every individual that it has F*. Finite knowers can certainly know (via the U. S. Constitution) *that* every president is over the age of 35. But, of course, one has this knowledge without knowing *of* every president (including those one has never heard of, let alone the as yet unborn) that each individual one of them is over the age of 35—something one cannot do without knowing who they individually are.

9.4 Surd Facts and Unknowability

One cannot provide concrete examples of specific facts that are unknowable for finite knowers in view of the aforementioned circumstance that a claim to factuality automatically carries a claim to knowledge in its wake. However, while we cannot know *what* is such a fact, one can certainly establish *that* there are such things.

Given any collection of items, there are two importantly different kinds of general properties: those that all members of the collection DO have in common, and those that all members of the collection MUST have in common. The latter are the *necessity-geared* general features of the collection, the former its *contingency-geared* features. Thus, that all prime numbers greater than 2 are odd is a necessity-geared feature of these primes. Or consider the set of *all* post-Washington U. S. presidents. That all of them are native-born and that all of them are over 35 years of age is a necessity-geared feature of the collection in view of our Constitution's stipulations. However, that all were the favored candidates of a political party will (if indeed true) be a contingently geared feature of the collection that is in no way necessitated by it constituting characterization.

Now, the crucial consideration for present purposes is that the necessary features of a collection must inhere in (and be derivable from) the generalities that

---

[128] To be sure, the prospect of inductively secured knowledge of laws is a philosophically controversial issue. But this is not the place to pursue it. For the author's view of the matter, see his *Induction* (Oxford: Blackwell, 1980).

govern the collection at issue as a matter of principle. But its contingent features will be *surd* in that they cannot be established on the basis of general principles. When and if they actually hold, this can only be ascertained through a case-by-case check of the entire membership of the collection. And this means that *finite knowers can never decisively establish a surd/contingent general feature of an infinite collection.* Whenever a generality holds for a collection on a merely contingent basis, this is something that we finite intelligences can never determine with categorical assurance since their determination of facts require an item-by-item check, which is *ex hypothesi* impracticable for us.

Whenever a situation of this kind actually obtains—which for all we know to the contrary is often the case—then we can never manage to ascertain all the facts regarding an unsurveyable totality! Confirmed knowledge of the matter is beyond our reach here. The best and most that we can ever do here is to employ inductive, plausible, or probabilistic reasoning in a way that leaves the issue beclouded with a shadow of doubt.

Consider an illustration. The *New York Times* is an English-language newspaper. And as such, it is a necessary feature of the *Times* that throughout the history of its publication, mostly English words appear on its front page. This circumstance is inherent in the general principle (the "laws") of the matter. With these general principles in hand we can settle the issue of front-page vocabulary. With such law-constrained facts—let us call them *nomic*—we certainly do not need to carry out a case-by-case check through every issue, and knowledge reacts on the general principles of the situation. And a *nomic* property of something is a necessary feature for its kind: one that everything of its type not only does but must exhibit as a member of that particular "natural kind."

However, it must also be presumed to be a fact that as long as the paper exists, every issue of the *New York Times* will be such that the word THE occurs more than ten times on its front page. This is almost certainly a fact. But to determine that it is actually so, a case-by-case check becomes unavoidable. Such a fact—one whose determination cannot be settled by general principles (laws) but whose ascertainment requires a case-by-case check—is generally characterized as *surd*. And such a property of something is contingent: it cannot be accounted for on the basis of the general principles at issue.

Consider now a set of objects of a certain sort S that is infinite or interminably open-ended (lions, say, or sunrises at Acapulco). And let P be a surd/contingent property of some S-item X which, while in principle applicable to S-members, is nevertheless unique to X—that is, is such that no other S-member actually has P. But now note that this uniqueness could only be determined on a case-by-case check across the whole range of S. That X is unique within S in point of P-possession is (by hypothesis) a truth which no finite intelligence could ascertain, seeing that an item-by-item canvass of an infinite/indefinite range is beyond its capacity. Such truths illustrate the prospect of truths beyond the cognitive grasp of finite knowers.

Of course, "unknowably true" is a *vagrant* predicate—one that has no determinate address in that it admits of no identifiable instance. Instantiating this sort of thing can only be done at the level of schematic generality and not that of concrete instantiation. But we can convince ourselves—for good reason —that there indeed are such things, even though it is in principle impracticable to provide examples of them.

To begin with, there is the prospect of what might be called the *weak limitation* inherent in the circumstance that there are certain issues on its agenda that science cannot resolve *now*. However, this condition of weak limitation is perfectly compatible with the circumstance that *every* question raiseable at this stage will *eventually* be answered at such future juncture. And so, a contrasting way in which the question-resolving capacity of our knowledge may be limited can envisage the following, more drastic situation:

> *Strong Limitation (The Existence of Insolubilia).* There will (at some juncture) be then-posable questions which will *never* obtain answer, meaningful questions whose resolution lies beyond the reach of science altogether—questions that will remain ever unsolved on the cognitive agenda.

Such strong limitation envisions the existence of immortal questions—insolubilia that admit of no resolution within any cognitive corpus we are able to bring to realization.

However, for there to be *insolubilia* it is certainly not necessary that anything be said about the current *availability* of the insoluble question. The prospect of its actual identification *at this or indeed any other particular prespecified historical juncture is wholly untouched*. Even a position which holds that there indeed *are* insolubilia certainly need not regard them as being identifiable at the present state of the art of scientific development. One can accordingly also move beyond the two preceding theses to the yet stronger principle of:

> *Hyperlimitation (The Existence of IDENTIFIABLE insolubilia).* Our present-day cognitive agenda includes certain here-and-now specifiable and scientifically meaningful questions whose resolution lies beyond the reach of science altogether.

After all, to identify an insoluble problem, we would have to show that a certain inherently appropriate question is such that its resolution lies beyond every (possible or imaginable) state of future science. This task is clearly a rather tall order. Its realization is clearly difficult. But not in principle impossible.

Observe, to begin with, that even if we agree with Peirce that science is en route to a completion, we may well always—at *any* given time—remain at a remove from ultimacy. For as long as the body of knowledge continues to grow, there will still remain scope for the possibility of insolubilia. Even an asymptotically completable science can accommodate a fixed region of unresolvability, as long as the scope of that science itself is growing. That is, even if the *fraction* of unresolved questions converges asymptotically to zero, the *number* of unresolved questions may be ever-growing in the context of an expanding science. For consider the figures of Table 1.

Table 1:

No. of questions on the agenda	100	1,000	10,000	10^k
Fraction of unresolved questions	1/2	1/4	1/8	$(1/2)^{k-1}$
No. of unresolved questions	50	250	1,250	$10^k \times (1/2)^{k-1}$

These figures indicate that there is room for irrelevant questions even within a science ever-improving so as to approach asymptotic completeness. And this points towards a prospect that is well worth exploring.

9.5 Identifying Insolubilia

To elucidate the prospect of identifying scientific insolubilia, let us resume the theme of the progressive nature of knowledge, and continue the earlier considerations of second-order questions about future knowledge. Specifically, let us focus even more closely upon the historicity of knowledge development.

It lies in the very nature of the situation that the detailed scope of our ignorance is—for us at least—hidden away in an impenetrable fog of obscurity. The limits of one's information set unavoidable boundaries to one's predictive capacities. In particular, we cannot foresee what we cannot conceive. Our questions—let alone answers—cannot outreach the limited horizons of our concepts. Having never contemplated electronic computing machines as such, the ancient Romans could also venture no predictions about their impact on the social and economic life of the twenty-first century. Clever though he unquestionably was, Aristotle could not have pondered the issues of quantum electrodynamics. The scientific questions of the future are—at least in part—bound to be conceptually inaccessible to the inquirers of the present. The question of just how the cognitive agenda of some future date will be constituted is clearly irresolvable for us now. Not only can we not anticipate future discoveries now, we cannot even prediscern the questions that will arise as time moves on and cognitive progress with it.[129] We are cognitively myopic with respect to future knowledge. It is, in principle, infeasible for us to say now what questions will figure in the erotetic agenda of the future, let alone what answers they will engender.

But, of course, all of these are, by hypothesis, issues that will resolve themselves in the fullness of time. We have not as yet identified an insolubilia that can never be satisfactorily resolved.

To address this question, consider, however, the thesis:

(*T*) It will always be the case that there will come a time when all of the ever-resolved questions then on the agenda will be resolved within 100 years.

And now let Q^* be the question: "Is (*T*) true or not?" It is clear that to answer this question one way or the other, we would need to have cognitive mastery over the question agenda of all future times. And, as emphasized above, just this is something that we cannot manage to achieve. By their very nature as such, the discoveries of the future are unavailable at present. Thus, Q^* illustrates the sort of case we are looking for: it affords an example of a specific and perfectly meaningful question that we are in effect always and ever unable to resolve convincingly—irrespective of what the date on the calendar happens to read.

And we can move even further in this direction. For, after all, scientific inquiry is a venture in innovation. Present science can never speak decisively for future science, and present science cannot predict the specific discoveries of future inquiry. Accordingly, claims about what someone will achieve overall—and thus just where it will be going in the long run—are beyond the reach of attainable knowledge at this or any other particular stage of the scientific "state of the art." And on this basis, the thesis "There are nondecidable questions that science will never resolve—even were it to continue *ad indefinitum*"—the Insolubilia Thesis as we may call it—is something whose truth status can never be settled in a decisive way. And since this is so, we have it that this question itself is self-instantiating: it is a question regarding an aspect of reality (of which, of course,

---

[129] Of course, these questions already exist—what lies in the future is not their existence but their presence on the agenda of active concern.

science itself is a part) that scientific inquiry will never—at any specific state of the art—be in a position to settle decisively.

It should be noted that this issue cannot be settled by supposing a mad scientist who explodes the superbomb that blows the earth to smithereens and extinguishes all organic life as we know it. For the prospect cannot be precluded that intelligent life will evolve elsewhere. And even if we contemplate the prospect of a "big crunch" that is a reverse "big bang" and implodes our universe into an end, the project can never be precluded that at the other end of the big crunch, so to speak, another era of cosmic development awaits.

Of course, someone may possibly be minded to complain as follows:

> You are not giving me what I want. For let us distinguish between a base-level question in which no (essential) inference to questions and question agendas is made and a meta-level question in which there is an ineliminable reference to questions and question agendas. What I want is an example—a definitively specified instance—of an insolubilium at the base-level of substantive questions about the real world.

To such a complainer, one can respond as follows:

> In its own way, your complaint is well taken. But it is worthwhile to look in a somewhat different light at this very question that you have just raised, viz. "Are there any base-level factual insolubilia." The reality of it is that it is somewhat beyond difficult and impossible to imagine that this is an issue that could be settled convincingly one way or the other in any state of actually available information. And so, this question itself is a pretty good candidate for an insolubilium—though, to be sure, not at the base-level.

Clearly, that complaint cannot accomplish its intended mission.

9.6 Relating Knowledge to Ignorance

Facts can lie outside a person's cognitive reach for various reasons. These include:
- The individual just is not smart enough to figure it out.
- The information needed for its determination simply is not available.

As to the former, there are puzzles and mathematical problems that will do the trick for most of us. And as to the latter, there is the matter of just how many elephants were alive in Caesar's day. But this sort of thing is not at issue here. For there are also facts that are unknowable in principle—for anyone and everyone as a matter of inexorable necessity. It is to this, decidedly radical, issue of inevitable ignorance that the present deliberations will be addressed.

Their concern is not with what we *do not* know, but with what we *cannot* know. And the questions that will preoccupy it are not just questions we cannot answer, but questions which, in the very nature of things, no one can possibly answer.

The idea of *necessary* or *demonstrable* unknowability admits of three construals:
- *logical* unknowability demonstrable on the basis of abstract considerations of epistemic logic;
- *conceptual* unknowability demonstrable on the basis of an analysis of the salient concept and ideas at issue;
- *in-principle* unknowability on the basis of the fundamental principles that delineate some area of inquiry or deliberation.

Thus, it is *logically* demonstrable that one cannot know that such-and-such a particular fact is among those one does not know. It is *unconceptually* impossible to know a certain idea that has fallen into total oblivion, or to know of a particular event that has left no trace of its occurrence. And it is *in-principle* impossible to know when and by whom the word "dog" was first used in English. These issues of necessary unknowability deserve special attention.

Among the facts that are unknowable are those which relate to the future contingencies of choice and chance. No one can presently identify those who will be killed in next year's automobile accidents, nor can one presently identify those whom you will meet en route to the store when next you shop. And this sort of thing holds *vis-à-vis* the past as well. No one can identify those who are alive today because a certain automobile speed limit was lowered or a certain driver-training program was instituted last year.

This last example takes us into the realm of "but-for" deliberation and here some special considerations come to the fore. For such facts root in counterfactual hypotheses. Thus, it may be a fact about the world that John would be dead if he had not jumped out of the way of that onrushing bus. But such iffy "facts" also lie outside the range of our present concern for unknowable fact.

And for very good reason. Thus, consider the question: "Would X be alive today if Y had not introduced his mother to his father?" Well, they could have met in other ways, so that their marriage and X's subsequent birth would be wholly unaffected. But then again, maybe not. And even if X was born on schedule, maybe the particular manner of his parents first meeting set in motion a set of events that prevented X's being killed five days ago. The whole question dissolves in an uncharted sea of possibilities and there is no practicable way to navigate in such waters.

So, what is one to make of reasoning of the following format:

- If *p* were true, then *XYZ* would be an unknowable fact.
- For ought we know, *p* might be true.

Therefore: For ought we know, *XYZ* is an unknowable fact.

This inference may look plausible, but it is invalid. The only validly derivable conclusion is:

Therefore: For ought we know, *XYZ might be* an unknowable fact.

But this "might be" conclusion here eviscerates the reasoning. For a might-be fact just is not a fact—any more than a might-be inheritance is an inheritance or a might-be disaster is a disaster.

Granted, one can readily—and quite plausibly—say things on the order of:

If *XYZ* were a fact, then we could never know it.

Hypothetical unknowability is certainly a prospect. For instance:

If this entire universe of ours were merely a subatomic particle in some unimaginably vast meta-universe, then we could never learn about the things that go on there.

But here we are erecting a house of cards on the sand of supposition. What we have is not an unknowable fact but a fact about unknowability—a *conditionally unknowable fact relative to a counterfactual supposition*. This sort of thing is not relevant to the present range of deliberations. Our concern is with unknowable *facts* and not with the unknowable *possibilities* at issue in mere suppositions.

Possibility-mongering does not come to grips with the issues at stake here. Our present concern is with the actualities (and in a way, even the inevitabilities) of unknowable fact, not with its possibilities. It is thereby unknowability *as matters stand* that concerns us. What would—or might be—unknowable if certain weird conditions obtained is not a matter of present concern.

For present purposes, however, all this is immaterial. Our present concern is with *actual facts*. Unknowability in the context of hypothetical or conjectural possibilities is something else again, beside the point of present concern.

One can certainly know *that* something or other is possible, but that which is *merely* possible but not actual for this very reason is something that one cannot know to be so.[130]

9.7 Unknowability

The great American philosopher C. S. Peirce wrote:

> For my part, I cannot admit the proposition of Kant—that there are certain impassable bounds to human knowledge... The history of science affords illustrations enough of the folly of saying that this, that, or the other can never be found out. Auguste Comte said that it was clearly impossible for man ever to learn anything of the chemical constitution of the fixed stars, but before his book had reached its readers the discovery which he had announced as impossible had been made. Legendre said of a certain proposition in the theory of numbers that, while it appeared to be true, it was most likely beyond the powers of the human mind to prove it; yet the next writer on the subject gave six independent demonstrations of the theorem.[131]

The present discussion will argue that, notwithstanding the plausibility of Peirce's considerations, there indeed are some impassable bounds to human knowledge.

To be sure, there is a perverse sense in which there are no statements whose truth statuses are undecidable and no questions that are unanswerable. For you can, of course, decide for or against a statement by merely flipping a coin. And you can answer every question by the simple algorithm that if the question asks *Why?* you answer "Because God wants it that way"; if the question asks *When?* you say "Yesterday"; if the question asks *Where?* you say "In Paris," and so on. You need never be at a loss for words. But, of course, what is wanted in these matters is not just a decision but a rationally grounded decision, and not just an answer—even one that happens to be correct—but one whose correctness can be made manifest. The crux throughout is a matter of rational cogency.

There are two modes of personal ignorance: the culpable and the inevitable. Culpable ignorance exists when one should know something but doesn't; inevitable ignorance exists where there just is no possible way of knowing something.

---

130 $K\Diamond p$ is perfectly coherent, nevertheless $\Diamond p$ & $\sim p$ is inconsistent with Kp (seeing that $Kp \to p$).

131 Charles S. Peirce, *Collected Papers*, ed. by Charles Hartshorne and Paul Weiss, vol. 6 (Cambridge, MA: Harvard University Press, 1929), sect. 6.556.

The necessary unknowability that concerns us here invariably falls into the latter range.

Here, we are not interested in questions whose unanswerability resides merely in the contingent fact that certain information is not in practice accessible. The present deliberations do not concern the contingent cognitive limitations of individuals, but rather those deeply intractable issues that no one can possibly resolve as a matter of principle rather than contingent circumstance. (No one knows what Columbus felt when first making land fall in "the new world"—but that is so simply because there is no way in which we can secure the needed information here and now.) The crux, rather, is a matter of the inevitable inhabitability of questions that are unanswerable as a matter of principle.

Now, when some fact is said to be unknowable, the question will immediately arise: For whom? And there are various prospects here, specifically:
- for a given individual
- for humans in general
- for finite intelligent beings at large

It will, ultimately, be this last and strongest mode of unknowability that constitutes the focus of these present deliberations.

As regards those facts that are unknowable only for a particular individual, consider an example. There are (surely) various facts that you do not know. But the truth of a specific claim of the format "F is a fact that I do not know" is something you cannot possibly know. To do so, you would have to know that F is a fact—which is exactly that what is now being denied. "What is an example of a fact that you do not know?" is a question you cannot possibly answer correctly (though others will have no difficulty with it).[132] For "F is a fact I do not know" is self-contradicting in its claim to F's factuality. And much the same holds of the claim "B is a belief I (now) hold mistakenly." Such contentions are self-negating. What the one hand gives, the other takes away.

But more far-reaching, there are also facts that no one can possibly know—issues whose resolution lies beyond the power of anyone and everyone. Given human finitude—both at the level of individuals and collectively—there will be some facts which nobody actually knows so that the now-generalized question "What is an example of a fact that nobody knows?" will be unanswerable. For while it doubtless has an answer, it will nevertheless be one that no one can ap-

---

132 There is, of course, no earthly reason why you cannot know that F is a fact that I do not know. It's just that I cannot possibly manage it. And this is so not for factual reasons relative to my stupidity but for conceptual reasons relating to the nature of the knowledge-claim that would be at issue.

propriately provide, since that such-and-such a particular fact is universally unknown to be so is something that no one can possibly know.

Yet while it is obviously impossible to provide examples of unknowable facts, it would take considerable hubris to deny that such facts exist. Thus, if no intelligent being in the cosmos happens to know that a certain fact obtains, then nobody can know that this particular circumstance is so. Even as our personal ignorance lies outside our personal ken, so our collective ignorance lies outside our collective ken as well.

Can anything general be said regarding just what it is that those unknowable facts are about?

The principal categories of classical ontology are:
- *transcendentalia:* God, angels, the extra-mundane
- *realia:* real things existing in the world
- *absracta:* abstract conceptual items, especially mathematical objects
- *possibilia:* unrealized possibilities
- *fictionalia:* fictional objects

Now, as already noted, fictionalia fall outside the range of present deliberations because our topic is to be unknowabiltiy in relation to matters of mundane fact. And this also puts transcendentals aside of our present concerns, notwithstanding the fact that theologians here generally insisted upon the unknowability of God. Moreover, as just noted for the same reason, possibilia also fall outside our scope. Then too we shall not here address (more than illustratively) the issue of unknowable abstract/mathematical fact and issues of indemonstrability in the abstract sciences where knowledge proceeds through demonstration.[133] Our present focus is to be on issues of unknowability about reality—about the facts of the world.

9.8 Unknowable Facts vs. Unanswerable Questions

An important indicator of limits to knowledge lies in the consideration that not only are there questions that cannot be answered cogently, but there will also be questions that a given person cannot even pose. Julius Caesar could not have wondered if his sword contained tungsten or if Rutherford B. Hayes won the U. S. presidency legally. The very concepts needed to form such question are out-

---

[133] On the mathematical issues, see Gregory J. Chaitin, *The Unknowable* (Singapore and New York: Springer, 1999).

9.8 Unknowable Facts vs. Unanswerable Questions

side the conceptual horizons of people at some times and places—or possibly of people at all times and places. And just such conceptual horizons afford a key pathway to the unknowable.

There are bound to be regions of our ignorance to which knowledge can gain no access, seeing that it is beyond the limits of possibility for anyone to know the details of their ignorance. To elucidate this idea, it is instructive to adopt an erotetic—that is, question-oriented—view of knowledge and ignorance.

It can be supposed, without loss of generality, that the answers to factual questions are always complete propositions. Thus, consider such examples as:

Q. "Who is that man?"
A. "Tom Jones."

Q. "When will he come?"
A. "At two o'clock."

Q. "What prime numbers lie between two and eight?"
A. "Three, five, and seven."

Throughout, the answers can be recast in the form of completed propositions, respectively: "That man is Tom Jones"; "He will come at two o'clock"; "Three, five, and seven are the prime numbers between two and eight." So, we shall have it here that proper answers to questions are given via complete propositions.

Furthermore, it must be acknowledged that *answering* a question is not simply a matter of giving a response that happens to be correct. For a proper answer must not just be correct but credible: it must have the backing of a rationale that renders its correctness evident. For example, take the question of whether the mayor of San Antonio had eggs for breakfast yesterday. You say yes, I say no—though neither of us has a clue. One of us is bound to be right. But neither one of us has managed to provide an actual answer to the question. One of us has made a verbal response that happens to be correct, but neither of us has given a cognitively appropriate answer in the sense of the term that is now at issue. For that would require the backing of a cogent rationale of credibility; merely to guess at an answer, for example, or to draw it out of a hat, is not really to provide one.

Reverting to our main them, recall those emphatically unanswerable questions are those which a particular individual or group is unable to answer.

And looking beyond this, we can also contemplate the prospect of globally intractable questions such that no one (among finite intelligences at least) can

possibly be in a position to answer them correctly. These questions have an appropriate answer but for reasons of general principle no one—no finite intelligence at least—can possibly be in a position to provide it. An example of such globally unanswerable questions can be provided by nontrivial but yet inherently uninstantiable predicates along the lines of:
- "What idea is there that has never occurred to anybody?"
- "What occurrence is there that no one ever mentions?"

There undoubtedly are such items, but of course they cannot be instantiated, so that these accordingly, then, are bound to be questions which ask for examples that are inherently unanswerable.[134]

As these considerations indicate, questions regarding the limits of our factual knowledge are particularly intractable. And indeed, the issue of the extent of our cognitive incapacity is itself perhaps the most dramatic and fateful token of the limits of human knowledge.

---

134 This issue here is one of so-called "vagrant predicates" that have no known address.

10 On Existence, Reality, and Facts

10.1 Is Man the Measure?

But how is the view of reality in terms of causal productivity related to the issue of knowledge? Clearly, whatever can be *known* by us humans to be real must, of course, for that very reason actually be real. But does the converse hold? Is the real for that very reason also automatically knowable? Is it appropriate to join C. S. Peirce who, in rejecting "incognizables," insisted that whatever is real must be accessible to cognition—and indeed must ultimately become known?

Is humanly cognizable reality the only sort of reality there is? Some philosophers certainly say so, maintaining that there actually is a fact of the matter only when "we [humans] could in finite time bring ourselves into a position in which we were justified either in asserting or in denying [it]."[135] On such a view, all reality is inevitably *our* reality. What we humans are not in a position to domesticate cognitively—what cannot be brought home to us by (finite!) cognitive effort—simply does not exist as a part of reality at all. Where we have no cognitive access, there just is nothing to be accessed. On such a perspective, we are led back to the *homo mensura* doctrine of Protagoras: "Man is the measure of all things, of what is, that it is, of what is not, that it is not."

However, in reflecting on the issue in a modest mood, one is tempted to ask: "Just who has appointed us to this exalted role? How is it that *we humans* qualify as the ultimate arbiters of reality as such?"

Regarding this doctrine that what is real must be knowable, traditional realism takes an appropriately modest line. It insists on preserving, insofar as possible, a boundary line of separation between ontology and epistemology; between fact and knowledge of fact, between truth-status possession and truth-status decidability with respect to propositions, and between entity and observability with respect to individual things. As the realist sees it, reality can safely be presumed to have depths that cognition may well be unable to plumb.

To be sure, it is possible to reduce the gap between personal and objective cognition by liberalizing the idea of what is at issue with cognizers. Consider the following series of metaphysical theses: *For something to be real in the mode of cognitive accessibility it is necessary for it to be experientiable by:*
1. oneself
2. one's contemporary (human) fellow inquirers

---

135 Michael Dummett, "Truth," *Proceedings of the Aristotelian Society. New Series* 59 (1958–1959), p. 160.

3. *us humans (at large and in the long run)*
4. *some actual species of intelligent creatures*
5. *some physically realizable (though not necessarily actual) type of intelligent being—creatures conceivably endowed with cognitive resources far beyond our feeble human powers*
6. *an omniscient being (i.e., God)*

This ladder of potential knowers is critically important for construing the idea that to be is to be knowable. For here the question "By whom?" cannot really be evaded.

The idea of an experiential idealism that equates reality with experientiality is one that can accordingly be operated on rather different levels. Specifically, the "i-th level" idealist maintains—and the "i-th level" realist denies—such a thesis at stage number i of the preceding six-entry series. On this approach, the idealist emerges as the exponent of an experience-productive theory of reality, equating truth and reality with what is experientially accessible to by "us"—with different, and potentially increasingly liberal, constructions of just who is to figure in that "us group" of qualified cognizers. But, of course, no *sensible* idealist maintains a position as strong as the egocentrism of the first entry on the list. Equally, it is presumably the case that no *sensible* realist denies a position as weak as the deocentrism of the last. The salient question is just where to draw the line in determining what is a viable "realistic/idealistic" position.

Let us focus for the moment upon the third entry of the above listing, the "man is the measure," *homo mensura* doctrine. By *this* standard, both Peirce and the Dummett of the preceding quotation are clearly *homo mensura* realists, seeing that both confine the real to what we humans can come to know. But this is strange stuff. Of course, what people can *know* to be real constitutes (*ex hypothesi*) a part or aspect of reality at large. That much is not in question. But the bone of contention between *homo mensura* realism and a sensible idealism is the question of a surplus—of whether reality may have parts or aspects that outrun altogether the reach of human cognition. And on this basis, the *homo mensura* doctrine is surely problematic. For in the end, what we humans can know cannot plausibly be seen as decisive for what can (unqualifiedly) be known.

Undoubtedly, a mind that evolves in the world by natural selection has a link to reality sufficiently close to enable it to secure *some* knowledge of the real. But the converse is decidedly questionable. It is a dubious proposition that the linkage should be so close that *only* what is knowable for some species of actual being should be real—that reality has no hidden reserves of fact that are not domesticable within the cognitive resources of existing creatures—let alone one particular species thereof. Accordingly, it seems sensible to adopt the "idealistic" line only at the penultimate level of the above listing and to be a realist short of that. Essentially, this is the position of the causal commerce realism espoused at the outset of the present discussion. As such a position sees it, the most plausible form of idealism is geared to that next-to-last position which takes the line that "to be real is to be causally active—to be a part of the world's causal commerce." For since one can always hypothesize a creature that detects a given sort of causal process, we need not hesitate to equate reality with experientiability in principle. We thus arrive at an idealism which achieves its viability and plausibility through its comparative weakness in operating at the next-to-last level, while at all of the earlier, more substantive, levels our position is effectively realistic. The result is a doctrinal position that is a halfway-house compromise that combines an idealism of sorts with a realism of sorts.

A conservative idealism of this description holds that what is so as a "matter of fact" is not necessarily cognizable by "us" no matter how far—short of God!—we extend the boundaries of that "us-community" of inquiring intelligences. On the other hand, one cannot make plausible sense of "such-and-such a feature of nature is real but no possible sort of intelligent being could possibly discern it." To be real is to be in a position to make an impact somewhere on something of such a sort that a suitably equipped mind-endowed intelligent creature could detect it. What is real in the world must make some difference to it, that is *in principle* detectable. Existence in this world is coordinated with perceivability in principle. And so, at this point, there is a concession to idealism—albeit one that is relatively weak. Since to be physically real is to be part of the world's causal commerce, it is always in principle possible for an intelligent sentient being of a suitable sort to enter into this causal situation so as to be able to monitor what is going on. Accordingly, *being* and *being knowable in principle* can plausibly be identified.

But in any case, traditional *homo mensura* realism is untenable. There is no good reason to indulge a hubris that sees our human reality as definitive on grounds of being the only one there is. Neither astronomically nor otherwise are we the center around which all things revolve. After all, humans have the capacity not only for knowledge but also for imagination. And it is simply too easy for us to imagine a realm of things and states of things of which we can obtain no knowledge because "we have no way to get there from here," lacking the essential means for securing information in such a case.

10.2 Realism and Incapacity

Charles Sanders Peirce located the impetus to realism in the limitations of man's will—in the fact that we can exert no control over our experience and, try as we will, cannot affect what we see and sense. Peirce's celebrated "Harvard Experiment" of the Lowell Lectures of 1903 makes the point forcibly:

> I know that this stone will fall if it is let go, because experience has convinced me that objects of this kind always do fall; and if anyone has any doubt on the subject, I should be happy to try the experiment, and I will bet him a hundred to one on the result... [I know this because of an unshakable conviction that] the uniformity with which stones have fallen has been due to some *active general principle* [of nature] ... Of course, every sane man will adopt the latter hypothesis. If he could doubt it in the case of the stone—which he can't—and I may as well drop the stone once and for all—I told you so!—if anybody doubt this still, a thousand other such inductive predictions are getting verified every day, and he will have to suppose every one of them to be merely fortuitous in order reasonably to escape the conclusion that *general principles are really operative in nature*. That is the doctrine of scholastic realism.[136]

In this context, however, it is important to distinguish between mental *dependency* and mental *control*. Peirce is clearly right in saying that we cannot *control* our conviction that the stone will fall, that, do what we will, it will remain. Nevertheless, this circumstance could conceivably still be something that *depends on us*—exactly as with the fearsomeness of heights for the man with vertigo. If the *unconscious* sphere of mind actually dictates how I *must* "see" something (as, for example, in an optical illusion of the Müller-Lyer variety), then I evidently have no *control*. But that does not *in itself* refute mind-dependency—even of a very strong sort. There is always the prospect that we are deluding ourselves in these matters—that the limitations at issue appertain only to our *conscious* powers, and not to our mental powers as such.[137]

This prospect blocks C. S. Peirce's argument in the way already foreseen by Descartes in the *Meditations:*

> I found by experience that these [sensory] ideas presented themselves to me without my consent being requisite, so that I could not perceive any object, however desirous I might be, unless it were present... But although the ideas which I receive by the senses do not depend on my will I do not think that one should for that reason conclude that

---

[136] Charles S. Peirce, *Collected Papers*, ed by Charles Hartshorne and Paul Weiss (Cambridge MA: Harvard University Press, 1934), vol. 5, sect. 5.64–67.
[137] On the other hand, there is also the fact that we can control the content and the outcome of our dreams as little as those of conscious experience.

they proceed from things different from myself, since possible some facility might be discovered in me—though different from those yet known to me—which produced them.[138]

The fact of it is that we may simply delude ourselves about the range of the mind's powers: lack of control notwithstanding, dependency may yet lie with the "unconscious" sector of mind. The traditional case for realism based on the limits of causal control through human *agency* thus fails to provide a really powerful argument for mind-independence.

However, a far more effective impetus to realism lies in the limitations of man's *intellect*, pivoting on the circumstances that the features of real things inevitably outrun our cognitive reach. In placing some crucial aspects of the real together outside the effective range of mind, it speaks for a position that sees mind-independence as a salient feature of the real. The very fact of fallibilism and limitedness—of our absolute confidence that our putative knowledge does not and cannot do full justice to the real truth of what reality is actually like—is surely one of the best arguments for a realism that turns on the basic idea that there is more to reality than we humans do or can know. Traditional scientific realists see the basis for realism in the accuracy and extent of our scientific knowledge; the present metaphysical realism, by contrast, sees its basis in our realization of the inevitable *shortcomings* of our knowledge—scientific knowledge included.

Such an epistemic approach accordingly preempts the preceding sort of objection. If we are mistaken about the reach of our cognitive powers—if they do not adequately grasp "the way things really are"—then this very circumstance itself clearly *bolsters* the case for the sort of realism now at issue. The cognitive intractability of things is something about which, in principle, we cannot delude ourselves altogether, since such delusion would illustrate rather than abrogate the fact of a reality independent of ourselves. The very inadequacy of our knowledge is one of the most salient tokens there is of a reality out there that lies beyond the inadequate groupings of mind. It is the very limitation of our knowledge of things—our recognition that reality extends beyond the horizons of what we can possibly know or even conjecture about it—that betokens the mind-independence of the real.

But a qualification is in order here. One must be careful about what the presently contemplated sort of argument for realism actually manages to establish. For it does *not* establish outright that a stone—be it Peirce's or Dr. Johnson's

---

[138] René Descartes, *Meditations*, No. VI, in: *Philosophical Works*, vol. 1., ed. by Elizabeth S. Haldane and G. R. T. Ross (Cambridge, MA: Cambridge University Press, 1911), pp. 187–189.

or the geologist's—is something mind-independently real. Rather, what it shows is that our conception of a "stone"—indeed, our conception of any physical object—is one of something that is mind-independently real, possessed of a nature extending beyond the realm of our minds. And so, the realism underwritten by these deliberations is not in fact a squarely *ontological* doctrine, but a realism nevertheless geared to our conceptual scheme for thinking about things. As indicated above, the present position is a halfway-house compromise: a metaphysical realism that is unproblematically compatible with an idealism of sorts.

10.3 Cognitive Dynamics

But there is yet another way of substantiating our point. For the preceding considerations related to the limits of knowledge that can be rationalized on a fixed and given conceptual basis—a fully formed, developed language. But in real life, languages are never fully formed and a conceptual basis is never "fixed and given." Even with such familiar things as birds, trees, and clouds, we are involved in a constant reconceptualization in the course of progress in genetics, evolutionary theory, and thermodynamics. Our conceptions of things always present a moving rather than a fixed object of scrutiny and this historical dimension must also be reckoned with.

Any adequate theory of inquiry must recognize that the ongoing process of information acquisition at issue in science is a process of conceptual innovation, which always leaves certain facts about things wholly outside the cognitive range of the inquirers of any particular period. Cicero did not know—and, in the then extant state of the cognitive arts, could not have known—that lemons contain citric acid. There will always be facts (or plausible candidate facts) about a thing that we do not know because we cannot even conceive of them in the prevailing order of things. To grasp such a fact means taking a perspective of consideration that as yet we simply do not have, since the state of knowledge (or purported knowledge) is not yet advanced to a point at which such a consideration is feasible. Any adequate world-view must recognize that the ongoing progress of scientific inquiry is a process of conceptual innovation that always leaves various facts about the things of this world wholly outside the cognitive range of the inquirers of any particular period.

The language of emergence can perhaps be deployed usefully to make the point. But what is at issue is not an emergence of the features of things, but an emergence of our knowledge about them. Blood circulated in the human body well before Harvey; substances containing uranium were radioactive before Becquerel. The emergence at issue relates to our cognitive mechanisms of conceptualization, not to the objects of our consideration in and of themselves. Real-world objects must be conceived of as antecedent to any cognitive interaction—as being there all along, "pregiven" as Edmund Husserl put it. Any cognitive changes or innovations are to be conceptualized as something that occurs on our side of the cognitive transaction, and not on the side of the objects with which we deal.[139]

The prospect of substantive change can never be eliminated in this domain. The properties of any real are literally open-ended: we can always discover more of them. Even if we were (surely mistakenly) to view the world as inherently finitistic—espousing a Keynesian principle of "limited variety" to the effect that nature can be portrayed descriptively with the materials of a finite taxonomic scheme—there will still be no *a priori* guarantee that the progress of science will not lead *ad indefinitum* to changes of mind regarding this finite register of descriptive materials. And this conforms exactly to our expectation in these matters. For where the real things of the world are concerned, we not only expect to learn more about them in the course of scientific inquiry, *we expect to have to change our minds about their nature and modes of comportment.* Be the items at issue elm trees, or volcanoes, or quarks, we have every expectation that in the course of future scientific progress, people will come to think about their origin and their properties differently from the way we do at this juncture.

This cognitive opacity of real things means that we are not—and will never be—in a position to evade or abolish the contrast between "things as we think them to be" and "things as they actually and truly are." Their susceptibility to further elaborative detail—and to changes of mind regarding this further detail—is built into our very conception of a "real thing." To be a real thing is to be something regarding which we can always, in principle, acquire more and possibly discordant information. This view of the situation is supported rather than impeded once we abandon the naive cumulativist/preservationist view of knowledge acquisition for the view that new discoveries need not supplement but can displace old ones. We realize that people will come to think differently about things from the way we do—even when thoroughly familiar things are at issue—recognizing that scientific progress generally entails fundamental changes of mind about how things work in the world.

---

139 One possible misunderstanding must be blocked at this point. To learn about nature, we must interact with it. And so, to determine a feature of an object, we may have to make some impact upon it that would perturb its otherwise obtaining condition. (The indeterminacy principle of quantum mechanics affords a well-known reminder of this.) It should be clear that this matter of physical interaction for data acquisition is not contested in the ontological indifference thesis here at issue.

In view of the cognitive opacity of real things, we must never pretend to a cognitive monopoly or cognitive finality. This recognition of incomplete information is inherent in the very nature of our conception of a "real thing." It is a crucial facet of our epistemic stance towards the real world to recognize that every part and parcel of it has features lying beyond our present cognitive reach—at any "present" whatsoever.

Much the same story holds when our concern is not with physical things, but with types of such things. To say that something is copper or magnetic is to say more than that it has the properties we think copper or magnetic things have, and to say more than that it meets our test conditions for being copper or being magnetic. It is to say that this thing is copper or magnetic. And this is an issue regarding which we are prepared at least to contemplate the prospect that we have got it wrong.

Certainly, it is imaginable that natural science will come to a stop, not in the trivial sense of a cessation of intelligent life, but in Charles Sanders Peirce's more interesting sense of eventually reaching a condition after which even indefinitely ongoing effort at inquiry will not—and indeed actually cannot—produce any significant change. Such a position is, in theory, possible. But we can never know—be it in practice or in principle—that it is actually realized. We can never establish that science has attained such an omega-condition of final completion: the possibility of further change lying "just around the corner" can never be ruled out finally and decisively. Thus, we have no alternative but to presume that our science is still imperfect and incomplete, that no matter how far we have pushed our inquiries in any direction, regions of *terra incognita* yet lie beyond.

10.4 Conceptual Basis of Realism as a Postulate

The skeptical tendency of these remarks is of a very restricted sort, however. It is not a fact-skepticism but a concept-skepticism. For to tell the truth is one thing, but to tell the whole truth another. And the former is certainly possible without the latter. The fact that our knowledge of the world is incomplete clearly does not mean that it is incorrect.

But in this regard, it is important to distinguish between a true *statement* and a true *conception*. The informative incompleteness of a statement does not preclude its truth. If the only thing I know about you is that you dislike peaches, so be it—I am still in possession of a fact about you and the statement at issue is a genuine truth. However, having a true *conception* of something is far more demanding. On the positive side, it requires that we have all of the important facts about you straight—that we know all of the *important* truths that are relevant

10.4 Conceptual Basis of Realism as a Postulate

here. And on the negative side, it means that the things that we accept about you —important or not— are all true.

Accordingly, while immediate information about something is perfectly compatible with knowing a true fact about it, it is not compatible—or not likely to be compatible—with knowing a true conception of it, seeing that the things we do not know may well include some important details.

The fact is that as long as our information about something is incomplete, we can never know that our conception of it is correct. For to know this would require that none of the unknown facts about it are important, that what we do not know does not matter substantially for the correctness of our conception—its adequacy overall. And this sort of knowledge about what we do not know is in principle unavailable.

The concept-skepticism at issue here is closely bound up with a realism.

The metaphysical realism of objective fact is the doctrine that the world exists in a way that is substantially independent of the thinking beings it contains that can inquire into it, and that its nature—its having whatever characteristics it does actually have—is also comparably knowledge-transcending. In saying of something that it is "a real thing," an object existing as part of the world's furniture, we commit ourselves to various (obviously interrelated) points:

1. *Self-subsistence.* Being a "something" (an entity or process) with its own unity of being. Having an enduring identity of its own.
2. *Physicality or reality.* Existing within the causal order of things. Having a place on the world's physical scene as a participant of some sort.
3. *Publicity or multilateral accessibility.* Admitting universality of access. Being something that different investigators proceeding from different points of departure can get hold of.
4. *Autonomy or independence.* Being independent of mind. Being something that observers find and learn about, rather than create in the course of their cognitive endeavors.

In natural science, we try to get at the objective matters of fact regarding physical reality in ways that are accessible to all observers alike. (The "repeatability of experiments" is crucial.) And the salient factor enters in with that fourth and final issue: autonomy. The very idea of a thing so functions in our conceptual scheme that real things are thought of as having an identity, a nature, and a mode of comportment wholly indifferent to and independent of the cognitive state of the art regarding them—and potentially even very different from our own current conceptions of the matter.

The conception of a thing that underlies our discourse about the things of this world inherently involves tentativeness and fallibilism—the implicit recognition that our own personal or even communal conception of particular things may, in general, be wrong, and is in any case inadequate. At the back of our thought about things there is always a certain wary skepticism that recognizes the possibility of error. The objectivity of real existents projects beyond the reaches of our subjectively conditioned information. There is wisdom in Hamlet's dictum: "There are more things in heaven and on earth, Horatio..." The limits of our knowledge may be the limits of *our* world, but they are not the limits of *the* world. We do and must recognize the limitations of our cognition.

And so we cannot justifiably equate reality with what is known to us, nor equate reality with what is expressible in our language. And what is true here for our sort of mind is true for any other sort of finite mind as well. It is inherent in our conception of physical reality that any physically realizable sort of cognizing being can only know a part or aspect of the real.

This "objectivity" in the sense of mind-transcendence is pivotal for realism. A fact is objective in this mode through obtaining independently of whatever thinkers may think about relevant issues, so that changes merely in what is thought by the world's intelligences would leave it unaffected. With objective facts (unlike those which are merely a matter of intersubjective agreement), what thinkers think is never reality-determinative.[140]

Realism, accordingly, has two indispensable and inseparable constituents: the one existential and ontological, and the other cognitive and epistemic. The former maintains that there indeed is a real world—a realm of thought-transcendent objective physical reality. The latter maintains that we can to some extent secure adequate descriptive information about this mind-independent realm. This second contention obviously presupposes the first. But how can that first ontological thesis be secured?

Metaphysical realism is clearly not an inductive inference secured through the scientific systematization of our observations. Rather, it represents a regulative presupposition that makes science possible in the first place. If we did not assume from the very outset that our sensations somehow relate to an extramental reality, we could clearly make no use of them to draw any inference whatever about "the real world." The realm of mind-independent reality is something we cannot *discover*—we do not learn that it exists as a result of inquiry and investigation. How could we ever learn from our observations that our mental experience is itself largely the causal product of the machinations of a mind-independent matrix, that all those phenomenal appearances are causally rooted in a

---

[140] Compare deliberations about realism with those regarding objectivity in Chapter 9 above. The same pragmatic rationale is at work in both contexts.

physical reality? This is obviously something we have to suppose from the very outset. What is at issue is, all too clearly, a *precondition* for empirical inquiry—a presupposition for the usability of observational data as sources of objective information. That experience is indeed objective, that what we take to be evidence *is* evidence, that our sensations yield information about an order of existence outside the experiential realm itself, and that this experience constitutes not just a mere phenomenon but an appearance of something extra-mental belonging to an objectively self-subsisting order, all this is something that we must always *presuppose* in using experiential data as "evidence" for how things stand in the world.

We do not learn or discover in the course of experience that there is a mind-independent physical reality; we have no alternative but to *presume or postulate* it. Realism represents a postulation made on *functional* (rather than *evidential*) grounds: we endorse it in order to be in a position to learn by experience at all. As Kant clearly saw, objective experience is possible only if the existence of such a real, objective world is *presupposed* from the outset rather than being seen as a matter of *ex post facto* discovery about the nature of things.[141]

To be sure, once we have made a start by accepting an objective reality and its concomitant causal aspect, more or less by sheer postulation, then principles of inductive systematization, of explanatory economy, and of common cause consilience can work wonders in exploiting the phenomena of experience to provide the basis for plausible claims about the nature of the real. But we indispensably need that initial existential presupposition to make a start. Without a commitment from the very outset to a reality to serve as a ground and object of our experience, its cognitive import will be lost. Only on this basis can we proceed evidentially with the exploration of the interpersonally public and objective domain of a physical world order that we share in common.

Of course, that second descriptive (epistemic) component of realism stands on a very different footing. Unlike its *existence*, reality's *nature* is something about which we can only make warranted claims through examining it. Substantive information must come through inquiry—through evidential validation. Once

---

[141] Kant held that we cannot experientially learn though perception about the objectivity of outer things, because we can only recognize our perceptions as *perceptions* (i.e., representations of outer things) if these outer things are supposed as such from the first (rather than being learned or inferred). As he summarizes in the "Refutation of Idealism": "Idealism assumed that the only immediate experience is inner experience, and that from it we can only *infer* outer things—and this, moreover, only in an untrustworthy manner...But in the above proof it has been shown that outer experience is really immediate..." (Immanuel Kant, *Critique of Pure Reason*, tr. by Norman Kemp Smith [New York: Random House, 1958], B276).

we are willing to credit our observational data with objectivity, and thus with evidential bearing, then we can, of course, make use of them to inform ourselves as to the nature of the real. But that initial presumption has to be there from the start.

Let us examine this basic reality postulate somewhat more closely. Our standard conception of inquiry involves recognition of the following facts: (1) The world (the realm of physical existence) has a nature whose characterization in point of description, explanation, and prediction is the object of empirical inquiry; (2) The real nature of the world is in the main independent of the process of inquiry which the real world canalizes or conditions; and (3) In virtue of these considerations, we can stake neither total nor final claims for our purported knowledge of reality. Our knowledge of the world must be presumed incomplete, incorrect, and imperfect, with the consequence that "our reality" must be considered to afford an inadequate characterization of "reality itself."

Our commitment to realism thus centers on a certain practical *modus operandi*, encapsulated in the precept: "Proceed in matters of inquiry and communication on the basis that you are dealing with an objective realm, existing quite independently of the doings and dealings of minds." Accordingly, we standardly operate on the basis of the "presumption of objectivity" reflected in the guiding precept: "Unless you have good reason to think otherwise (that is, as long as *nihil obstat*), treat the materials of inquiry and communication as veridical—as representing the nature of the real." The ideal of objective reality is the focus of a family of effectively indispensable regulative principles—a functionally useful instrumentality that enables us to transact our cognitive business in the most satisfactory and effective way.

And so, the foundations of objectivity are not provided by the findings of science. They precede and underlie science, which would itself not be possible without a precommitment to the capacity of our senses to warrant claims about an objective world order. Mind-transcendence is not a *product* of inquiry; we must precommit ourselves to it to make inquiry as we understand it possible. It is a necessary *(a priori)* input into the cognitive project and not a contingent *(a posteriori)* output thereof. The objective bearing of experience is not something we can preestablish; it is something we must presuppose in the interest of honoring Peirce's pivotal injunction never to bar the path of inquiry.

What we learn from science is not *that* an unobservable order of physical existence causally undergirds nature as we observe it, but rather *what* these underlying structures are like. Science does not (cannot) teach us that the observable order is explicable in terms of underlying causes and that the phenomena of observation are signs or symptoms of this extra- and sub-phenomenal order of existence; we must acknowledge this prior to any venture in developing an empirical science. It is something we must accept *a priori* to hold of any world in which observation as we understand it can transpire. (After all, observations are, by their very nature, the results of interactions.) What science does teach us (and metaphysics cannot) is what the descriptive character of this extra-phenomenal order can reasonably be supposed to be in the light of our experience of it. The substance of the factual realm is its concern. But the nature and status of this realm in the wider scheme of things is on the problem-agenda not of the scientist but of the philosopher.

Bibliography

Adams, Robert M. "Theories of Actuality." *Nous* 8 (1974), pp. 211–231.
Alston, William P. "Yes, Virginia, There is a Real World." *Proceedings and Addresses of the American Philosophical Association* 52 (1979), pp. 779–808.
Archimedes. *The Works of Archimedes*. Tr. by Thomas Heath. Cambridge: Cambridge University Press, 1897.
Aristotle. Categories and De Interpretatione: Translated with Notes and Glossary. Ed. by John L. Ackrill. Oxford: Clarendon Press, 1963.
Armstrong, David M. *Belief, Truth and Knowledge*. Cambridge: Cambridge University Press, 1973.
Armstrong, David M. *A Combinatorial Theory of Possibility*. Cambridge: Cambridge University Press, 1989.
Ashworth, E. Jennifer. *Language and Logic in the Post-Medieval Period*. Dordrecht: Reidel, 1974.
Beeley, Philip. "Leibniz on the Limits of Human Knowledge." *The Leibniz Review* 13 (December 2003), pp. 93–97.
Bradley, Francis H. *Appearance and Reality*. Oxford: Clarendon Press, 1893.
Burnet, John. *Early Greek Philosophy*. London: Adam and Charles Black, 1892; ^{4}1930.
Cameron, Alastair G. W. (ed.) *Interstellar Communication: A Collection of Reprints and Original Contributions*. New York and Amsterdam: W. A. Benjamin, 1963.
Casey, Edward S. *Imagining: A Phenomenological Study*. Indianapolis: University of Indiana Press, ^{2}2000.
Cassirer, Ernest. Determinism and Indeterminism in Modern Physics: Historical and Systematic Studies of the Problems of Causality. New Haven: Yale University Press, 1956.
Chaitin, Gregory J. *The Unknowable*. Singapore and New York: Springer, 1999.
Chihara, Charles. *The Worlds of Possibility: Modal Realism and the Semantics of Modal Logic*. Oxford Clarendon Press, 1998.
Clement, Saint. *Stromata*. Berlin: Akademie Verlag, 1960.
Cowley, Robert (ed.). *What If?* New York: G. P. Putnam's Sons, 1999.
Davidson, Donald. "The Very Ideas of a Conceptual Scheme." *Proceedings and Addresses of the American Philosophical Association* 47 (1973–1974), pp. 5–20.
Delaney, Cornelius F. "Peirce on 'Simplicity' and the Conditions of the Possibility of Science." In: Linus J. Thro (ed.). *History of Philosophy in the Making*. Washington, D.C.: University Press of America, 1982, pp. 177–194.
Descartes, René. *Meditations*. In: *Philosophical Works*, vol. 1. Ed. by Haldane, Elizabeth S. and G. R. T. Ross. Cambridge, MA: Cambridge University Press, 1911.
Dole, Stephen H. *Habitable Planets for Man*. New York: Blaisdell, 1964; New York: American Elsevier, ^{2}1970.
du Bois-Reymond, Emil. "The Limits of Our Knowledge of Nature." *Popular Scientific Monthly* 5 (1874), pp. 17–32.
du Bois-Reymond, Emil. On the Limits of Scientific Knowledge as Ueber Die Grenzen des Naturerkennens: Die Sieben Welträtsel—Zwei Vorträge. 11th ed., Leipzig: Veit, 1916.
Dummett, Michael. "Truth." *Proceedings of the Aristotelian Society. New Series* 59 (1958–1959), pp. 141–162.

Dyson, Freeman. "Mathematics in the Physical Sciences." In: Committee on Support of Research in the Mathematical Sciences (ed.). *The Mathematical Sciences*. Cambridge, MA: MIT Press, 1969, pp. 97–115.
Eddington, Arthur. *The Nature of the Physical World*. New York: Macmillan; Cambridge: Cambridge University Press, 1928.
Edwards, Paul (ed.). *The Encyclopedia of Philosophy*. New York: Macmillan, 1967.
Einstein, Albert. *Lettres à Maurice Solovine*. Paris: Gauthier-Villars, 1956.
Fecher, Vincent J. *Error, Deception, and Incomplete Truth*. Rome: Officium Libri Catholici, 1975.
Ferguson, Niall. *Virtual History*. New York: Basic Books, 1999.
Galilei, Galileo. *Dialogo sopra i due massimi sistemi del mondo*. In: *Le Opere di Galileo Galilei*, vol. 7. Florence: Barbèra, 1897.
Gray, Thomas. "Ode on a Prospect of Eton College." London: R. Dodsley, 1747.
Grim, Patrick. "There Is No Set of All Truths." *Analysis* 44 (1984), pp. 206–208.
Haeckel, Ernst. *The Riddle of the Universe—at the Close of the Nineteenth Century*. Tr. by Joseph McCabe. New York and London, 1901.
Harré, Rom. *Principles of Scientific Thinking*. Chicago: University of Chicago Press, 1970.
Hartshorne, Charles. *Anselm's Discovery*. La Salle, IL: Open Court, 1965.
Hempel, Carl G. "Problems and Changes in the Empiricists Criterion of Meaning." *Révue Internationale de Philosophie* 4 (1950), pp. 41–63.
Hesse, Mary. *Revolutions and Reconstructions in the Philosophy of Science*. Bloomington, IN: University of Indiana Press, 1980.
Horowitz, Tamara and Geoffrey J. Massey (eds.). *Thought Experiments in Science and Philosophy*. Savage, MD: Rowman & Littlefield, 1991.
Huang, Su-Shu. "Life Outside the Solar System." *Scientific American*, 202/4 (April 1960), pp. 55–63.
Hugly, Philip and Charles Sayward. "Can a Language Have Indenumerably Many Expressions?" *History and Philosophy of Logic* 4 (1983), pp. 112–126.
Huntford, Roland. *The Last Place on Earth*. New York, 1985.
Huygens, Christiaan. *Cosmotheoros: The Celestial Worlds Discovered—New Conjectures Concerning the Planetary Worlds, Their Inhabitants and Productions*. London, 1698; reprinted London: F. Cass & Co., 1968.
James, William. "The Sentiment of Rationality." In: *The Will to Believe and Other Essays in Popular Philosophy*. New York and London: Putnam, 1897, pp. 78–79.
Jefferson, Thomas. *Notes on the State of Virginia*. New York and London: Penguin, 1999.
Kant, Immanuel. *Critique of Pure Reason*. Tr. by Norman Kemp Smith. New York: Random House, 1958.
Kirk, Geoffrey S. and John E. Raven. *The Presocratic Philosophers*. 2nd ed. with the collaboration of M. Schofield. Cambridge: Cambridge University Press, 1983.
Kirk, Geoffrey S. *Heraclitus: The Cosmic Fragments*. Cambridge: Cambridge University Press, 1954.
Kretzman, Norman and Eleonore Stump. *The Cambridge Translation of Medieval Philosophical Texts*. Vol. 1: *Logic and Philosophy of Language*. Cambridge: Cambridge University Press, 1988.
Kuhn, Thomas S. "A Function for Thought Experiments in Science." In: Ian Hacking (ed.). *Scientific Revolutions*. Oxford: Oxford University Press, 1981, pp. 6–27.

Leibniz, Gottfried Wilhelm. *De l'horizon de la doctrine humaine*. Ed. by Michael Fichant. Paris: Vrin, 1991.
Leibniz, Gottfried Wilhelm. *Philosophische Schriften*. Ed. by Carl I. Gerhardt. Vol. 7. Berlin: Weidmann, 1890.
Lewis, C. I. *An Analysis of Knowledge and Valuation*. La Salle, IL: Open Court, 1962.
Mach, Ernst. "Ueber Gedankenexperimente." In: *Erkenntnis und Irrtum*. Leipzig: J. A. Barth, 1906, pp. 183–200.
Machlup, Fritz. *The Production and Distribution of Knowledge in the United States*. Princeton: Princeton University Press, 1962.
Maimonides, Moses. *The Guide for the Perplexed*. Tr. by Chaim Rabin. Indianapolis and Cambridge: Hackett.
McKinnon, Edward A. (ed.). *The Problem of Scientific Realism*. New York: Appleton-Century-Crofts, 1972.
Moore, G. E. *Some Main Problems of Philosophy*. London: Allen and Unwin, 1953.
Peirce, Charles Sanders. *Collected Papers*. Ed. by Charles Hartshorne and Paul Weiss. Cambridge, MA: Harvard University Press, 1929–1934.
Plantinga, Alvin. The Nature of Necessity. Oxford: Clarendon Press, 1974.
Popper, Karl R. *Objective Knowledge*. Oxford: Clarendon Press, 1972.
Prantl, Carl. *Geschichte der Logik im Abendlande*, vol. 4. Leipzig: S. Hirzel, 1955.
Purcell, Edward. "Radioastronomy and Communication through Space." In: Alistair G. W. Cameron (ed.). *Interstellar Communication: A Collection of Reprints and Original Contributions*. New York and Amsterdam: W. A. Benjamin, 1963, pp. 121–143.
Rees, Martin. *Just Six Numbers*. New York: Basic Books, 2000.
Rescher, Nicholas. *Baffling Phenomena*. Savage, MD: Rowman & Littlefield, 1991.
Rescher, Nicholas. *Cognitive Economy*. Pittsburgh: University of Pittsburgh Press, 1989.
Rescher, Nicholas. *Empirical Inquiry*. Totowa, NJ: Rowman & Littlefield, 1982.
Rescher, Nicholas. *Epistemic Logic*. Pittsburgh: University of Pittsburgh Press, 2005.
Rescher, Nicholas. "Extraterrestrial Science." *Philosophia Naturalis* 21 (1984), pp. 400–424.
Rescher, Nicholas. *Induction*. Oxford: Basil Blackwell, 1980.
Rescher, Nicholas. "Leibniz's Quantitative Epistemology." *Studia Leibnitiana* 36 (2004), pp. 210–230.
Rescher, Nicholas. *Limits of Science*. Pittsburgh: University of Pittsburgh Press, 2000.
Rescher, Nicholas. *Metaphysics*. Amherst, NY: Prometheus, 2006.
Rescher, Nicholas. *Methodological Pragmatism*. Oxford: Basil Blackwell, 1977.
Rescher, Nicholas. *Peirce's Philosophy of Science*. Notre Dame and London: Notre Dame Press, 1976.
Rescher, Nicholas. *Presumptions*. Cambridge: Cambridge University Press, 2006.
Rescher, Nicholas. *Scientific Realism*. Dordrecht: D. Reidel, 1987.
Russell, Bertrand. *Introduction to Mathematical Philosophy*. London: Allen & Unwin, 1919.
Sagan, Carl. *Cosmos*. New York: Random House, 1980.
Schrödinger, Erwin. *What is Life?* Cambridge: Cambridge University Press, 1945.
Sellars, Wilfred. *Science Perception and Reality*. London: Humanities Press, 1963.
Seneca, *Natural Questions*. Vol. 2: Books 4–7. Cambridge, MA: Harvard University Press, 1972.
Shklovskii, Iossif S. and Carl Sagan. *Intelligent Life in the Universe*. San Francisco, London, and Amsterdam: Holden-Day, 1966.

Simpson, George G. "The Nonprevalence of Humanoids." *Science* 143 (1964), pp. 769–775, Chapter 13 of *This View of Life: The World of an Evolutionist*. New York: Harcourt Brace, 1964.

Strawson, Peter F. "Truth," *Proceedings of the Aristotelian Society*. New Series 59 (1958–1959), pp. 141–162.

Suppe, Frederick. "Facts and Empirical Truth." *Canadian Journal of Philosophy* 3 (1973), pp. 197–212.

Suppe, Frederick (ed.). *The Structure of Scientific Theories*. Urbana: University of Illinois Press, ²1977.

Surowiecki, James. *The Wisdom of Crowds*. New York: Anchor Books, 2005.

Vaihinger, Hans. *Philosophie des Als ob*. Berlin: Reuther & Reichard, 1911.

Wigner, Eugene P. "The Unreasonable Effectiveness of Mathematics in the Natural Sciences." *Communications on Pure and Applied Mathematics* 13 (1960), pp. 1–14.

Zipf, George K. *Human Behavior and the Principle of Least Effort*. Cambridge, MA: Addison-Wesley, 1949.

Index

Adams Robert M., 25, 25n23, 180
Alston, William P. 47n53, 180
Anaximander of Miletus 67
Aquinas, St. Thomas 128
Archimedes 72, 72n62, 180
Aristotle 44, 61, 81n75, 83, 157, 180
Armstrong, David M. 15, 16n10, 17, 17n11, 33, 34n29, 85n78, 180
Ashworth, E. Jennifer 150n132, 150n123, 180
Augustine, Saint 132

Beeley, Philip 72n63, 180
Bosanquet, Bernard 62
Bradbury, Ray 110
Bradley, Francis H. 68, 68n60, 82, 180
Burley, Walter 24–25
Burnet, John 42n42, 42n43, 42n44, 43n45, 43n46, 43n47, 43n48, 44n49, 44n50, 44n51, 48n54, 180
Butler, Joseph 153
Bywater, Ingram 42n42

Cameron, Alastair G. W. 104n92, 111n94, 112n95
Cantor, Georg 79
Carnap Rudolf 30
Casey, Edward S. 34N31, 180
Cassirer, Ernest 151n124, 180
Castella, George 134n109
Cervantes, Miguel de 28
Chaitin, Gregory J. 164n133, 180
Chihara, Charles 36, 36n32, 38, 180
Clement, Saint 180
Comte, Auguste 162

Davidson, Donald 22n20, 180
Delaney, Cornelius F. 2n2, 18-
Descartes, René 170, 180
Diels, Hermann 42n42
Dionysius 43
Dole, Stephen H. 101, 101n86, 180
Doyle, Arthur Conan 3237, 37n34

du Bois-Reymond, Emil 150–151, 151n124, 180
Dummett, Michael 167n135, 168, 180
Dyson, Freeman 142n117, 181

Eddington, Sir Arthur 103, 103n89, 181
Einstein, Albert 39, 113, 136, 136n113, 181

Fecher, Vincent J. 17n12, 181
Ferguson, Niall 44n52, 181

Galilei, Galileo 142,142n117, 181
Galton, Francis 132
Gödel, Kurt 73
Goodman, Nelson 30
Gray, Thomas 130n106, 181
Grim, Patrick 79, 79n73, 181

Haeckel, Ernest 151–152, 151n125, 152n126, 181
Handy, Rollo 151n125
Harré, Rom 90n83, 181
Hartshorne, Charles 19n16, 25–26, 25n22, 181
Hegel, G. W. F. 68
Hekataios 44
Hempel, Carl G. 66n59, 181
Heraclitus of Ephesus 42–44, 48, 149
Hesiod 44
Hesse, Mary 137, 137n115, 181
Hippolytus 40n38
Homer 37, 44
Horowitz, Tamara 44n52
Huang, Su-Shu 103n88, 181
Hugly, Philip 74n65, 181
Hume, David 30
Huntford, Roland 3n5, 181
Husserl, Edmund 173
Huygens, Christiaan 114, 115n96, 181

James, William 4n6, 181
Jefferson, Thomas 121, 121n100, 181

Kant, Immanuel   10, 19n15, 37, 48, 50, 116, 118, 118–119n99, 149, 162, 177, 177n141, 181
Kepler, Johannes   142n117
Kirk, Geoffrey S.   40n38, 41n39, 41n40, 41n41, 42n42, 43n45, 181
Koyré, Alexandre   113
Kretzman, Norman   24n21, 181
Kuhn, Thomas S.   40n37, 181

Leibniz, Gottfried Wilhelm   19n15, 72–73, 72n63, 72n64, 76, 76n70, 182
Lewis, C. I.   20, 20n17, 182

Mach, Ernest   39, 40n36, 182
Machlup, Fritz   2n4, 182
Maimonides, Moses   53n57, 182
Massey, Gerald   44n52
Meinong, Alexius   32
Mittelstrass, Jürgen   142n117
Moore, G. E.   87, 87n80, 182

Nansen, Fridtjof   3n5
Newton, Isaac   94, 136
Nietzsche, Friedrich   48

Occam, William of   6

Pascal, Blaise   114
Pearman, J. P. T.   103–104
Peirce, Charles Sanders   2, 2n2, 2n3, 38n35, 55, 139, 162, 162n131, 167–168, 170, 170n136, 171, 174, 178, 182
Plantinga, Alvin   36, 36n33, 182
Plato   10, 19n14, 48
Popper, Karl   137, 137n114, 182
Prantl, Carl   150n123, 182
Protagoras   167
Purcell, Edward   98n85, 182
Pythagoras   44

Quine, W. V. O.   30

Raven, John E.   40n38, 41n39, 41n40, 41n41, 42n42, 43n45, 181
Rees, Martin   26n24, 182
Rescher, Nicholas   72n64, 182
Robert, Christian P.   134n109
Royce, Josiah   68
Russell, Bertrand   32–33, 33n27, 36, 182

Sagan, Carl   101, 101n86, 103n90, 103n91, 106, 115n97, 182
Sayward, Charles   74n65, 182
Schofield, Malcolm   40n38, 181
Schrödinger, Erwin   136, 136n110, 182
Sellars, Wilfred   90n83, 182
Seneca   1, 182
Shakespeare, William   37
Shklovskii, Iossif S.   103n90, 103n91, 106, 115n97, 182
Simpson, George G.   104n93, 183
Solovine, Maurice   136
Spinoza, Baruch   68, 135
Strawson, Peter F.   21n18, 183
Stump, Eleonore   42n21, 181
Suppe, Frederick   47n53, 183
Surowiecki, James   132n108, 183

Tarski, Alfred   71
Teilhard-de-Chardin   103
Thales   43
Themistius   53

Vaihinger, Hans   30, 30n26, 183

Wigner, Eugene   136, 136n111, 136n112, 183
Wittgenstein, Ludwig   76

Xenophanes of Colophon   40–44

Zipf, George K.   6n8, 183

www.ingramcontent.com/pod-product-compliance
Lightning Source LLC
Chambersburg PA
CBHW020331170426
43200CB00006B/346